'A' Level L

GW00372135

Barry Jones

BA (London)
Barrister, formerly Headmaster, Avonhurst School, Bristol

Third Edition

THE M & E HANDBOOK SERIES

Pitman Publishing
128 Long Acre, London WC2E 9AN

A Division of Longman Group UK Limited

First published in 1981
Second edition 1984
Third edition 1991
Reprinted 1992

© Longman Group UK Ltd 1991

British Library Cataloguing in Publication Data
Jones, Barry
  'A' Level law. – 3rd ed. – (M & E handbook series)
  I. Title II. Series
  349.41

ISBN 0 7121 0842 4

Founding Editor: P.W.D. Redmond

Printed and bound in Singapore

Contents

Part two The law of contract

Part three The law of torts

Part four The criminal law

Preface

The passage of time since the publication of the previous edition, coupled with the enhanced format of the M & E Handbook series, has necessitated an almost total rewriting of this book. Every endeavour has been made to include recent developments and, in order to accommodate changes in the examination syllabuses, a new Part three on Torts has been added.

It is an old axiom that a legal textbook is akin to a photograph of the Clapham omnibus as it thunders past and, to the best of my knowledge, the law is stated as at 1 January 1991. The uniformity in presentation is intended to facilitate learning but, as evidenced by the cross-referencing, the individual sections cannot be in any way looked upon as mutually exclusive. Every chapter should be read through, with a view to acquiring a general picture of its scope and content. Thereafter all of the separate topics need to be studied in detail and only then should the Progress Test be tackled — and ultimately checked against the sectional references.

With synopses of approximately 500 illustrative cases, it is hoped that this book will be of value to 'A' Level candidates, to students pursuing courses in the English Legal System, Contract, Torts or Criminal Law, and also to those who simply wish to acquire a general introduction to law.

1991   BJ

Table of cases

Table of statutes

Part one

The English legal system

1
The origins of law

The nature of law

1. The meaning of law

'The law' is difficult to define as it may be used to describe a
scientific fact (e.g. the law of gravity), a particular system (e.g. the
law of England) or a recognised legal area (e.g. the law of contract).
Nevertheless, more generally, it connotes a series of *rules* (each
called 'a law') which govern people's behaviour. In their turn, the
rules may sometimes be supplemented by certain established
principles and common examples in English law are the maxims
ignorantia juris neminem excusat ('ignorance of the law excuses no
man'), likewise *ex turpi causa non oritur actio* ('a legal action does
not arise from a base cause' — e.g. a contract to commit a crime
is unenforceable); *see also* 1:5(d). In examining the meaning of law,
it is of value to consider:

(a) *The relevance of morality.* The value-concepts of right and wrong
form the basis of *morality* and, although this is closely interwoven
with *religion*, a distinction must be drawn between the two — as the
one concerns a relationship between people, whereas the other
establishes it between mankind and some higher power. Nowadays
the law regards some kinds of behaviour (e.g. parking offences) as
criminal although, in general, they may not be looked upon as
morally wrong. Likewise, other forms of conduct (e.g. adultery)
may be morally condemned but not legally prohibited. Yet again,
some practices considered to be immoral (e.g. lying) are illegal
only in certain circumstances (as in the case of perjury or
misleading trade descriptions). It has sometimes been argued that
the law should proscribe all immoral acts, as failure to do so would

ultimately cause the disintegration of society. The impracticality of this, however, stems from the plurality of cultures and values in our society (whereby there is a total lack of consensus over particular moral issues, e.g. abortion), as well as from the evolutionary nature of morality (whereby what is immoral and criminal at one moment might not be so shortly afterwards). As *deviance* (the breaking of rules) can be said to be created by the very framing of those rules, one should examine the manner in which any particular moral attitude (as opposed to a competing one) becomes embodied in the law. Often it simply reflects the views of a restricted section of society (politicians, judges, etc) at one moment. Legislation of morality 'for its own sake' is notably exemplified by the so called *victimless crimes*, which involve only the participants themselves (e.g. smoking cannabis). There is thus a school of thought to the effect that, although morality and law are interrelated, there are some aspects of human behaviour which may be considered immoral but which should not be legally proscribed so long as they do not harm other people (e.g. homosexual practices between consenting adults in private).

(b) *The concept of justice.* Justice, the ultimate goal towards which the law should strive, is but one segment of morality because, although unjust acts (e.g. unjustifiably punishing one child more than another) may be considered immoral, the converse is not true and immoral acts (e.g. cruelty to children) cannot be described as unjust. 'Fairness' is the closest synonym to justice, a vital function of which is the attainment of equality. Some lawyers tend to be concerned only with *formal justice* — i.e. fairness in the *application* of valid law and the *conduct* of trials — whereby like cases are treated alike under existing rules which are generally and impartially applied. Laymen, however, are more prone to take entirely subjective views on *substantive justice* — i.e. fairness in the *substance* of the law and in the *outcome* of trials.

2. The essentials of the law

The most important basic rules which a society needs to lay down, in order to guide the conduct of its members, probably relate to:

(a) *The control of harmful activities.* As a marker of boundaries of 'acceptable conduct', the law should provide sanctions for breaches thereof. Nowadays, therefore, punishment is imposed for offences against the person, offences against property and offences against the state — whilst there is redress for breaches of contract and torts.

(b) *The protection of freedom.* The maintenance of social order must be reconciled with the preservation of individual *freedom,* an objective sought by most people and consequently deserving of legal protection. It is, however, difficult to interpret as it is a normative word and valuational in concept — since preference for a particular system, as offering greater freedom than others, stems from the fact that it is free in those things which the observer values most. Respect for rights and freedoms of some people must give rise to certain limitations on the freedom of others, who become subject to corresponding obligations and duties. In this way *relative freedom* is sought but, in a society with a plurality of cultures and values, there will always be areas of disagreement as to what conduct is 'acceptable' and which activities are 'harmful'. The role of the state should therefore be that of protecting freedoms of highest general value, bearing in mind that freedom is situational in time and place, being subject to new interpretations and modifications as conditions and circumstances alter. *See also* Chapter 8.

(c) *The balancing of interests.* The American jurist Roscoe Pound (1870–1964) considered that the main function of law is to maximise the fulfilment of the *interests* of the community; and he defined an interest as *a demand or desire or expectation which human beings, either individually or in groups . . . . seek to satisfy.* Nevertheless, different interests may easily conflict with each other and, in order to decide which should prevail, comparisons and evaluations must be made. These necessitate an assessment of the values of society, with the result that legal decisions can be influenced by an ideology. In some countries (e.g. the USA and the Federal Republic of Germany) attempts have been made to identify certain 'preferred values', which override lesser ones in the event of conflict, but they relate only to a particular period of time and cannot give rise to any permanent order of priority. With regard to contemporary English values, 'national and social safety override all other considerations and sanctity of the person is superior to sanctity of property but, beyond this, the pattern is kaleidoscopic and not hierarchical'. (R.W.M. Dias: *Jurisprudence*).

Examples of competing interests exist in respect of *freedom of speech* (possibly conflicting with the protection of personal reputation, state security or racial harmony), *enjoyment of property* (possibly conflicting with a neighbour's similar interest), *right of employment* (possibly conflicting with an employer's right to dismiss) and the *right of political protest* (possibly conflicting with the preservation of public order).

The nature of the common law

3. The development of the common law

From 1066 William I effected a policy of centralisation which led to one government for the whole of the country, one legal system and one body of law. Being the national law, as opposed to previous local laws and customs, it can be called *common law* but, confusingly, this term has two other possible meanings. In the first place, it can connote the law applied in the common law courts described below and, secondly, it is now most commonly used to describe the decisions of *all* courts (including those of equity — 1:5). After the Norman Conquest the chief central administrative organ was the *Curia Regis* ('Court of the King'), which dealt with legislation and also important trials. As time went on, it took over much of the administration of justice from existing local courts but the resultant increase in its work-load created a need for delegation. Gradually, therefore, its judicial functions were divided amongst the following courts, all of which existed until 1875:

(a) *The Court of Exchequer.* This broke away from the Curia Regis in the reign of Henry I (1100–1135) and its officials were termed Exchequer Barons. Originally their jurisdiction was purely fiscal (e.g. deciding questions between the Crown and the taxpayer). From about 1320 the court gained common law jurisdiction by the use of the writ *quominus*, whereby a plaintiff could plead the fiction that he was a debtor of the King and could not repay his debt because of the defendant's failure to pay him. *Fictions* have played a significant part in English law and are statements or suppositions known to be untrue but not permitted to be denied, in order to overcome difficulties and to secure substantive justice. Up until the mid-sixteenth century, the court dealt mainly with financial matters but thereafter it enjoyed a broader common law jurisdiction.

(b) *The Court of Common Pleas.* Justices of the Curia Regis originally travelled throughout the country with the King and eventually a distinction developed between *pleas of the Crown* (involving the King) and *common pleas* (between subject and subject), with the latter being judged from 1178 by specially appointed justices. In 1215 Magna Carta provided that the *Court of Common Pleas* should not travel with the King but should be held in a certain place (usually Westminster). It enjoyed exclusive jurisdiction in *real actions* (i.e. those concerning land) and also debt; thus in the medieval period it had a monopoly of important work. However, it was less popular than the Courts of Exchequer or King's Bench (*below*), as its judgments were subject to review by the latter and it did not have recourse to fictions.

(c) *The Court of King's Bench.* This separated from the Curia Regis in 1230 and for a time it heard cases concerning the King (or important persons entitled to be judged only by the King). It travelled the realm until 1400, after which it remained at Westminster. From the fifteenth century it enjoyed criminal jurisdiction over ordinary cases and indictments, also matters removed from inferior courts by the writ of *certiorari*. It likewise gained an important supervisory role mainly through the prerogative writs of *habeas corpus, prohibition* and *mandamus* (*see* 7:2(f) and 8:10).

4. The development of other jurisdictions

Other forms of jurisdiction exercised by courts which existed until 1875 developed as follows:

(a) *The development of appellate jurisdiction.* In the reign of Edward II (1307–1327) the practice arose whereby informal meetings of the King's Bench and Common Pleas judges took place in a chamber at the Exchequer, to discuss cases of particular importance or complexity. This gave rise to the idea that such gatherings constituted courts and a statute of 1357 established a *Court of Exchequer Chamber,* to amend errors in the Court of

Exchequer. From 1366 jurisdiction over errors by the common law courts was vested in Parliament and subsequently became limited to the House of Lords. Up till the sixteenth century errors by the Court of King's Bench could still be amended only by Parliament, which rarely met; consequently in 1585 a new Court of Exchequer Chamber was established. This comprised any six or more of the Common Pleas justices and Exchequer Barons, who heard error from the King's Bench in certain types of cases. Further appeal thence lay to Parliament and it was still made to the House of Lords in proceedings not mentioned in the Act. In 1830 the two courts thus created were merged in a Court of Exchequer Chamber, wherein judges of any two of the common law courts heard appeals against decisions by the third one, with appeal thence lying to the House of Lords.

(b) *The development of divorce jurisdiction.* A significant effect of the Norman Conquest was the establishment of *canon law* (based on that of Rome), administered by ecclesiastical courts. These granted decrees of divorce which did not completely sever the marriage bond or permit remarriage. In 1533–34, following the Reformation, the system was radically altered and canon law was subordinated to the law of the state. Particularly after 1700 divorce permitting remarriage began to be granted by private Act of Parliament but this procedure was cumbersome and costly. Under the Matrimonial Causes Act 1857, the *Divorce and Matrimonial Causes Court* was created to grant divorce by judicial process.

(c) *The development of probate jurisdiction.* Jurisdiction relating to the grant or revocation of *probate* (the judicial authentication of an effective will made by someone who has died *testate*) or *letters of administration* (granted when a person has died *intestate* — i.e. not leaving a valid will) developed in the ecclesiastical courts. It remained therein until it was transferred to the *Probate Court* under the Court of Probate Act 1857.

(d) *The development of maritime jurisdiction.* After the Battle of Sluys (1340) the admirals and their deputies held courts at the main sea ports, mainly to prevent or punish piracy and to deal with *prize* matters (i.e. property captured from an enemy at sea). Early in the fifteenth century the courts were amalgamated to form one *High Court of Admiralty*, which gained criminal jurisdiction under the Offences at Sea Act 1536, whilst its civil jurisdiction extended to all mercantile and shipping cases. Opposition came from the common law courts, which envied the profit of its business, and by 1660 the influence of the court had greatly diminished. However, its prize jurisdiction had been left untouched and this became important in the Napoleonic wars. In 1834 the criminal jurisdiction was transferred to the Central Criminal Court but statutes of 1840 and 1861 enlarged the court's jurisdiction and it dealt with the increasing volume of litigation in shipping, collision and salvage cases.

The nature of equity

5. The development of equity

In addition to providing only one remedy (damages), the common law courts also developed extremely restrictive *forms of action*. These required proceedings to be commenced with *original writs* which were obtained from the Chancellor and which were quite separate from the *judicial writs* subsequently issued to bring parties before the court, settle subsidiary questions and enforce judgment. Different causes of action gave rise to individual original writs and, in its turn, each original writ attracted towards it certain judicial writs and particular procedures. Outside these forms of action, no action lay and no remedy could be acquired. Persons who were unable to obtain redress for a wrong consequently commenced presenting petitions to the King, as the 'fountain of justice' and, as time went on, these were passed to the Chancellor for a report. This practice became increasingly formal and by 1377 petitioners were addressing themselves directly to the Chancellor. In 1474 the first decision was given on the Chancellor's sole authority and herein lies the inception of the *Court of Chancery*. Being normally an ecclesiastic, the Chancellor granted remedies in the name of reason, right and conscience. In practice, he issued a decree in the form of a declaration of rights — or of an order to the defendant — and, if the latter failed to comply, he was sent to prison until he decided to 'purge' his conscience. This type of justice came to be known as *equity* and originally there were no binding rules, with each Chancellor giving judgment in a way that satisfied his own conscience; consequently, there was considerable criticism concerning the possible outcome of cases. However, the Chancery Court gained such a volume of business that *Vice-Chancellors* had to be appointed, also *Masters in Chancery*, who handled minor matters. At the beginning of the eighteenth century there commenced a systematisation of rules, based on precedent, and this eliminated the arbitrary nature of decisions. Unlike the common law, equity is not a complete system in itself but it is a valuable supplement, comprising certain rules devised to cover particular situations. Sir Henry Maitland's statement that 'Equity is a gloss on the Common Law' greatly understates its significance, in view of the following important contributions that it has made:

(a) *The introduction of new remedies.* Whereas the common law remedy of damages was (and still is) awarded to a successful plaintiff *as of right*, equity introduced new remedies which were (and still are) *discretionary* — it being up to the court's discretion whether or not the remedy should be awarded. These include the *injunction, decree of specific performance* and *declaratory judgment* (7:2(b) – (d)) which were all unknown to the common law — whilst, conversely, the Chancery Court could not award damages until 1858. The fact that equitable remedies are to this day capable of adaptation and expansion has been illustrated in *Mareva Compania Naviera SA* v. *International Bulk Carriers SA* (1975). This case gave rise to what is termed a *Mareva Injunction* — a court order to a third party (e.g. a bank), requiring that the assets of a party to a dispute should be frozen, if they might possibly be removed from the court's jurisdiction (e.g. taken out of the country). In a like manner, the case of *Anton Piller KG* v. *Manufacturing Processes Ltd* (1976) has created the *Anton Piller Order*. This can be granted by the court, at a private hearing, to require a defendant to permit the searching of his premises (and the seizure of any relevant material or documents) by the plaintiff's representatives.

(b) *The introduction of new rights.* Rights created by equity include the recognition and enforcement of equitable interests in property; the concept of trusts (enforcing the obligation of trustees to beneficiaries); the equity of redemption in mortgages (enabling borrowers to retain the security for their debts after the due date for repayment); the appointment of receivers (persons nominated by the court to control property affected by proceedings, until the rights of parties have been determined); the doctrine of promissory estoppel (9:4(d)); actions for rescission on terms and rectification (in respect of mistake in contract — 11:5); equitable relief in cases of fiduciary relationship (13:2(c)); actions for rescission (in respect of misrepresentation in contract — 13:3(b)); the creation of constructive trusts (15:2(b)); and equitable assignment of rights (15:5(b)).

(c) *The introduction of new procedures.* Equity was not bound by the complicated forms of action, cases were heard in English (instead of Latin), and it developed new procedures unknown to the common law — e.g. the use of *subpoena* (4:3(a)), *discovery of documents* and *interrogatories* (*see* 6:2(c) – (d)).

(d) *The development of maxims.* These summarise general principles upon which the courts of equity founded their decisions and they are sometimes used nowadays for the justification of judicial rulings. Principal examples include: equity will not suffer a wrong to be without a remedy; equity follows the law; where there is equal equity, the law shall prevail; where the equities are equal, the first in time prevails; he who seeks equity must do equity; he who comes to equity must come with clean hands; delay defeats equities; equity looks to the intent, rather than to the form; equity looks on that as done which ought to be done; equity imputes an intention to fulfil an obligation.

6. The fusion of law and equity

By the nineteenth century equity had become as rigid as the common law itself; moreover, the multiplicity of courts created conflicts of jurisdiction, different bodies of law, distinct procedures and uncertainty as to the appropriate court in which to bring proceedings. Reforms were effected by the Court of Chancery Act 1851 (which created a *Court of Appeal in Chancery*, as an intermediate appellate tribunal between the Chancery Court and the House of Lords), the Common Law Procedure Acts 1852–54 and the Chancery Amendment Act 1858, all of which tended to bring in line the procedures of common law and equity. Finally, concurrent administration was achieved with the Supreme Court of Judicature Acts 1873–75, which brought about:

(a) *The abolition of existing courts.* From 1875 the following courts ceased to exist: Exchequer; Common Pleas; Queen's Bench; Exchequer Chamber; Divorce and Matrimonial Causes; Probate; High Court of Admiralty; Chancery; and Appeal in Chancery.

(b) *The establishment of the Supreme Court.* The above courts were absorbed into a unified *Supreme Court of Judicature,* which was to consist of the *Court of Appeal* (exercising the jurisdiction of the former courts of Exchequer Chamber and Appeal in Chancery) and the *High Court.* The latter originally comprised five Divisions but in 1880 these were reduced to three — *Queen's Bench Division, Chancery Division* and *Probate, Divorce and Admiralty Division.* The last-named was replaced (under the Administration of Justice Act 1970) by the *Family Division,* and Admiralty work was transferred to the Queen's Bench Division.

(c) *The fusion of administration.* Hitherto anyone seeking an equitable and also a common law remedy (e.g. an injunction as well as damages) had to bring proceedings in two different courts. For the future, however, law and equity were to be administered by all judges in all courts — thus complete relief could be obtained in one only. In this way, matters of administration *but not principles* were fused, as the Acts have *not* abolished the distinction between equitable and legal rights. Furthermore, whereas damages are awarded to a successful plaintiff *as of right,* equitable remedies have remained *discretionary.*

(d) *The establishment of common procedures.* The Acts abolished the forms of action and introduced new rules of procedure, whereby, in particular, that relating to the issue of writs and other stages of litigation was much simplified.

The rule of law

7. The concepts of the rule of law

In his *Introduction to the Study of the Law of the Constitution* (published in 1885), Professor A.V. Dicey considered 'a fundamental principle of the British Constitution' to be the *rule of law.* This he resolved into three main concepts: *the absolute supremacy of regular law* (with no one being made to suffer except for a distinct breach of law); *equality before the law* (with everyone being subject to the ordinary law of the land); and *the growth of the constitution from the ordinary law* (with individual rights arising from judicial decisions, as opposed to formal documents). Dicey's treatment of the subject is now considered to be largely outmoded but the rule of law is an important concept and not easy to define

— being a term which is all too often loosely used in political rhetoric. In general, however, it can be taken to imply a number of principles which would be generally accepted as fundamental to the application of the law (based on the essentials outlined in 1:2) in a democratic society. The extent to which the rule of law exists in any state can therefore be best assessed by examining:

(a) *The impartiality of the law.* It is essential, as Dicey propounded, that everyone should be subject to the ordinary law of the land — though certain exceptions do exist in Britain (e.g. in respect of diplomatic immunity). Although the government maintains and enforces law and order, it must itself be subject to the law — thus 8:**8–12** outline the ways in which control is exercised over administrative functions —

> *R* v. *Secretary of State for Transport, ex parte Greater London Council* (1985): In respect of the transfer of London Regional Transport from the GLC to the Minister, the Court of Appeal held that the GLC had been denied natural justice (8:**12**) in its representations, that the Minister had behaved 'irrationally and improperly' and that *certiorari* (8:**10**) was appropriate to quash his order.

(b) *The certainty of the law.* It is essential that everyone should be aware of the possible consequences of his acts. Persons should therefore be prosecuted only for offences which were specifically defined prior to the date when they were allegedly committed. For this reason, penal legalisation which is retrospective in effect or imprecisely worded (e.g. a 1935 German Act imposing sanctions for conduct 'deserving of punishment according to fundamental conceptions of a penal law and sound popular feeling') would contravene the rule of law.

(c) *The enforcement of the law.* It is essential that there should be certainty of the law being enforced if it is violated; that fair trials should be held in public; that judgments should be given in accordance with the law — and not the needs of policy; that decision-making should conform to the rules of natural justice (8:**12**); that facilities for appeals should be available ; also that punishments should be humane.

(d) *The availability of the law.* It is essential that recourse to the law should not be precluded by inability to meet the cost. In Britain, publicly-financed legal advice, assistance and aid (including representation in court) are available to persons of limited means (**7:5**).

(**e**) *The independence of the law.* It is essential that the judiciary should be independent of the executive and legislature (**5:2**). In Britain, judges are not political appointees and, as shown above, they can enforce the law against the government.

(**f**) *The substance of the law.* It is essential that, even if administered in accordance with the above principles, the laws of a country should not lack universal fairness — on account of bias, intolerance, jealousy or a desire to benefit certain minority interests. Such a situation is not unimaginable in Britain, in view of its 'unwritten' constitution and sovereign Parliament (which largely implements the policies of a majority government). It is therefore questionable whether there should not be greater safeguards against the possible abuse of executive and legislative power — a matter examined further in **8:1**. As shown in **2:1(b)**, the sovereignty of Parliament (which Dicey considered to be 'the very keystone of the British Constitution') means that Parliament has the right to make or unmake any law whatsoever. From a practical point of view, however, laws cannot be made if they would prove unenforceable — through being repugnant to the moral sense of the people; it can consequently be said that Parliament enjoys *legal* but not *political* sovereignty. Just as the government has to obey the law, so do the people; thus those who strongly oppose any particular law should nevertheless obey it, albeit adopting every legal means to get it reformed.

Progress test 1

1. Compare and contrast law and morality. (**1**)

2. Distinguish between law and justice. (**1**)

3. How does the law control activities defined as 'harmful' ? (**2**)

4. What is meant by 'relative' freedom ? (**2**)

5. Examine the nature and balancing of interests.   **(2)**

6. Trace the development of the common law courts prior to 1873.   **(3)**

7. Assess the contribution of equity to the civil law.   **(5, 6)**

8. What do you understand by the rule of law?   **(7)**

2
The sources of law

The emergence of law

1. The legal sources of law

With regard to English law, the word 'source' can have four main connotations. First, there is the *literary source* — i.e. the records in which the law is to be found (e.g. statutes and law reports); secondly, there is the *formal source* — i.e. the authority which gives force to the rules of law (Parliament); thirdly, there is the *historical source* — i.e. the causes which induced the creation of the law (e.g. religious beliefs, moral standards, political pressure, etc); and, fourthly, there is the *legal source* — i.e. the means by which the law is brought into existence. English courts will recognise and apply only law that has originated from the following legal sources:

(a) *The recognition of custom.* Anglo-Saxon customs constitute the oldest source of English law and a distinction can be drawn between those which were general and those which were local in nature. *General custom* implies the body of rules which were obeyed throughout the realm but, by the fourteenth century, most of them had been absorbed into case law by court decisions. *Local custom* implies rules and traditions obeyed by the inhabitants of a particular locality and the possibility of its recognition today is outlined in 2:**2.**

(b) *The enactment of legislation.* In some countries (e.g. the USA) which have 'written' constitutions (i.e. embodied in formal documents), the courts have the power to declare invalid the provisions of any enacted legislation which they consider to be inconsistent with the constitution. There are no such limitations on the law-making ability of the British Parliament, which enjoys legal *sovereignty* — as, theoretically, it can make or repeal legislation on any topic — thereby creating what is termed *statute law*. To sustain future sovereignty, Parliament has always been subject to one legal restriction, in that, technically, it cannot enact any unrepealable provision which would bind its successors. Nevertheless, many treaty obligations impose restraints upon enacting legislation which would be inconsistent with them. In this respect, the strongest argument over the erosion of parliamentary sovereignty (also that of the jurisdiction of the House of Lords) has centred upon the subjection of the United Kingdom to European Community law (2:4–5). This stems from the European Communities Act 1972 and European Communities (Amendment) Act 1986 — both of which could constitutionally be repealed — though such an action would be seen as a serious breach of a treaty. Acts (or statutes) are initiated as *bills*, which are of three main types:

(*i*) *The public bills.* These relate to the public as a whole and they are introduced by the government in either the House of Commons or the House of Lords. The procedure for their enactment is outlined in 3:**1**.

(*ii*) *The private members' bills.* These are simply public bills which are introduced by back-bench MPs or peers (instead of by the government).

(*iii*) *The private bills.* These relate to particular localities, bodies or persons, and their enactment involves special procedures. Public bills which affect private interests are sometimes termed *hybrid*.

A second attribute of sovereignty is that Parliament alone enjoys the power to make all law but, through pressure of business and lack of time, it cannot adequately discharge this function and, consequently, it statutorily delegates law-making authority (*see* 3:3).

(c) *The decisions of the courts.* By the doctrine of *stare decisis* ('the standing of decisions'), courts must follow rules and principles enunciated in the decisions of superior courts (also sometimes their own previous decisions). As shown in 1:**3**, case law originating in all courts may be termed *common law* and this principle of *judicial precedent* is examined in 3:**4**.

(d) *The law of the European Communities.* Under the Treaty of Accession, signed in Brussels in 1972 and ratified in Britain by the European Communities Act 1972, the United Kingdom joined the

European Communities on 1st January 1973. Though the word 'community' is commonly used, the plural is strictly correct, on account of the fact that the body comprises three organisations — the European Coal and Steel Community (ECSC), the European Atomic Energy Community (Euratom) and the European Economic Community (EEC or 'Common Market'). Currently there are 11 other member nations: France, Germany, Italy, Belgium, the Netherlands, Luxembourg, Denmark, Republic of Ireland, Hellenic Republic, Spain and Portugal. The legislatures of member states cannot make enactments (and have to 'harmonise' existing ones) that are inconsistent with Community law. This is outlined in 2:4–5 and the organisation should not be confused with the *Council of Europe,* which comprises 25 nations and is described in 8:1.

2.   The recognition of custom

There are divergent opinions as to whether custom is actually law until it is recognised by the courts and, in order to gain recognition and enforcement, a local custom must fulfil the following requirements:

(a) *It must apply to a definite locality.* E.g. a shire, borough, parish or manor.

(b) *It must have been exercised from 'time immemorial'.* This was fixed at 1189 (under the Statute of Westminster 1275) but nowadays it is merely necessary to prove that a custom goes back as far as living memory —

> *Mercer* v. *Denne* (1905): M claimed a customary right
> for the fishermen of Walmer to dry their nets on D's land,
> proving user for 70 years — and, by reputation, even
> longer. D pleaded that, at times since 1189, the land had
> been under the sea but judgment was given for M.

(c) *It must have been continuously exercisable,* without lawful interruption. It need not have been continuously *exercised* but at all times it must have been possible to exercise it lawfully —

> *Wyld* v. *Silver* (1963): A private Enclosure Act of 1799
> entitled the inhabitants of a parish to hold an annual 'fair or
> wake' on certain land but they had not exercised the right

within living memory, and the owner wished to build upon it. An injunction was granted to restrain him from doing so.

(d) *It must have been exercised peaceably, openly and as of right,* i.e. 'not by violence, stealth or entreaty' (*nec vi, nec clam, nec precario*). The need for permission to be granted would invalidate an alleged custom —

> *Mills* v. *Corporation of Colchester* (1867): CC owned an oyster fishery and had, since the time of Elizabeth I, held courts at which, on payment of a fee, they granted fishing licences to inhabitants of certain parishes, who had been apprenticed to licensed fishermen. M had the qualifications and was willing to pay the fee but CC refused to grant him a licence. It was held that the inhabitants had never had such enjoyment *as of right*; therefore judgment was given for CC.

(e) *It must be reasonable.* The test is 'whether it is in accordance with the fundamental principles of right and wrong' —

> *Wolstanton Ltd* v. *Newcastle-under-Lyme Borough Council* (1940): The lord of a manor claimed the right to take minerals from under a tenant's land, in accordance with an alleged manorial custom, and without paying compensation for resulting damage. It was held that this was unreasonable.

(f) *It must be definite in nature and scope* —

> *Wilson* v. *Willes* (1806): The tenants of a manor claimed an alleged custom entitling them to take from the manorial common as much turf as they required for their lawns. It was held that this was too uncertain.

(g) *It must be recognised as binding* on those affected by it.
(h) *It must not contravene statute law or the common law.*
(i) *It must not be inconsistent with other customs*; conflicting customs cannot all be good.

The law of the European Communities

3. The institutions of the European Communities
Charged with administering the Communities are the following institutions:

(a) *The European Council.* Although not recognised in the treaties as a Community institution, this is a politically significant forum of the 12 Heads of Government who meet twice-yearly to agree broad lines of policy (considered by ministers beforehand); also to discuss and resolve intractable Community disputes.

(b) *The Council of Ministers.* This comprises one minister from each member state — generally the Foreign Minister — though another may attend instead, dependent upon the subject-matter under discussion (e.g. agriculture). The presidency is held in rotation by each country for six months and, supported by a Committee of Permanent Representatives (COREPER — national officials of ambassadorial status), the Council of Ministers is the supreme decision-making body. Its decisions (normally resulting from proposals by the Commission (*below*) and considered by COREPER) are generally made by a 'qualified majority' — i.e. 54 votes, when each nation is allotted a quota and the United Kingdom has 10 out of a total of 76.

(c) *The Commission.* This comprises 17 Commissioners, representing (but totally independent of) the member states and appointed for four-year renewable terms. From among their number, a President is appointed by the European Council. Collectively, their decisions are taken by majority vote and, individually, they are responsible for defined areas of Community business (e.g. competition policy, fiscal harmonisation, regional policy, etc). Assisted by a large bureaucracy of 13,000 people divided into 27 directorates, the Commission initiates policy proposals for the Council of Ministers and oversees the implementation of Community law.

(d) *The European Parliament.* This comprises 518 members directly elected for five-year terms, with 81 United Kingdom MEPs representing specially created constituencies. They meet for about a week each month and sit, not as national delegations, but in European political groupings. The Parliament has no legislative power but its agreement must be obtained before new states can join the Communities, or association arrangements are made with non-member countries. It also has the right to address questions to the Council of Ministers and the Commission, about all aspects of the Community business. On receiving a Commission proposal, the Council reaches a common position by a qualified majority and, if adoption necessitates the co-operation of the Parliament, the decision is referred to that body — which can, by an absolute majority, propose amendments or effect outright rejection. Proposed amendments must be examined by the Commission, and the Council may then accept its revisions by a qualified majority, or amend by unanimous decision. If the Parliament rejects the common position outright, the Council can still vote it through, but only unanimously. In extreme circumstances, the Parliament could dismiss the entire Commission, by passing a vote of censure with a two-thirds majority and more than half of the total numbers voting in favour.

(e) *The European Court of Justice (ECJ)*. This comprises 13 judges, appointed by agreement among the member states, for renewable periods of six years, with partial replacement every three years. The Court has a President, elected by his fellow judges; it sits in Luxemburg and it should not be confused with the European Court of Human Rights (8:1). When a case comes before the Court, there is first a written stage and the President nominates one judge as *juge-rapporteur*, to prepare a preliminary report and to decide whether there is need for *instruction* (an investigation or hearing of evidence, carried out by the Court, a chamber thereof, or the *juge-rapporteur*). Then follows oral argument, after which an Advocate-General submits provisional conclusions. Having deliberated in private, the judges deliver a single judgment, with dissent not disclosed.

(f) *The Court of First Instance (CFI)*. Inaugurated in 1989, this sits in Luxembourg and has 12 judges, each representing one member state. Its purpose is to reduce the work-load of the ECJ, by conclusively determining the *facts* of a case, thus enabling the ECJ to rule exclusively on points of *law*. Initially, it will be mainly concerned with competition law but it will also arbitrate in disputes between Community institutions.

4. The secondary legislation of the Communities

In addition to the decisions of the ECJ (*below*), EC law comprises *primary legislation* (created by the relevant treaties and national statutes), together with the following *secondary legislation*, which emanates from the Council of Ministers and Commission:

(a) *The regulations*. Having general application, these are binding in their entirety and *directly applicable* in all member states (i.e. *without reference to their legislatures*). When they are in draft form ('*projets de lois*'), they are examined in the House of Commons by the Select Committee on European Legislation, which decides whether they are of sufficient importance to justify debate. However, the *Fourth Report from the Select Committee on Procedure*, 1988–89, found the scrutiny arrangements to be unsatisfactory and proposed that there should be regular debates prior to each twice-yearly meeting of the European Council. It also recommended the establishment of five new Special Standing Committees (Agriculture, Trade and Industry, Treasury, Transport and Environment, General) on European Community Documents, with the power to take evidence from, and to question, ministers.

(b) *The directives.* These are binding on the member states to which they are addressed, in respect of the results to be achieved — but the method of implementation is left to the national authorities. They are appropriate measures where there is a need to modify existing national legislation, but this would continue to bind British courts until the ECJ or House of Lords rules that the directive is paramount.

(c) *The decisions.* These are binding in their entirety on *those to whom they are addressed* — i.e. not only member states but also corporate bodies and individual persons. They are generally appropriate for implementing EC law, granting exceptions or authorisations, imposing fines or obligations, etc.

There are also 'recommendations' and 'opinions' which have no binding force.

5.   The judicial decisions of the Communities
The decisions of the ECJ relate mainly to:

(a) *Proceedings against member states.* These may be brought by the Commission for alleged violation of EC law, also by other member states, provided that they first refer the matter to the Commission. e.g. —

> *EC Commission v. United Kingdom (no.60/86)* (1989): The Court held that the prohibition of vehicles on British roads, unless equipped with a dim-dip lighting device (under the Road Vehicles Lighting Regulations 1984) contravened a Council directive. Manufacturers who followed

harmonisation requirements could not be unilaterally compelled to comply with additional regulations and the United Kingdom had thus failed to fulfil its obligations under the treaty.

(b) *Proceedings against EC institutions.* These may be brought by member states, other EC institutions and, in certain circumstances, by corporations or private persons. The procedure may be used to 'appeal for an annulment' of a regulation, directive or decision; to obtain a judgment to the effect that the EC Council or Commission had failed to act, when required to do so by a treaty; also to set aside (and possibly obtain compensation for damage caused by) an illegal act of an institution —

> *United Kingdom* v. *EC Council (no.131/86)* (1988): The United Kingdom sought the annulment of the Council Directive 86/113, which prescribed minimum standards for the protection of battery hens. The draft approved by the Council had contained a statement of reasons, which was subsequently altered by the general secretariat. The Court held that the Directive was void, because the amendments went beyond simple spelling and grammatical corrections.

> *EC Commission* v. *EC Council (no.45/86)* (1987): The Court held that the Council Regulations 3599/85 and 3600/85 (relating to tariff preferences for certain industrial and textile goods originating in third world countries) were void, as the precise legal basis upon which they were adopted was not stated.

(c) *Preliminary rulings.* When a case involving the validity and interpretation of the treaties (or acts of the institutions) reaches a national court from which there is no appeal (e.g. the House of Lords), it must first be referred to the ECJ for a *preliminary ruling*, unless the matter has previously been decided by the Court. When this judgment has been given, it is applied by the national court in deciding the case. Lower courts *may* (but do not have to) follow this procedure —

> *Marshall* v. *Southampton & South West Hampshire Area Health Authority (no. 152/84)* (1986): SWHAHA had terminated M's employment as she had passed the national pensionable age

(60 for women, 65 for men). She commenced proceedings in the Industrial Tribunal, claiming that her dismissal unlawfully contravened the Sex Discrimination Act 1975 and EC law. On appeal, the Court of Appeal sought a preliminary ruling from the ECJ, which held that such dismissal amounted to sex discrimination, contrary to the Council Directive 76/207. Subsequently, Parliament included a provision in the Sex Discrimination Act 1986, giving women the right of working until the same age as men, without prejudicing their pensions. In a like manner, as shown in 8:1(b), Parliament has enacted legislation resulting from decisions of the European Court of Human Rights.

Progress test 2

1.   What are the principal sources of English law?   **(1)**

2.   What is the significance of the sovereignty of Parliament?   **(1)**

3.   Outline the requirements for the recognition of a local custom.   **(2)**

4.   What is the importance of the European Communities Act 1972?   **(3, 4, 5)**

5.   Outline the nature of EC law which must be recognised in United Kingdom courts.   **(3, 4, 5)**

3
The creation of law

The creation of statute law

1. The enactment of statutes

A public bill introduced in the House of Commons is subject to the following procedure:

(a) *The first reading.* This is purely formal, with the Speaker calling the name of the sponsoring minister who bows from a seated position. The Clerk of the House reads out the short title of the bill, which can then be printed and published.

(b) *The second reading.* On the nominated day, the sponsoring minister moves 'that the bill be now read a second time' and he makes his main speech in favour of it. An opposition spokesman then speaks and the House debates the *main principles* of the bill. Alternative methods of achieving its purpose may be discussed but changes in its detailed provision are not permitted. Finally, the sponsoring minister (or another from the same department) sums up and the motion is normally carried. Non-controversial bills may have their second reading in a second reading committee.

(c) *The committee stage.* Most public bills now pass to a Standing Committee or Special Standing Committee — though some may be placed before a Committee of the Whole House. In each case, amendments (moved by any member of the committee) must be *in detail* and cannot affect the main principles (which were agreed at the second reading).

(d) *The report stage.* On completion of (c), the committee chairman reports the bill to the House — so that amendments can be considered, members not on the committee can put down amendments (subject to the Speaker's discretion), the government can propose changes or new clauses, and the bill can also be sent back to committee. Where a bill authorises any expenditure, a financial resolution is taken by the House at this stage. If the bill had its second reading in a second reading committee, the report stage may also be taken in that committee, which then reports to the House that it has considered the bill and whether it has been amended.

(e) *The third reading.* This enables the House to review the bill, as amended in committee or on report, but substantive alterations cannot be made.

(f) *The readings in the House of Lords.* The bill now goes through the same procedure in the House of Lords. However, the committee stage generally takes place in a Committee of the Whole House, as there are no standing committees — though sometimes suitable bills are sent to a Public Bill Committee. Even when no amendments have been made in committee, there may be a report stage and amendments can then be moved — also on the third reading. When the Lords make no amendment to a bill, it is presented for the Royal Assent but, if amended, it is returned to the Commons.

(g) *The considerations of the Lords' amendments.* The House of Commons considers the Lords' amendments and, if it disagrees with them, there is an exchange of messages between the two Houses. Should it prove impossible to resolve differences, the Commons could invoke the Parliament Acts 1911–1949, which limit the Lords' delaying power to one year, but this procedure has not been implemented since the passing of the 1949 Act.

(h) *The Royal Assent.* This is signified by letters patent under the great seal and signed by the monarch. Under the Royal Assent Act 1967, a bill is duly enacted if the assent is notified to each House separately by its Speaker or Acting Speaker. This has replaced a traditional ceremony which is normally used only at the end of a parliamentary session. Some statutes become effective immediately, some at a date specified in their text and others by *commencement orders*. These are in the form of statutory instruments (3:**3**), which may activate all or part of an Act and, as an example, the Easter Act 1928 (to make a fixed date for Easter) has never been brought into force.

2. The interpretation of statutes
It has been estimated that over 50 per cent of cases in the Court

of Appeal (and over 75 per cent in the House of Lords) relate to the interpretation of statutes. In this connection, the first function of a judge is to decide whether a statute is ambiguous and, if he does reach this conclusion, he must then determine which (if any) of a number of (often conflicting) rules should be applied. Reference may not be made to the parliamentary debates preceding the passing of the Act, or to its marginal notes (which are not inserted by parliamentary authority) but *see* **3:7(c)**. In general, interpretation is effected in accordance with the following principles:

(a) *The statutory provisions.* Consolidating previous legislation, the Interpretation Act 1978 prescribes the manner in which certain words or expressions are to be interpreted. *Unless the contrary intention appears in a particular statute*, words importing the masculine gender include the feminine (and vice versa); words in the singular include the plural (and vice versa); the measurement of any distance relates to a straight line on a horizontal plane; an expression of time connotes Greenwich Mean Time; a 'month' means a calendar month; to 'swear' includes to affirm and declare; a 'person' can be a body of persons (*see* **5:7**); 'writing' covers typing, printing, lithography, photography and any other modes of representing or reproducing words in a visible form. Where one statute repeals another and is then itself repealed, the original one is not revived. Where an Act empowers the making of delegated legislation, expressions in it have the meaning that they bear in the enabling Act. All of these provisions may nevertheless be confuted by a contrary intention —

> *Rolloswin Investments* v. *Chromolit Portugal* (1970): It was held that a limited company was *not* a 'person' within the meaning of the Sunday Observance Act 1677, as it was incapable of public worship and also a creature of law unknown in 1677.

(b) *The literal rule.* Initially the words of a statute must be applied according to their 'ordinary, plain and natural meaning'. Thus, if hardship results and there is no ambiguity, the only remedy is an amending statute (*see also* **3:6(b)**), —

> *Mesure* v. *Mesure* (1960): Under the Matrimonial Causes Act 1950, as amended, five years' continuous treatment for

mental illness was a ground for divorce, at the petition of the spouse. Mrs M had been in a mental hospital from 1952–59 but, for 11 weeks in 1955, she was in a sanatorium being treated for tuberculosis. It was held that no divorce could be granted, as the mental treatment was not continuous.

(c) *The golden rule.* This permits the literal application of words to be modified if it would lead to 'an absurdity or repugnancy or inconsistency with the rest of the instrument' —

Maddox v. *Storer* (1963): The Road Traffic Act 1960 made it an offence to drive at over 30 mph a vehicle 'adapted to carry more than seven passengers'. The appellant had been convicted of driving a minibus (originally constructed to carry 11 passengers, and not altered) at more than 30 mph. The offence was held to be proved as 'adapted' was taken to mean 'suitable or apt' (rather than 'altered so as to be apt').

(d) *The mischief rule.* If the literal of golden rules fail to assist the judge, he may seek the aid of the mischief rule, enunciated in *Heydon's Case* (1584). This entitles him to consider: the common law before the passing of the Act; the mischief and defect for which the common law failed to provide; and the remedy resolved by Parliament for curing the defect —

Elliott v. *Grey* (1960): Under the Road Traffic Act 1930, it was an offence for a car to be 'used on the road' without a valid insurance policy. The Court of Appeal held that a jacked-up car, with its battery removed, was being 'used on the road' as it could create a hazard.

(e) *The ejusdem generis rule.* This means that, where particular words are followed by general ones, the general words must be limited to the same kind as the particular —

Gregory v. *Fearn* (1953): The Sunday Observance Act 1677 provided that 'no tradesman, artificer, workman, labourer *or other person whatsoever* shall do or exercise any worldly labour, business or work of their ordinary callings upon the Lord's Day'. The Court of Appeal held that the words 'or other person whatsoever' must be construed *ejusdem generis* with those that precede them; thus the provisions did not apply to an estate agent (who was not a tradesman because he did not buy and sell things).

(f) *The presumptions of interpretation.* Unless a statute contains express provisions to the contrary, it may be presumed that: it applies to the United Kingdom as a whole; it does not bind the Crown; it does not restrict individual liberty or deprive anyone of property; it does not have retrospective effect; it does not infringe international law; it does not make any major constitutional change; it does not impliedly repeal another Act.

3. The delegation of legislative authority

As stated in 2:1(b), pressure of business and lack of time compel Parliament to delegate law-making authority — e.g. to local authorities (which issue by-laws) and to other bodies, such as the British Railways Board. However, by far the greatest delegation is to ministers, who are often empowered by statutes to issue *Statutory Instruments (SIs)*. These are particularly appropriate for framing regulations which require technical expertise (e.g. building construction, health, etc) or which may need to be easily and speedily amended (e.g. specifying financial limits) or which can be quickly introduced in a state of emergency. The widespread use of SIs may be appreciated from the fact that the number made in 1989 totalled nearly 2,500, compared with 46 statutes passed. Moreover, they are often subject to criticism as they receive far less publicity than Acts and they can place extensive legislative power in ministerial hands; there is consequently a need for:

(a) *The parliamentary control of delegated legislation.* The Statutory Instruments Act 1946 introduced a uniform procedure for numbering, printing, publishing and citing SIs. It also provided that most of them (i.e. those other than ones of a purely local nature) cannot come into force until 'laid' in both Houses — and, if this is not possible, the matter must be notified to the Lord Chancellor and the Speaker. Enabling Acts specify the manner in which a SI shall become effective — and this may be in three ways. In the first place, non-contentious and relatively unimportant Instruments (e.g. Commencement Orders) come into force on the date stated therein, without any special parliamentary procedure. Secondly, some SIs are subject to *negative resolutions*, whereby an

Instrument comes into force on the date stated unless either House (the Commons only in respect of SIs concerning financial matters) passes a motion calling for its annulment within a certain time (usually 40 sitting days). Thirdly, there are SIs subject to *affirmative resolutions,* whereby an Instrument *cannot* come into force unless a motion approving of it is passed within a specified period (usually 28 or 40 days). Only SIs of special importance are subject to this procedure — e.g. those imposing taxation or modifying the provisions of an existing statute. Instruments subject to negative or affirmative resolutions can only be annulled or approved — as neither House has the power of amendment, unless the enabling Act provides otherwise. In the Commons, debates on annulment or approval may take place on the floor of the House; more commonly, however, such matters are referred instead (on a motion by a minister) to one of the standing committees on Statutory Instruments (each usually comprising 17 members), provided that there are less than 20 objections. Scrutiny is also effected by a joint committee, comprising seven members from each House with a chairman from the Commons. It cannot consider the merits of any Instrument and it simply ensures that the exercise of the Minister's powers has been proper and within the provisions of the enabling Act. It reports on any imposition of a charge on the public revenue, any unjustifiable delay in publication or laying before Parliament, any exceeding of statutory authority, any 'unusual or unexpected' use of the powers, any need for elucidation, or any defect in drafting.

(b) *The judicial control of delegated legislation.* As shown in 2:1(b), the validity of a statute cannot be challenged in the courts. However, this protection does not apply to a SI (or any other form of delegated legislation), which can be declared void, invariably on the ground that its provisions are *ultra vires* — i.e. beyond the powers delegated in the enabling Act (*see* 8:11) —

> *R* v. *Secretary of State for Social Services, ex parte Cotton* (1985): Under the Supplementary Benefits Act 1976 the Secretary of State made a Statutory Instrument (SI 1985 No. 613), enabling him to fix the maximum amount of supplementary benefit payable to young people in board and lodging accommodation, the maximum period for which it would be payable and the geographical limits of the

board and lodging areas. The Court of Appeal held that
these provisions exceeded the powers granted by the Act.

The creation of the common law

4. The doctrine of judicial precedent

If a case to be decided is one without precedent (i.e. unlike any
previous case), the judge must decide it according to general
principles of law. By so doing, it can be said that he lays down an
original precedent, which later judges will follow if they encounter
a similar case. Some authorities consider that judges merely *declare*
the law (*jus dicere*), while others hold that they actually *make* it (*jus
dare*). It is contended that this implies that the facts of a case were
previously governed by no law, and it is like arguing that a piece
of land is valueless until it has been sold. The two opinions may be
resolved by saying that, in any proceedings, it can be assumed that
there is somewhere a rule of law which will cover the facts in
dispute but, once the judgment has been rendered, it may be
admitted that the new decision has modified the law. It should also
be emphasised that the judges' role in interpreting statutes has
given rise to a large body of case law. When a judgement is
delivered in court, the *ratio decidendi* (reason for the decision) is
stated and it is this that creates a *binding precedent* which *must* be
applied by the courts, described in 4:**11**, as follows:

(a) *The House of Lords.* Like all United Kingdom courts, this is
bound by the decisions of the European Court of Justice (2:**5**).
Formerly, the House regarded itself as being bound by its own
previous decisions but, under the *Practice Statement (Judicial
Precedent)* (1966), it can depart from previous decisions where it
appears right to do so.

(b) *The Court of Appeal (Civil Division).* This is bound by the
decisions of the House of Lords and also by *its own previous decisions.*
However, it was ruled in *Young* v. *Bristol Aeroplane Co* (1944) that
the Court would not be so bound if there were conflictions in the
previous decisions or if a previous decision was made *per incuriam*
(in error). In *Davis* v. *Johnson* (1979), by a majority of three to two,
the Court held that it could overrule any of its previous decisions
— with the Master of the Rolls, Lord Denning, arguing that
precedent comprised rules of *practice* (as opposed to law),

consequently the House of Lords could not stop the Court of Appeal from adopting its own practices; the Lords nevertheless rejected this contention.

(c) *The Court of Appeal (Criminal Division).* This is bound by decisions of the House of Lords and basically by *its own previous decisions.* However, in *R* v. *Newsome* (1970) Widgery, LJ said that a court of five judges might depart from an earlier view expressed by a court of three. The two Divisions of the Court of Appeal do not bind each other.

(d) *The Divisional Courts of the High Court.* These are bound by decisions of the House of Lords, the Court of Appeal and *their own previous decisions,* subject to the exceptions in *Young* v. *Bristol Aeroplane Co* (1944).

(e) *The ordinary courts of the High Court.* These are bound by decisions of the House of Lords, the Court of Appeal and Divisional Courts of the same Division. In *Huddersfield Police Authority* v. *Watson* (1947), Lord Goddard, CJ said that, as a matter of comity, a judge of first instance would follow the judgment of a fellow-judge, unless he was convinced that it was wrong. In *Colchester Estates* v. *Carlton Industries* (1984), Nourse, J stated that, if a decision by a judge of the High Court has been fully considered, but not followed, by another judge of the High Court, it is in the interests of certainty that the second decision should normally be considered as having settled the matter.

(f) *The county courts.* These are bound by decisions of the House of Lords, Court of Appeal and High Court.

(g) *The Crown Court and magistrates' courts.* These are bound by decisions of the House of Lords, Court of Appeal, Divisional Court of the Queen's Bench Division and High Court (in civil matters).

5.   The terminology of precedent

In the practical application of judicial precedent, the significance of the following terms needs to be appreciated:

(a) *Distinguishing.* The binding precedent of a higher court may sometimes be evaded by distinguishing — i.e. by finding some material differences between the facts of the earlier case and those of the one being decided.

(b) *Reversing.* A precedent may be reversed when a higher court allows an appeal *in the same litigation,* disagreeing with a point of law which decided the matter in the court below. This is illustrated at 5:**1(b)** in *Gouriet* v. *Union of Post Office Workers* (1977).

(c) *Overruling.* A precedent may be overruled when, *in a later case,* a higher court decides a similar matter differently. This does not, however, affect the decision in the earlier case because, under the maxim *res judicata* (in full — *res judicata pro veritate accipitur* — 'a thing adjudicated is received as the truth'), once an issue between parties has been litigated and decided, it cannot be raised again between the same parties —

> *Re Waring, Westminster Bank* v. *Burton Butler* (1948): Under a will, annuities (yearly payments of a certain sum of money) were left to A and B. In 1942, A was a party in an appeal to the Court of Appeal, which ruled that income tax must be deducted from the annuity. In 1946, in a similar case involving different parties, the House of Lords overruled the 1942 decision. Consequently, both A and B applied to the High Court to determine whether tax should be deducted from their annuities. It was held that only A was liable to deduction, on account of the 1942 case, which could not be re-opened.

6. The merits and demerits of judicial precedent
In examining precedent, consideration should be given to:

(a) *The advantages of the system.* The common law provides much greater detail than would be possible with a purely enacted system. Statutes assume the existence of the common law and are addenda and errata to it; they would be meaningless if it were swept away. On the other hand, when statute and common law conflict, it is the former that prevails — on account of the sovereignty of Parliament. Precedent also creates precision and consistency in the application and development of the law. It thus provides some degree of certainty, upon which people can base their conduct. Many continental systems have only persuasive precedent (*below*). Moreover, it can be said that precedent is based on factual situations of a practical nature and it creates flexibility — as a general *ratio decidendi* can be applied to numerous circumstances. It also has an aptitude for growth, as the needs of society alter.

(b) *The disadvantages of the system.* Critics argue that precedent restricts the discretion of judges; also that 'distinguishing' can lead to over-subtlety and artificiality. Not all decisions are reported — but this does not affect their validity as precedent; consequently, the law can be difficult to find, despite the introduction of computerised facilities. The common law also lacks ability to correct its own defects. Bad decisions are binding until reversed or overruled; sometimes, therefore, amendment has to be effected by a statute (which supervenes on account of the sovereignty of Parliament) —

> *Bowles* v. *Bank of England* (1913): B claimed from the Bank the sum of £52, which had been deducted as income tax, in accordance with a budget resolution in the House of Commons, prior to the passing of the Finance Bill. It was held that there could be no taxation without the authority of a statute, so the deduction was illegal. Parliament then passed the Provisional Collection of Taxes Act 1913, which gave temporary effect to House of Commons taxation resolutions.

7.   The forms of persuasive precedent

In addition to the binding form described above, there is also *persuasive* precedent, which need not be followed but which may be worthy of the court's consideration. It generally originates from:

(a) *The decisions of English courts not binding the one concerned*, also those of the Judicial Committee of the Privy Council, Scottish, Commonwealth and United States courts —

> *Westward Television Ltd* v. *Hart* (1968): In this tax case, the Court of Appeal held that the decision of the Scottish Court of Session in another case should be followed.

(b) *The obiter dicta of English judges.* The term *obiter dicta* covers explanations, illustrations, etc, said 'by the way' and not necessary to the decision of the case being tried.

(c) *The writings of leading authorities.* These have no binding force in themselves but they sometimes influence the decisions of judges. Theoretically, no living writer should be cited in an English court as an authority but, in practice, judges accord due weight to the opinions of eminent contemporaries —

R v. *Local Commissioner for Administration for the North & East Area of England* (1979): Local commissioners (8:**8(c)**) are statutorily empowered to investigate complaints of *maladministration* by local authorities and it was necessary for the Court of Appeal to determine the meaning of this word. Lord Denning MR adopted the definition suggested by Mr R.H.W. Crossman, Lord President of the Council, when relevant legislation was being considered in the House of Commons. Being prohibited from referring to the official reports of parliamentary debates (3:**2** *above*), the Master of the Rolls acquired the quotation from the writings of a leading constitutional lawyer.

(**d**) *The rules of Roman law.* Persuasive authority has been accorded to Roman law, notably Justinian's Digest, e.g. —

Tucker v. *Farm & General Investment Trust* (1966): In this case, relating to animals acquired on hire purchase terms, the Court of Appeal followed the Roman rule as to the ownership of the progeny.

The instigation of reform

8. The reform of the law

Law reform is initiated principally by the government, wherein proposed legislation is agreed by the Cabinet, drafted by the relevant ministry and considered by two main Cabinet Committees. The *Legislation Committee* examines draft bills (to ensure that they comply with Cabinet decisions) and watches their progress through Parliament. The chairman is the Lord President of the Council and meetings are generally attended by the Leader of the House of Commons and the departmental minister concerned. The *Future Legislation Committee* considers projected bills and prepares the programme for each parliamentary session. Private members' bills (2:**1(b)**) can also reform the law if they become statutes (e.g. the Control of Smoke Pollution Act 1989). In respect of law reform, the government is assisted by the following three part-time advisory committees and also a full-time Law Commission:

(**a**) *The Statute Law Committee (SLC).* Founded in 1868, this is presided over by the Lord Chancellor and the 24 members include the Attorney-General and the Lord Advocate (5:**1(b)**). It is concerned primarily with the form (rather than the content) of statutes and it therefore deals with *consolidation* (the amalgamation of existing Acts), rather than *codification* (the amalgamation of statute and case law). One example of its work has been the Taxes Management Act 1970.

(b) *The Law Reform Committee (LRC)*. Constituted in 1945 (from the former Law Revision Committee, created in 1934), this reports to the Lord Chancellor on civil law and it comprises five judges, four practising barristers, two solicitors and three academic lawyers. One example of its work is the Occupiers' Liability Act 1957 (18:**5**) and more recently its report on limitation periods led to the Latent Damage Act 1986.

(c) *The Criminal Law Revision Committee (CLRC)*. Created in 1959, this reports to the Home Secretary on criminal law. Its eighth and thirteenth reports led to the Theft Acts 1968 and 1978 (26:**1–9**), whilst a working paper on *Offences Relating to Prostitution* gave rise to the Criminal Justice Act 1982, which *inter alia* abolished imprisonment for women convicted of soliciting.

(d) *The Law Commission*. Constituted under the Law Commission Act 1965, this comprises two legal practitioners, two academics and a High Court judge as chairman, with a research staff and parliamentary draftsmen. Its duties comprise a continuous review of the law, codification, as well as recommendations for the repeal of obsolete enactments and the elimination of anomalies. It issues annual reports which are laid before Parliament and, unlike the advisory committees but subject to the Lord Chancellor's veto, it can itself decide what subjects to investigate. In practice, it issues working papers containing tentative proposals to interested parties and, in the light of their responses, it produces final reports — sometimes with draft legislation. To date it has made over 80 major reform recommendations, 80 per cent of which have resulted in legislation. Subjects have included the consolidation of family law (Family Law Reform Act 1969), the control of exclusion clauses in contract (14:**6**), liability in tort for interference with goods (19:**4**) and the law of blasphemy. Its report on *Conspiracy and Criminal Law Reform* led to the Criminal Law Act 1977, and its working paper *Offences against Public Order* resulted in the Public Order Act 1986, with the new statutory offence of riot.

Progress test 3

1. Describe the procedure for the enactment of a public bill.
(1)

2. Outline the rules governing the interpretation of statutes.
(2)

3. Consider any ways of improving the interpretation of statutes. **(2)**

4. Why and to whom does Parliament delegate legislative powers ? Assess the advantages and disadvantages of this system. **(3)**

5. Explain how the doctrine of judicial precedent operates. **(4)**

6. Do judges make the law — or merely declare it ?
(2, 4, 5, 6)

7. Examine the composition and functions of the Law Commission. **(8)**

8. Do you consider that existing arrangements for law reform are adequate ? **(8)**

4

The institutions of the law

The courts of first instance

1. The structure of the courts

The word 'court' can, in fact, have two possible connotations — as, in addition to being a place where justice is administered, it can also mean the judge(s) officiating there. Every court exercises *jurisdiction*, a term that can also have two meanings — it can signify either the power of the court to hear particular proceedings or, alternatively, the geographical area within which its jurisdiction can be enforced. The jurisdiction exercised by any court may be *original* (or *first instance* — i.e. the hearing of cases for the first time) or *appellate* (i.e. the hearing of appeals from lower courts). Basically the courts of England and Wales fall into two categories:

(a) *The courts of criminal jurisdiction*. These deal with infringements of the criminal law of the state (ranging from minor parking offences to murder, etc). First instance jurisdiction is exercised in the magistrates' courts and Crown Court (*below*).

(b) *The courts of civil jurisdiction*. These are concerned mainly with *litigation* — i.e. *actions* (legal disputes) between private parties, mostly in respect of contracts (*see* Part Two) and torts (*see* Part Three). As shown below, magistrates' courts deal with a few civil matters but first instance jurisdiction is exercised mainly in the county court and High Court.

2. The characteristics of criminal proceedings

The significant aspects of criminal proceedings are that:

(a) *The proceedings are initiated with a summons or a warrant.* A *summons* is a document from a court office requiring a person to attend before the court. A *warrant* is issued by a magistrate, after a written information upon oath, and it is addressed to a police officer, ordering him to bring the person named before the court. Warrants are used for serious offences or where a summons is ignored. Witnesses can be compelled to attend a magistrates' court by means of a summons or warrant but, in the Crown Court, a *witness summons* or *witness order* is used.

(b) *The Crown prosecutes the defendant,* with a view to *punishment.* Thus the form of citing cases is, e.g., *R* v. *Smith* (1990), where R stands for *Rex* (King) or *Regina* (Queen) and Smith is the defendant. Under the Prosecution of Offences Act 1985, most prosecutions are instituted by the *Crown Prosecution Service* (CPS), which employs a large number of barristers and solicitors, organised in local areas, each headed by a Chief Crown Prosecutor, and appointed by the *Director of Public Prosecutions* (DPP — 5:**1(c)**). The latter deals only with the most complex and sensitive cases (e.g. political, terrorist, official secrets, company fraud and race relations prosecutions). Having investigated a criminal offence, the police refer the matter to the CPS, which determines whether there shall be a prosecution. The decision is taken in the light of a Code, issued by the DPP, which provides that prosecutions shall not be brought unless 'there is a realistic prospect of a conviction'. Even when this exists, the question must then be considered as to 'whether the public interest requires a prosecution'. Other matters that must be taken into account include the likely penalty, the age and physical or mental condition of the alleged offender, the attitude of a complainant, etc. Prosecutions may also be instituted by government departments (e.g. the Commissioners of Customs and Excise) and by private persons — though, in these cases, it may be necessary to obtain consent and the DPP can take over the conduct of the prosecution at any stage.

(c) *The defendant is presumed to be innocent until proved guilty.* The prosecution must prove *beyond reasonable doubt* (which does not mean 'beyond the shadow of a doubt') that a criminal offence was committed and that the defendant was guilty of it. The onus normally rests on the prosecution throughout the trial and, in the relatively few circumstances where the burden of proving a fact rests on the defence, the standard of proof is 'on a balance of probabilities'.

(d) *The case cannot be discontinued,* without the leave of the court or a *nolle prosequi* entered by the Attorney-General (*see* 5:**1(b)**).

(e) *The Crown may pardon a crime.*

3.   The characteristics of civil proceedings
The significant aspects of civil proceedings are that:

(a) *The proceedings are initiated with a summons or writ.* County court proceedings are commenced with a *summons* (6:**4**) and the attendance of witnesses can be compelled with a *witness summons.* High Court proceedings are initiated with a *writ* (6:**2(a)**) and witnesses can be compelled to attend by the issue of a *subpoena* (a writ requiring attendance *under a penalty*).

(b) *The plaintiff sues the defendant,* seeking *redress.* Thus the form of citing cases is *Smith* v. *Brown* (1990), where Smith is the plaintiff and Brown the defendant.

(c) *There is generally no presumption favouring either party.* Civil cases are proved by *preponderance of evidence* and, at the beginning of a trial, the onus normally rests on the plaintiff. Nevertheless, as the case proceeds, the burden may shift and, even at the outset, it may sometimes rest on the defendant — e.g. where the maxim *res ipsa loquitur* applies in negligence (18:**7**).

(d) *The action may be withdrawn by the plaintiff at any time.*

(e) *The Crown cannot pardon a tort.*

Certain acts (e.g. causing injury or damage by careless driving) may give rise to both a criminal prosecution and also a civil action.

The courts of criminal jurisdiction

4.   The jurisdiction of the magistrates' court
In London and certain other places, courts are presided over by *stipendiary magistrates,* who are salaried barristers or solicitors of at least seven years' standing. In other magistrates' courts, however, there are 25,000 *Justices of the Peace* (JPs). They date back to the Justices of the Peace Act 1361 and they have no essential legal qualifications, but are simply required to undergo a short course of basic training. Furthermore, they are advised on matters of law and procedure by the *Clerk of the Court,* who should be a barrister or solicitor of at least five years' standing. JPs are

appointed on behalf of the Queen by the Lord Chancellor, to whom recommendations are made by local advisory committees. Any person or organisation may suggest candidates to an advisory committee which, in its turn, must ensure that each bench of magistrates is broadly representative of all sections of the community. JPs are paid only travelling, subsistence and financial loss allowances and, except in certain circumstances, they are transferred to a supplemental list at the age of 70. This administration of justice by lay men and women has been criticised on several grounds — notably the lack of uniformity in sentences. In 1989, e.g., a Consumers' Association survey showed that the average fine imposed for driving with excess alcohol was £44 in Carlisle and £317 in Billericay, Essex. Other criticisms relate to the absence of legal knowledge, with possibly a corresponding excess of influence by the clerks, a tendency to accept police evidence as indisputable, and the lack of suitable people with the necessary time to spare. On the other hand, merits derive from the close contact of JPs with everyday life and local conditions, the democratic value of associating lay persons with the administration of criminal law, the speedy provision of justice and economy for the state — bearing in mind that replacing lay magistrates with salaried judges would cost at least £100 million a year. Magistrates' courts exercise criminal jurisdiction in respect of offences committed by persons who have attained the age of 17 and, under the Magistrates' Courts Act 1980, these fall into three categories:

(a) *The offences triable only summarily.* Each year over a million relatively minor offences (representing more than 90 per cent of all crimes) are tried, without a jury, by benches of not less than three JPs. These decide whether the defendant is guilty and, if so, they award appropriate punishment. Many offences have stipulated penalties but, in the absence of these, the maximum is a fine of £2,000 and/or six months' imprisonment.

(b) *The offences triable only on indictment.* More serious offences are tried by a jury in the Crown Court where, as shown in 6:1(a), the proceedings commence with the reading of the *indictment*. This is a formal document specifying the offence(s) which the defendant is alleged to have committed; consequently they are known as *indictable* offences. Before they reach the Crown Court, however, a magistrates court must first carry out a preliminary investigation in what are called *committal proceedings*. The purpose of these is simply to determine whether a *prima facie* case (a case in which, *at first appearance*, there is some evidence in support of the charge) has been made out. If the magistrates decide that this is so, they commit the defendant (on bail or in custody) to the Crown Court for trial. The procedure differs from that of a summary trial in that there is no plea (e.g. 'not guilty') and, if discharged, the defendant may subsequently be charged again (*see* 6:**1(b)**). If all the evidence comprises written statements, and if the (or each) defendant is legally represented and does not plead that there is no case to answer, then the Magistrates' Courts Act 1980, s. 6, permits the court to commit the defendant(s) for trial without itself considering the evidence. To avoid prejudicing a subsequent trial, s. 8 of the same Act (as amended by the Criminal Justice (Amendment) Act 1981) makes it an offence to publish or broadcast in Great Britain details of committal proceedings, other than certain bare facts, unless the defendant requests that the restriction be lifted (e.g. to publicise the need for witnesses).

(c) *The offences triable either way.* Certain specified offences may be tried either summarily or on indictment. In such circumstances, a magistrates' court must first allow the prosecutor and the defendant to make representations concerning the mode of trial. It must then consider the nature and circumstances of the alleged offence, whether the punishment which it could inflict would be adequate, and any other relevant matters. Where it appears that summary trial is the more suitable alternative, the court must explain to the defendant that either he can consent to be so tried, or he can elect trial by jury. It must also point out to him that, if he is tried summarily and convicted, he may be committed to the Crown Court for sentence, if his past record merits greater punishment than the magistrates can inflict.

Not more than three JPs (at least one of whom must be a woman), selected from a special panel, form a *juvenile court*. This hears charges against children (under 14) and young persons (14–17), though murder or offences for which long imprisonment is appropriate necessitate committal for trial. The parent or guardian of the juvenile must attend and may be required to pay any fine. The public is excluded, the police do not wear uniform and the words 'conviction' or 'sentence' must not be used. Media reports must not identify a juvenile unless the court or Home Secretary directs otherwise.

5. The jurisdiction of the Crown Court

Jurisdiction in the Crown Court, which was created by the Courts Act 1971, is exercised by High Court judges, circuit judges and recorders; however, for appeals and proceedings on committal for sentence, they sit with two to four JPs. Currently, High Court judges are appointed from barristers of at least 10 years' standing; circuit judges must also have been barristers of 10 years' standing (or recorders of three years' standing), whilst recorders, who act as part-time judges, are appointed from barristers or solicitors of at least 10 years' standing. The courts' service is divided into six circuits: Midland and Oxford, North-Eastern, Northern, South-Eastern, Wales and Chester, Western. Each of these has towns designated as first-, second-, and third-tier centres. First-tier centres deal with both civil and criminal cases and are served by all three types of judges. Second-tier centres deal with criminal matters only, and the same applies to third-tier centres which are served by circuit judges and recorders. For the purposes of trial, criminal cases may be classified as follows:

(a) *The class 1 offences.* These must be tried by a High Court judge and they include murder and also contravention of the Official Secrets Acts 1911–1989.

(b) *The class 2 offences.* These must be tried by a High Court judge, unless released by a presiding judge (the High Court judge assigned to have particular responsibility for a circuit). They include manslaughter, abortion, rape, sexual intercourse or incest with a girl under 13.

(c) *The class 3 offences.* These may be tried by a High Court judge, circuit judge or recorder and they comprise all indictable offences other than those in classes 1,2 and 4; they also include robbery or assault with intent to rob, wounding or causing grievous bodily harm with intent.

(d) *The class 4 offences.* These may be tried by a High Court judge, circuit judge or recorder (but generally one of the last two) and they are mainly the offences which are triable 'either way'. They also comprise causing death by reckless driving, burglary and offences under the Forgery and Counterfeiting Act 1981.

With 60 per cent of defendants triable either way opting for jury trial, Home Office research in 1988 showed that Crown Courts were seriously overloaded. In 1989 the Lord Chancellor stated that, whereas the number of adult offenders had risen by 16 per cent between 1979 and 1987, the number committed to the Crown Court had increased by 69 per cent. A one per cent rise necessitated three court rooms and full-time judges if delay in bringing cases to trial (on average about 14 weeks) was not to get worse.

The courts of civil jurisdiction

6.   The civil jurisdiction of magistrates' courts
Magistrates' courts enjoy limited civil jurisdiction, comprising mainly:

(a) *The hearing of domestic proceedings.* Under the Magistrates' Courts Act 1980, ss. 65–74, members of a special panel of justices form a domestic court. This is empowered to make orders for: financial provision for parties to a marriage and children of the family; the custody of children under the age of 18 (also the supervision of, and access to, them); the committal of children to the care of a local authority; the protection of a party to a marriage or a child of the family (attaching, if necessary, a power of arrest). The public is excluded from domestic proceedings and there are restrictions on media reports.
(b) *The recovery of statutory debts.* Certain creditors authorised by statute (e.g. the collectors of taxes) may pursue their debtors in the magistrates' courts. All other creditors must seek recovery in the county court.
(c) *The granting of licences.* These include public houses, betting shops, etc.

7.   The jurisdiction of the county court
Throughout England and Wales there is a network of small

courts, divided into districts, each of which has one or more circuit judges assigned to it. There is also a District Judge (prior to 1991, a registrar) who can hear cases not involving more than £500, as a Small Claims Court. Herein, and without the aid of solicitors, parties can inexpensively bring and defend actions. The jurisdiction of a county court is limited to causes of action arising within its locality and, under the County Courts Act 1984 it currently consists principally of:

(a) *The common law jurisdiction.* This comprises actions in contract and tort (excluding libel and slander).

(b) *The real property jurisdiction.* This comprises actions for the recovery of possession of land, also disputes as to *title* (right to ownership).

(c) *The equity jurisdiction.* This relates to the administration of estates; the execution, declaration and variation of trusts; the foreclosure and redemption of mortgages; the maintenance and advancement of minors; the dissolution of partnerships; also relief against fraud or mistake.

(d) *The probate jurisdiction.* This comprises actions concerning the grant or revocation of probate (1:**4(b)**).

(e) *The admiralty jurisdiction.* Some county courts have jurisdiction in respect of damage received (or caused) by a ship; loss of life or personal injury sustained from defects or wrongful acts by personnel in a ship; loss of, or damage to, goods carried; salvage, towage and pilotage of ships, aircraft, etc.

(f) *The divorce jurisdiction.* Some county courts have jurisdiction to hear undefended divorce actions, and cases concerning adoption and guardianship.

(g) *The discrimination jurisdiction. See* 8:**7(a)–(b)**.

8. The jurisdiction of the High Court
The High Court has its headquarters at the Royal Courts of Justice in London but, under the Courts Act 1971, it may sit anywhere in England and Wales — normally at 24 first-tier centres. Under the Supreme Court Act 1981, the High Court comprises the following three Divisions:

(a) *The Queen's Bench Division (QBD).* Dealing with all civil matters which do not come within the ambit of the other two Divisions, the QBD comprises a number of ordinary courts, together with some specialist ones. In each of the ordinary courts there is to be found one High Court judge, with occasionally (but rarely) a jury, mainly hearing actions in contract and tort. There is also an *Admiralty Court* (handling maritime matters — e.g. collisions at sea and salvage) and a *Commercial Court* (dealing with mercantile documents, insurance, banking, etc). Like the other two Divisions, the QBD has a *Divisional Court*, wherein two or three High Court judges sit together, without a jury, and deal principally with: criminal appeals from the magistrates' courts by way of *case stated* (4:**10(a)**); applications for *judicial review* (7:**2(e)** and 8:**10**) and the writ of *habeas corpus* (7:**2(f)**), also appeals from the Solicitors' Disciplinary Tribunal (5:**3**). The administrative staff of the Division is headed by a number of barristers, known as *Masters*.

(b) *The Chancery Division*. This is headed by the *Vice-Chancellor* and its jurisdiction covers: contentious probate cases, partnerships, mortgages, trusts, administration of deceased persons' estates, rectification and cancellation of deeds, land law, company law and revenue matters. Many of the cases are not disputes but rather proposed courses of action requiring judicial approval. Included in the Division is the *Patents Court* (hearing appeals from the Comptroller-General of patents, designs and trade marks), whilst the *Divisional Court* hears appeals from county courts in bankruptcy matters. The administrative staff of the Division is headed by a number of solicitors, known as *Chancery Masters*.

(c) *The Family Division*. This is headed by the *President* and its jurisdiction covers: matrimonial causes (notably defended and complex divorce cases); adoption; wardship; guardianship of minors; title to property in the dispute between spouses; validity of marriages; presumption of death; and granting of probate or letters of administration. The *Divisional Court* hear appeals from magistrates' courts and county courts in family law matters. The administrative staff of the Division is headed by registrars.

In 1988, the *Report of the Review Body on Civil Justice* stated that much of the work in the High Court (notably the QBD) was of 'middling or low' significance and that this delayed the hearings of more substantial cases. It therefore recommended an enhancement of the county court's jurisdiction — limited to £5,000 in contract and tort, £30,000 in equity and £15,000 in probate. The resulting Courts and Legal Services Act 1990 empowers the Lord Chancellor to redistribute civil court work, in phased stages, so that the High Court can be reserved for judicial review and other specialist cases, together with general cases of particular complexity. Accorded wider powers to grant remedies, county courts can then deal more speedily and cost-effectively with lesser cases.

9. The jurisdiction of the Restrictive Practices Court
Established by the Restrictive Trade Practices Acts 1956–76 and the Restrictive Practices Court Act 1976, this court is served by both judges and lay members and it judicially examines:

(a) *Commercial conduct detrimental to consumers' interests.* The Fair Trading Act 1973 created the Monopolies and Mergers Commission (MMC) and also the office of Director General of Fair Trading. If it appears to the Director that a course of conduct in a business is unfair to consumers (or detrimental to their interest), he must endeavour to obtain an assurance that it will be discontinued. Should he not receive such a promise (or should it be broken), he may bring proceedings in the Restrictive Practices Court.
(b) *Resale price maintenance.* The Resale Prices Acts 1964–1976 declared void any contractual conditions by suppliers to establish a minimum resale price of goods, unless they have been specifically exempted by the Restrictive Practices Court.

See also 11:**6** and 12:**1(a)**.

The Courts of Appeal

10. The courts of criminal appeal
Appeals may be made against the decisions of the above courts and, in such circumstances, the party appealing is known as the *appellant*, whereas the other is termed the *respondent*. From criminal courts, appeals lie as follows:

(a) *From the magistrates' court.* There is a general right of appeal to the Crown Court on a point of law or fact but, if the defendant has pleaded guilty, appeal lies only against sentence. The Crown Court may confirm, vary or reverse the decision appealed against *or* may remit the matter with its opinion to the original court *or* may make such other order as it thinks fit. If either party to a proceeding before justices wishes to question *either* a conviction on a point of law *or* the Crown Court's decision on an appeal, he may apply to have the *case stated* in a Divisional Court of the QBD; it is also possible to apply for judicial review in the Divisional Court.

(b) *From the Crown Court.* Appeals by convicted persons lie to the Court of Appeal (Criminal Division) and, if they are against *conviction* on solely *a question of law*, they lie *as of right*. However, if an appeal is against conviction on a matter of *fact* (or *mixed law and fact*), the leave of the Court of Appeal, or a certificate from the trial judge, is necessary. An appeal against *sentence* (where the penalty is not one fixed by law) lies only by leave of the Court of Appeal. Appeals are heard by not less than three judges and the Court of Appeal (Criminal Division), which is headed by the Lord Chief Justice, comprises *Lords Justices of Appeal*, together with judges of the QBD (who may sit at the request of the Lord Chief Justice, after consultation with the Master of the Rolls).

(c) *From the Court of Appeal.* Appeal lies to the House of Lords — but only with the leave of the House or of the court below, if the latter has certified that *a point of law of general public importance* is involved, and that it is one which ought to be considered by the House of Lords. Under the Appellate Jurisdiction Act 1876, appeals to the House are heard by the *Lords of Appeal*. These comprise the Lord Chancellor, ex-Lords Chancellor, *Lords of Appeal in Ordinary* (i.e. persons who have held high judicial office and who are appointed to assist in the appellate functions of the House), and any other peers who hold (or have held) high judicial office (e.g. the Lord Chief Justice and the Master of the Rolls). The quorum is three and each peer delivers a separate judgment, with the verdict being a majority.

In 1989 the Court of Appeal quashed the convictions of the 'Guildford Four' (sentenced in 1974 to life imprisonment for causing five deaths in the bombing of two public houses), after it became apparent that misleading evidence had probably been given by Surrey police officers at their trial. In 1990 a new inquiry was instituted into the convictions of the 'Birmingham Six' (also sentenced in 1974 to life imprisonment for causing 21 deaths in the bombing of two public houses), after it was alleged that evidence had been fabricated by former members of a disbanded West Midlands Serious Crimes Squad. Miscarriages of justice can most often be attributed to false confessions, wrongful identification, perjury, police misconduct or bad defence tactics. There has consequently been much discussion about the powers of the Court of Appeal, which can currently deal with cases only on the basis of the evidence and submissions put before it. It has even been suggested that the Court might be empowered to initiate its own enquiries — possibly by means of a team of investigators attached to it.

11. The courts of civil appeal

From the civil courts appeals lie as follows:

(a) *From the magistrates' court.* There is no general right of appeal in civil matters and any right that does exist must originate in the statute that empowers the magistrates to make a particular order (e.g. a Divisional Court of the Family Division hears appeals in respect of separation, maintenance and adoption orders). However, either of the parties in civil proceedings may request to have a *case stated* to a Divisional Court of the QBD, on the grounds that the magistrates have acted erroneously on a point of law or in excess of their jurisdiction (*ultra vires — see* 8:11).

(b) *From the county court.* As shown in 4:8(b), appeals in bankruptcy are heard by a Divisional Court of the Chancery Division, whilst those concerning guardianship of minors lie to a Divisional Court of the Family Division. Otherwise, appeals from the county court lie to the Court of Appeal (Civil Division); this is headed by the Master of the Rolls and comprises the Lords Justices of Appeal together with High Court judges (who may sit at the request of the Lord Chancellor).

(c) *From the High Court.* From any Division appeal lies to the Court of Appeal (Civil Division) but leave must be obtained if the appeal has already been determined by a Divisional Court. Under the

Administration of Justice Act 1969, s. 12, a judge of the High Court may give a certificate for an appeal from his decision to go direct to the House of Lords (by-passing the Court of Appeal — a procedure known as 'leap-frogging'), if it involves a point of law of general public importance. The certificate can be granted only if the point of law relates to the construction of an Act or statutory instrument, or if it is covered by a previous decision of the Court of Appeal or House of Lords, and provided that both parties consent.

(d) *From the Restrictive Practices Court.* Appeal on any question of law lies to the Court of Appeal (Civil Division) in England and Wales, the Court of Session in Scotland, or the Court of Appeal in Northern Ireland.

(e) *From the Court of Appeal (Civil Division).* Appeal lies to the House of Lords, by leave of the Court or of the House, and leave will be granted only if a point of law of general public importance is involved.

The alternatives to the courts

12. The system of administrative tribunals

Many claims and disputes are nowadays settled by special tribunals which are quite separate from the courts of law. There are in fact over 2,000, of more than 50 different types, and terminology is remarkably confusing — as not all are actually named as 'tribunals' (e.g. the General Commissioners of Income Tax, hearing appeals against tax assessments). Furthermore, they are sometimes referred to as 'statutory tribunals', despite the fact that a few (e.g. the Criminal Injuries Compensation Board) were not constituted by Act of Parliament. More commonly, they are often termed 'administrative tribunals' (implying that they handle disputes involving government departments or public authorities); nevertheless, some are concerned only with problems between individuals (e.g. Rent Tribunals and Industrial Tribunals). The courts would be overburdened if they had to decide all the constantly recurring and relatively trivial problems heard by tribunals; moreover, the resulting need to increase the judiciary would cause a lowering of standards. Tribunals are subject to the Tribunals and Inquiries Act 1971 (which consolidated similarly-named Acts of 1958 and 1966) and they can be contrasted with courts of law in the following ways:

(a) *The composition of tribunals.* This varies greatly but many comprise a chairman, a clerk (often a civil servant from the relevant government department) and a number of (normally) unpaid lay members. From experience, these generally acquire an expert knowledge of their particular subject-matter (not necessarily possessed by judges) and they may include persons with relevant qualifications (e.g. doctors or engineers). The 1971 Act requires that chairmen of specified tribunals must be selected from a panel of persons appointed by the Lord Chancellor, and no minister, other than the Lord Chancellor, may remove a member of a specified tribunal from office, except with the consent of the Lord Chancellor or the Lord President of the Court of Session in Scotland.

(b) *The procedure of tribunals.* Sittings may be in public or private; legal representation is generally allowed; evidence is rarely taken on oath; adjudication is impartial — but wide discretionary power can cause decisions to be unpredictable and inconsistent. The procedure is speedy, cheap, flexible and informal. Decisions are achieved quickly and delays are minimised; no fees are usually payable and the wide discretionary powers of a tribunal free it from the rigidity of judicial precedent. Litigious procedure does not provide the right atmosphere for the implementation of social schemes and the greater informality of a tribunal is less intimidating to the individual. Tribunals are not limited to considering only the information provided by the parties, but they can themselves play an active part in ascertaining facts.

(c) *The rights of appeal.* If requested to do so, tribunals must give reasons for their decisions and many have statutory provision for appellate procedure. Under the 1971 Act, if a party to proceedings before specified tribunals is dissatisfied in point of law, he may appeal to the High Court or require the tribunal to state a case for the opinion of the High Court. *Notwithstanding the provisions of any previous Act,* the High Court may supervise the proceedings of *any* tribunal by way of judicial review (8:**10**).

(d) *The supervision of tribunals.* Under the 1971 Act, supervision is exercised by a *Council on Tribunals.* This consists of 10 to 15 members appointed by the Lord Chancellor and the Secretary of State for Scotland, having also a Scottish Committee. The Parliamentary Commissioner (8:8(a)) is an *ex officio* member of both the Council and the Committee. The Council's jurisdiction covers England, Scotland and Wales, and its principal functions are: to review and report on the constitution and working of *certain* tribunals specified in a Schedule to the Act; to consider and report on matters referred to it concerning *any* tribunal; also to be consulted before procedural rules are made for any of the scheduled tribunals. However, *it has no say in the issues to be decided and it cannot overrule the decisions which are made.*

13. The process of arbitration

To provide an alternative to litigation, many commercial contracts contain an *arbitration agreement,* requiring dispute between the parties to be referred for determination to one or more persons called *arbitrators.* If one party to such an agreement starts proceedings in the ordinary courts, before submitting to arbitration, the other party may apply to the court to stay the action.

However, under the Consumer Arbitration Agreements Act 1988, s. 1, this does not apply to anyone who enters into a contract 'as a consumer' (i.e. not in the course of a business and where goods sold are ordinarily supplied for private use or consumption), unless he gave written consent to arbitration after differences arose *or* he has submitted to arbitration *or* the court makes an order. In addition to arbitration agreements, various statutes also provide for the settlement of specified kinds of disputes by arbitration — regardless of any objection by the parties. Although arbitrators' fees can be high, arbitration involves no court fee, expense in preparing pleadings or necessity for legal representation. Proceedings are private and informal, with the time and place of the hearing arranged to suit the convenience of the parties. No delay is incurred in waiting for the case to be called and the decision is immediate. Furthermore, the fact that an arbitrator can have special expertise in the subject-matter of a dispute can obviate the time-consuming calling of witnesses, necessary to provide a judge with basic information. Nevertheless, if the basis of a dispute is complex, normal court procedure might provide a more satisfactory solution; moreover, if the unsuccessful party challenges the arbitrator's decision (*see* **(d)** *below*), litigation could then ensue and negate financial economy. Arbitration can be contrasted with litigation in the following ways:

(a) *The appointment of arbitrators*. An arbitration agreement may specify arbitrators by name or supply a method of selection (e.g. appointment by a relevant trade association). Under the Administration of Justice Act 1970, provision is made for judges of the Commercial Court to act as arbitrators in commercial disputes. The circuit judges and district judges in county courts may also so act.

(b) *The procedure of arbitration*. Arbitrators are not judges or court officials but hearings must be conducted in a judicial manner, in accordance with the Arbitration Act 1950, which empowers arbitrators to administer oaths, and the parties to seek writs of subpoena. Where reference is made to two arbitrators, they may at any time appoint an *umpire* to settle differences between them — and they must do so immediately if they cannot agree. Where reference is made to three arbitrators, the decision of any two is binding, unless a contrary intention was expressed in the arbitration agreement. An arbitrator's decision is called an *award* and, if the unsuccessful party fails to comply with it, he can be sued on it — or the successful party can seek leave of the High Court for the award to become an order of the court. The Administration of Justice Act 1977 provides that, if the sum involved is within a county court's jurisdiction, it is recoverable as if payable under an order of that court. An application to the High Court would preclude one to the county court, and vice versa.

(c) *The determination of points of law*. Under the Arbitration Act 1979, a party may, at any time during the proceedings, and with the consent of the arbitrator or of all the other parties, apply to the High Court for the determination of a question of law. However, such an application will be entertained only if it might produce substantial savings in costs to the parties and provided that the question of law is one on which leave to appeal (*see* **(d)** *below*) would be likely to be given. Appeal from the High Court's decision lies to the Court of Appeal only with the leave of the High Court, which must certify that the point of law is one of general public importance, or one which should be considered by the Court of Appeal for some special reason.

(d) *The right of appeal.* In general, an arbitral award is final (*res judicata* — 3:5(c)). However, with the consent of all the other parties or with leave of the court, any party may appeal to the High Court on a question of law. Leave of the court will be granted only if the determination of the question could substantially affect the rights of one or more of the parties and (with certain exceptions), provided that they had not entered into an 'exclusion agreement', precluding a right of appeal. The High Court may confirm, vary or set aside an award, and also remit it with an opinion to the arbitrator for his reconsideration within three months. Appeal from the High Court's decision lies to the Court of Appeal on the same conditions as in **(c)** above.

Progress test 4

1. Compare and contrast the proceedings in criminal and civil courts of first instance. **(1, 2, 3)**

2. Comment critically upon the role of magistrates in the administration of justice. **(4,6)**

3. Outline the organisation and jurisdiction of the Crown Court. **(5)**

4. Consider the functions and value of the county courts. **(7)**

5. Critically examine the work of the High Court. **(8)**

6. Assess the role of the Court of Appeal. **(10, 11)**

7. A is charged with committing murder. Describe the courts before which A may appear, assuming he takes every opportunity of appealing against conviction. **(4, 5, 10)**

8. B purchased a motor-cycle from C and discovered it to be unroadworthy. Advise B as to the courts to which he may apply, in order to pursue a claim against C. **(7, 8, 11)**

9. Explain the role of tribunals in the English legal system and assess the importance of the Tribunals and Inquiries Act 1971. **(12)**

10. Assess the value of arbitration, as an alternative to judicial trial, and consider the extent to which the High Court exercises supervision over arbitration. **(13)**

5

The personnel of the law

The judicial and legal offices

1. The principal offices of the law

Three principal legal offices in England and Wales are described below and it should be appreciated that the Lord Chancellor and Law Officers are political appointees — i.e. leading lawyers who support the party in power and who lose office if there is a change of government; however, the Director of Public Prosecutions is non-political and does not lose office.

(a) *The Lord Chancellor.* The Lord Chancellor is appointed on the recommendation of the Prime Minister, who is not required to consult the House of Lords. As a member of the Cabinet, he is the government's chief legal and constitutional adviser. He is the holder of the Great Seal, which authenticates documents such as letters patent. In the legislature, he presides over the House of Lords (sitting on the woolsack) but, unlike the Speaker in the Commons, he may speak as a Minister of the Crown (standing at the despatch box) and he may also participate in debates (standing unwigged beside the woolsack). As head of the judiciary, he presides over the House of Lords, as the final Court of Appeal, and also the Judicial Committee of the Privy Council. He is president of the Supreme Court of Judicature, the Court of Appeal and the Chancery Division. He nominates the *puisne* ('younger', i.e. ordinary) High Court judges, circuit judges, recorders, Queen's Counsel and stipendiary magistrates. On behalf of the Crown, he appoints JPs and district judges. He is chairman of the committee that makes rules of procedure for the Supreme Court and he has responsibilities in respect of law reform (3:8), tribunals (4:12), legal aid (7:5) and also the organisation of the courts system, including the summoning of juries.

(b) *The Attorney-General.* The Attorney-General is one of the four *Law Officers of the Crown* — the other three being the Solicitor-General, the Lord Advocate (in Scotland) and the Solicitor-General for Scotland. They are appointed by letters patent and are normally members of the House of Commons (but not in the Cabinet). The Attorney-General's main functions are as follows:

(*i*) He advises the government on points of law and scrutinises draft bills.

(*ii*) He is an *ex officio* member of the Senate of the Inns of Court and the Bar (5:**3(a)**).

(*iii*) He sometimes prosecutes personally in important criminal cases. He supervises the work of the Director of Public Prosecutions and his consent is necessary before certain prosecutions (e.g. under the Official Secrets Acts 1911–1989) can be initiated.

(*iv*) He can stop trials on indictment by entering a *nolle prosequi* (an undertaking to forbear from proceeding).

(*v*) He is empowered by the Criminal Justice Act 1972, s. 36, to seek the opinion of the Court of Appeal (Criminal Division) on a point of law, after an acquittal on indictment. The matter can thence be referred to the House of Lords, and by this means the common law can be altered for the future — but the acquittal itself cannot be affected.

(*vi*) He can represent the Crown in civil proceedings and, in certain circumstances (e.g. the infringement of public rights), he may bring what is termed a *relator action* at the request and expense of a private person. This is a means of overcoming the problem of *locus standi* — i.e. the question as to whether or not someone has sufficient 'interest' (i.e. practical involvement) in a matter to be allowed by the court to sue for a remedy. Consent to a relator action is within the Attorney-General's discretion, the exercise of which is not subject to supervision by the courts —

Gouriet v. *Union of Post Office Workers* (1977): Two Post Office trade unions announced that they would be calling on their members to boycott mail for South Africa. As this appeared to constitute a criminal offence, G sought a relator action for an injunction and, when the Attorney-General refused his consent, G sued in his own name. Reversing the High Court decision of Stocker, J, the Court of Appeal held that he was entitled to do so and granted interim injunctions (7:**2(b)**). Reversing this decision, the House of Lords held that, as G did not have any special interest, he was not entitled to initiate proceedings in his own name.

(*vii*) He can refer to the Court of Appeal (with its leave) a Crown Court sentence which he considers to be too lenient (Criminal Justice Act 1988, ss. 35–6); any sentence which the Crown Court is empowered to pass could then be substituted for it.

(c) *The Director of Public Prosecutions (DPP).* The holder of this office must be a barrister or solicitor of at least 10 years' standing. He is appointed by the Home Secretary and aided by Assistant Directors, and a civil service staff. As shown in 4:**2(b)**, he heads the Crown Prosecution Service but also deals personally with complex and sensitive cases. The DPP is the only authorised prosecutor for certain offences against public order and good government (e.g. bribery and corruption, contravention of the Official Secrets Acts 1911–1989, etc) and his consent is necessary before some prosecutions (e.g. under the Bankruptcy Acts) can be initiated. When directed to do so by the Divisional Court or Court of Appeal, the DPP appears for the Crown or the prosecutor in criminal appeals from the Crown Court, Divisional Court or Court of Appeal. He may also take over the conduct of private prosecutions at any stage.

In addition to the Lord Chancellor and Attorney-General, another member of the government with responsibilities relating to the administration of justice is the Home Secretary. He is concerned principally with criminal law, public order, penal policy, the treatment of offenders and the prison service, the police, the protection of civil liberties, etc. It can therefore be seen that benefit might possibly be gained from combining currently divided responsibilities. In view of the fact that the Lord Chancellor's department is not subject to House of Commons' scrutiny, it has often been suggested that there is a need for a unified *Ministry of Justice*, with the responsible minister sitting in the Commons. The main arguments against such a department centre around the fact that it might lead to the administration of justice becoming too politicised.

2. The characteristics of the judiciary

The qualifications required of High Court judges, circuit judges and recorders have been outlined in 4:**5**. To ensure the impartial administration of the law, it is clearly desirable that the judiciary should enjoy a high degree of independence — notably in respect of:

(a) *The government.* As shown above, judicial appointments are made on the recommendation of the Lord Chancellor (the Prime Minister in the case of the Lord Chief Justice and the Master of the Rolls), but political considerations play no real part in the nominations — except with that of the Lord Chancellor himself and, to a certain extent, lay JPs. With the exception of the Lord Chancellor, all senior members of the judiciary retire at 75 and, up to that age, they hold office *quamdiu se bene gesserint* (during good behaviour), being removable only by the Monarch on an address by both Houses of Parliament. Circuit judges and recorders may be removed by the Lord Chancellor on the grounds of misbehaviour or incapacity. Once appointed, judges cannot be controlled by the government, or even required to implement its wishes; conversely, as already illustrated in 1:**7(a)** and 3:**3(b)**, they enforce the law against ministers and their departments.

(b) *The legislature.* Judges (but not JPs) are excluded from membership of the House of Commons. In order to preclude parliamentary criticism or control, judicial salaries are not subject to annual debate (unlike many other forms of national expenditure) and they are sufficiently high to avoid any question of corruption. Parliament will not debate any matter which is *sub judice* (awaiting, or in course of, trial) and, unless there is a substantive motion, 'reflections must not be cast in debate upon the conduct of judges' (Erskine May).

(c) *The public.* Under the Habeas Corpus Act 1679, judges may be sued for a penalty of £500 if they wrongfully refuse to issue a writ of *habeas corpus* (7:**2(f)**) in vacation but, with this exception, they are completely immune from civil or criminal proceedings in respect of acts done by them in the exercise of their judicial functions, and within the limits of their jurisdiction, even if they have acted maliciously or mistakenly —

> *Sirros* v. *Moore* (1974): Being mistaken as to his jurisdiction, a circuit judge refused an appeal against a deportation order and required the appellant to be detained. *Habeas corpus* was granted and the appellant sued the judge, as well as the arresting police officer, for false imprisonment. The Court of Appeal held that the detention was invalid, but that the judge, and police officers acting on his instructions, were immune from liability.

It is a common law offence of *contempt of court* to 'utter in court disparaging or offensive words to the judge, or to utter such disparaging remarks out of court, concerning judges of the superior courts in relation to their office or otherwise'. Contempt of court also covers failure to comply with an order of the court, and the Contempt of Court Act 1981 makes it a statutory offence to publish anything (by way of speech, writing, broadcast, etc) that tends to interfere with the course of justice in particular legal proceedings, regardless of intent to do so. This does not preclude fair and accurate reports of legal proceedings held in public, published contemporaneously and in good faith. The Act likewise makes it an offence to obtain, disclose or solicit details of a jury's deliberations; also, without leave, to bring a tape recorder into court, or to publish recordings made. *See* 8:6(c).

The profession of the law

3.   The branches of the legal profession

It is an important characteristic of the English legal system that lawyers are controlled by autonomous bodies and are therefore not state officials. A second vital facet is the fact that law reports are published by independent organisations. For over six centuries the legal profession in England and Wales has been divided into two distinct branches:

(a) *The barrister*. The training, call and professional practice of barristers are controlled by the *Senate of the Inns of Court and the Bar*. There are four Inns of Court — Lincoln's Inn, Inner Temple, Middle Temple, Gray's Inn. A barrister's training commences with an *academic stage*, which is completed by gaining a second-class honours degree in law (including six specified subjects). However, other graduates may qualify by gaining a recognised Diploma in Law. Having been admitted to one of the Inns of Court, students must then undertake a one-year *vocational stage* of training, carried out by the *Council of Legal Education* (appointed by, and subject to the control of, the Senate), which sponsors the *Inns of Court School of Law*. Having completed both stages, also having 'kept terms' (by dining 24 times in the hall of their Inn), students may then be 'called to the Bar' but, before they can practise, they must complete a year's *pupillage* in the chambers of an established barrister. Currently, barristers do not deal directly with their clients — but only through solicitors, by whom they are 'briefed'. They may plead in court at all levels, though some spend most of their time in chambers, drafting opinions. After a period of generally not less than 15 years, a barrister may apply to the Lord Chancellor to 'take silk' and become a Queen's Counsel (QC).

(b) *The solicitor.* The training, admission and professional practice of solicitors are controlled by the *Law Society*, under the Solicitors Act 1974. A solicitor's training commences with an *academic stage*, which is completed by acquiring an approved law degree. However, non-graduates over 25 with considerable experience and exceptional ability in an academic, professional, business or administrative field may qualify by passing an examination in eight law subjects. Having enrolled with the Law Society, students must then undertake a *professional stage* of training. This comprises a nine-month course for the final examination and service under *articles of clerkship* with a practising solicitor for two years. On fulfilling these requirements, candidates may apply to have their names placed on the roll but, in order to practise, they must obtain from the Law Society a practising certificate, which has to be renewed annually. Solicitors deal directly with their clients, from whom they receive 'instructions', and their work includes the conveyancing (legal transfer) of property, the drawing up and probate of wills, the preliminary conduct of litigation, the giving of legal advice on a wide variety of subjects, and the representation of clients in court. Hitherto, they have enjoyed a right of audience only in magistrates' and county courts, the Crown Court (on appeals or committals for sentence from magistrates' courts) and the High Court (in formal and unopposed proceedings). In their practices, solicitors generally employ clerks who are not under articles, but who can qualify for membership of the Institute of Legal Executives.

Currently, complaints against barristers are made to the *Professional Conduct Committee,* which refers *prima facie* cases to the Senate Disciplinary Tribunal, whose decisions are subject to pronouncement by the individual Inns. Barristers are not liable to actions for negligence by their clients in respect of work performed in court, or intimately connected with it. Complaints against solicitors are investigated by the *Solicitors Complaints Bureau* and serious cases of misconduct are referred to the *Solicitors Disciplinary Tribunal.* Complainants wishing to pursue negligence claims can be put in touch with a Negligence Panel, which should overcome the problem of solicitors possibly being unwilling to act in litigation against fellow-solicitors. A *lay observer* has hitherto handled allegations by complainants who are still dissatisfied after going through the Bureau, whilst a *Solicitors Compensation Fund* makes payments when solicitors misappropriate clients' money. In 1989 complaints to the Bureau totalled 18,000 (with discipline imposed in about 2,000 cases), the lay observer had a backlog of 400 cases at the end of the year and the Compensation Fund paid out £14.6 million.

4.   The reform of the legal profession

The Courts and Legal Services Act 1990 has made provisions in respect of:

(a) *The rights of audience.* Existing rights of barristers and solicitors are preserved, and their respective professional organisations (the General Council of the Bar and the Law Society) are specifically authorised to grant these rights. Decisions on the extension of rights of audience can be taken by the Lord Chancellor and the four senior judges, following advice from an *Advisory Committee on Legal Education and Conduct.* This is an independent body, chaired by a senior judge and comprising two practising barristers, two practising solicitors, two teachers of law and eight lay members.

(b) *The conducting of litigation.* Professional bodies can be given the power to grant to practitioners the right to conduct litigation. Decisions as to which bodies should have this right are taken by the Lord Chancellor and the four senior judges on advice by the

Advisory Committee. The question as to whether any person should be granted a right of audience or a right to conduct litigation is determined by whether he has qualifications appropriate to the court or proceedings in question, and also whether he belongs to a professional or other body which has rules for standards of conduct appropriate for the proper and efficient administration of justice. With the exception of family and criminal law cases, restrictions have been removed in respect of clients' ability to negotiate 'no win – no fee' agreements with their legal advisers.

(c) *The applications for probate.* The sole rights of barristers and solicitors to prepare applications for the grant of probate are subject to relaxation. Most banks, building societies and insurance companies could undertake such business, provided that they agree to have a complaints-handling system conforming to requirements specified by the Lord Chancellor. The latter can extend the right to other suitable bodies on the advice of the Advisory Committee, and after consultation with the President of the Family Division.

(d) *The right to conveyancing.* The right to conveyancing (hitherto enjoyed by solicitors) can be extended to banks, building societies and insurance companies, subject to safeguards against unfair competition and conflicts of interest. New practitioners have to be approved by an *Authorised Conveyancing Practitioners Board* and must comply with statutory requirements, including regulations made by the Lord Chancellor concerning competence and conduct. Appeals against rejection by the Board are heard by a *Conveyancing Appeal Tribunal,* whence appeal on a point of law lies to the High Court. The Board is required to institute a system of dealing with individual complaints against practitioners.

(e) *The appointments to the judiciary.* Eligibility criteria for judicial appointments are being revised to reflect the scope for the grant of extended rights of audience to practitioners other than barristers.

(f) *The investigation of complaints.* A *Legal Services Ombudsman* has been appointed to monitor the way in which the different professional bodies investigate complaints — with the ability to recommend (but not award) compensation. The barristers' immunity from actions in respect of work in court is being extended to all advocates.

The adjudication of fact

5.   The functions of juries

A clear distinction must be drawn between *law* and *fact*. For example, if a person is charged with theft, it is a question of *law* as to what constitutes theft (26:1) and whether the alleged conduct would amount to theft. Conversely, it is a question of *fact* as to whether a theft has actually been committed and, if so, whether it is the defendant who has committed it. In all trials where there is a jury, the judge gives decisions on points of law, whereas the jury decides on matters of fact (in the light of the law determined by the judge). Juries are to be found in:

(a) *The criminal courts.* Indictable offences are tried in the Crown Court by juries of 12 persons, who may receive allowances for subsistence, travel, loss of earnings, etc. Under the Juries Act 1974, as amended, anyone between the ages of 18 and 70 who is registered as an elector, and who has resided in the United Kingdom, Channel Islands or Isle of Man for at least five years since the age of 13, is liable for jury service unless he or she is ineligible, disqualified or excused as of right. Persons who are *ineligible* include: judges, magistrates, barristers, solicitors, court officers, coroners, police, prison and probation officers, priests of any religion, vowed members of religious communities and certain sufferers from mental illness. Persons who are *disqualified* (under the Juries (Disqualification) Act 1984) include anyone who has in the preceding 10 years served any part of a sentence of imprisonment, youth custody or detention, *or* received a suspended prison sentence, detention order or community service order, *or* who has been placed on probation in the preceding five years. Persons who are *excusable as of right* include: members and officers of the Houses of Parliament, full-time serving members of HM Forces, registered and practising members of the medical, dental, nursing, veterinary and pharmaceutical professions and anyone who has served on a jury within the preceding two years. If, through death, illness or discharge, the number of jurors is reduced, the Juries Act 1974, s. 16, permits the trial to continue, provided that the number remaining is not less than nine. This does not apply in the case of murder unless both the prosecution and the defence assent. The verdict of a jury is explained in 6:1(h).

(b) *The civil courts.* High Court juries comprise 12 persons, selected as for criminal cases and with similar provisions for majority verdicts. The Supreme Court Act 1981, s. 69, provides that jury trial may be ordered, on the application of any party to the action, in cases of fraud, defamation, malicious prosecution and false imprisonment. In other cases, the court has a discretion to order that an action be tried by a jury — though, in practice, this is seldom done and generally cases are heard by a judge alone. There are no juries in the Chancery Division or in the Admiralty Court, but either party may apply for a jury in probate or defended divorce cases. In county courts, juries comprise eight members but are not normally encountered.

6. The criticisms of jury trial

It is claimed that, in criminal trials, the jury system provides disinterested adjudication at a time when judges are sometimes seen as representing a limited social background. Juries are also thought to be free from the kind of prejudice which a judge may acquire from constant contact with the courts. Yet another argument is that a jury provides an effective check on the arbitrary use of power by the state; nevertheless the system does not lack criticism — notably in respect of:

(a) *The composition of juries.* With no literacy requirement for jury service, the criterion is simply an understanding of spoken English and this would clearly be insufficient in any cases involving documents. In 1986 the *Report of the Fraud Trials Committee* (under the chairmanship of Lord Roskill) recommended that complex fraud cases should be tried, not by a judge and jury, but by a Fraud Trials Tribunal, comprising a judge and two lay-members with appropriate professional qualifications. In 1990, however, it was contended that the effectiveness of a jury in such circumstances was vindicated by the conviction of the four defendants in the lengthy *Guinness* trial. Sometimes discretion to excuse potential jurors is exercised too widely, with long cases often tried by predominantly unemployed and retired persons. Even the statutory requirements for disqualification are not fully effected — with Government research having revealed that 5 per cent of jurors have criminal records. As shown in 6:**1(c)**, the defence or prosecution can challenge any prospective juror 'for cause' (e.g.

involvement in the case, disqualification, physical incapacity, etc.). Additionally, the prosecution can prevent a person from sitting as a juror by exercising in open court the right to request a 'stand by'. Another practice, utilised generally by the prosecution, is that of 'jury checks' (or 'vetting') whereby, in cases involving national security and terrorism, the panel of jurors is subjected to a limited investigation. Both stand by and jury checks must comply with guidelines issued by the Attorney-General (*Practice Note (Jury: Stand by : Jury checks) (1983)* updated 1989). One proposition which has been canvassed, but which has received little support, is that of forming panels of professional jurors.

(b) *The decisions of jurors.* Allowing for pleas of guilty and acquittals on a judge's direction, juries return verdicts in about 30 per cent of Crown Court cases. It is not impossible for individual jurors to be swayed by ignorance, boredom with the whole process, prejudice against other social groups, antagonism towards the police, disagreement with the law or sentiments about a particular defendant. Verdicts are not always explicable but no firm evidence is available concerning the deliberations upon which they are based (*see* 5:2(c)). A popular impression is that juries are 'too prone to acquit' — a belief reinforced by a Home Office publication *Managing Criminal Justice* which suggested that acquittals by magistrates are about half those of juries. However, an Oxford Penal Research Unit Study in 1972 attributed a high proportion of acquittals to the inadequacy of the prosecution, rather than perverseness by the jury. In 1979 research in Birmingham by John Baldwin and Michael McConville categorised 36 per cent of acquittals and 5 per cent of convictions as 'questionable', with trial judges being in agreement with 85 per cent of the verdicts. Emphasising the significance of disagreement between judge and jury, research in Chicago in 1966 by Harry Kalven and Hans Zeisel covered 3,576 cases and yielded a total agreement rate of 75.4 per cent. Of the remaining 24.6 per cent, 5.5 per cent represented hung juries, while approximately 19 per cent related to acquittals and 3 per cent to convictions.

The law of persons

7. The concepts of legal personality

In law, the term 'person' means any entity which is capable of having rights and obligations (notably the ability to sue, to be sued and to own property). There are two classes — *natural persons* (human beings) and *artificial* or *juristic persons* (corporations). A clear distinction must therefore be drawn between:

(a) *The corporation.* A corporation comprises a body of persons with an existence, a name, rights and duties distinct from those of the individuals who form it from time to time. A relatively rare type consists of only one human being (e.g. a bishop) and it is then termed a *corporation sole*, which can own property and which (unlike the human office-holder) cannot die; new corporations sole must be created by statute. Much more common are corporations comprising more than one member and these are of three main kinds: chartered, statutory and registered. *Chartered corporations* are created by the grant of a royal charter (e.g. the BBC, the Law Society, the universities); *statutory corporations* are constituted by Act of Parliament (e.g. local authorities), whilst *registered corporations* are formed by registration in accordance with the Companies Acts (e.g. limited companies). Registration necessitates depositing two documents with the Registrar of Companies; these are a *Memorandum of Association* (showing the capital and objects of the company) and *Articles of Association* (showing the rules governing the company and its members). Together with the accounts, the Memorandum and Articles are open to public inspection. The term 'limited' indicates limitation of liability in the event of winding-up etc. It is possible for a company to be *limited by guarantee* — in which case, if it should be wound up, the liability of the members is limited to a sum of money (often £1). However, most registered companies are *limited by shares* — whereby, on a winding-up, the liability of each member (i.e. shareholder) is limited to the value of his shares; consequently, if these have been fully paid for, he has no further obligation. Under the Companies Act 1985, as amended, the minimum number of people who may form a company is two and there are two main types of limited companies — *private* and *public*. A company will be in the first category unless its allotted share capital is at least £50,000 and the Memorandum of Association states it to be public and includes 'public limited' (plc) in the company name. The contractual capacity, and the tortious and criminal liability of corporations, are outlined at 10:**3**, 17:**3(b)** and 22:**6(b)**. The fact that a limited company is separate from the shareholders has been illustrated in —

> *Salomon* v. *Salomon & Co Ltd* (1897): S converted his boot business into a seven-member limited company, which purchased the firm from him partially by way of £10,000 in debentures (documents in evidence of the debt, giving him right of repayment before other creditors). Owing to a strike in the trade, the company was wound up, with assets of £6,000 and debts to S; also £7,000 due to other creditors. These claimed that, as S & Co Ltd was really the same person as S, he could not owe money to himself and that they should be paid first. Reversing the decision of the Court of Appeal, the House of Lords held that, as the company had a separate identity in law, S was entitled to the £6,000.

(b) *The unincorporated association.* This may be a club, society, partnership, trade union, etc — none of which has a legal personality distinct from that of the members. Though such bodies can be subject to corporation tax, uniform business rate, etc, the law tends to regard them as groups of individuals. As shown in 17:3(d), however, certain members can be deputed to sue or be sued as representing the membership as a whole. The fact that a firm does not include 'Ltd' or 'plc' in its name indicates that it has a single proprietor or is a partnership (a 'relationship which subsists between persons carrying on a business in common with a view of profit'); the use of the words '& Co' has no legal significance. In a partnership, the partners are agents for the firm, which is legally liable for breaches of contract or torts committed by a partner on its behalf. Every partner is normally liable for the firm's debts, to the whole extent of his property. It is, however, possible to create a *limited partnership* (which must be registered under the Limited Partnerships Act 1907), whereby a partner's liability may be restricted to an agreed sum — provided that there is at least one 'general' partner with unlimited liability. Dissolution of a partnership may be effected by bankruptcy, the decision or death of a partner, or an order made by a court. The contractual and tortious liabilities of unincorporated associations are further examined in 10:4 and 17:3(c) – (e).

Progress test 5

1. Consider the role of the Lord Chancellor in the English legal system. **(1)**

2. Explain the functions of the Attorney-General and the Director of Public Prosecutions in the administration of justice. **(1)**

3. Describe the system of appointment of High Court judges and circuit judges. How can they be removed? **(1, 2)**

4. Explain the extent of judicial immunity. **(2)**

5. Consider the different functions of barristers and solicitors. **(3)**

6. Are the courts and legal services in England adequate for the country's needs? **(3, 4)**

7. In what courts are juries mainly found? Are they necessary? **(5)**

8. Outline the system of jury trial in criminal cases. What criticisms might be made of it? **(6)**

9. 'A corporation is an artificial legal person.' Explain this statement. **(7)**

10. Give examples of unincorporated associations and examine their legal position. **(7)**

6

The procedures of the law

The procedure of the Crown Court

1. The trial procedure of a criminal prosecution

As shown in 4:4(b), anyone accused of an indictable offence is first brought before a magistrates' court for committal proceedings and, if there is found to be a *prima facie* case, he or she is remanded (on bail or in custody) to the Crown Court, where the procedure is as follows:

(a) *The arraignment.* The defendant is 'put up to plead' at the bar of the court (i.e. called by name to the front of the dock); the clerk reads out the indictment and asks: 'How say you, are you guilty or not guilty?' To this the defendant must reply personally and not through counsel.

(b) *The pleas.* Several courses of action are now open to the defendant. In the first place he may *plead guilty*. The court will then hear the facts of the case from the prosecution, as well as evidence of character and pleas in mitigation, after which it passes sentence. In serious cases the defendant may be advised to withdraw a guilty plea. If there are several charges and possibly a long hearing, there may be a question of *plea-bargaining*, whereby the prosecution has agreed to withdraw the most serious charge(s) in return for the defence pleading guilty to one or more of the less serious. This practice does not exist to the same extent as in America, but it is open to abuse and has been criticised by the Court of Appeal. Secondly, the defendant may *stand mute* (i.e. say nothing). In this case, a jury may be empanelled to determine whether he is 'mute of malice' (deliberately silent) or 'by visitation of God' (e.g. deaf and dumb). If he is found to be mute of malice, a plea of not guilty is entered for him but, if he is found to be mute by visitation, the question of his fitness to plead must then be considered. Thirdly, the defendant may plead *autrefois acquit* or *autrefois convict*, i.e. that he cannot be tried for a crime in respect of which he has previously been acquitted or convicted. Fourthly, of course, the defendant may plead *not guilty*, whereat the procedure outlined in the following sections then ensues.

(c) *The swearing of the jury.* Before the oath is administered, the defence or prosecution may challenge any juror *for cause* (e.g. involvement with the case or the defendant). After the jury has been sworn, the defendant is 'put in charge of the jury' and the clerk addresses them, stating the nature of the charge(s).

(d) *The case for the prosecution.* The indictment is then 'opened', i.e. counsel for the prosecution addresses the jury and tells them what evidence he proposes to adduce — but he should regard himself as assisting the jury in arriving at the truth, rather than as an advocate pressing for a conviction. On concluding his address, he calls his witnesses, who are 'examined-in-chief' (by the prosecuting counsel), cross-examined (by the defending counsel) and possibly re-examined (by prosecuting counsel). At the end of the prosecution case, defending counsel may submit that there is no case to answer.

(e) *The case for the defence.* If the submission that there is no case to answer is either refused or not made, defending counsel then 'opens' his case and calls his witnesses for examination-in-chief, cross-examination and re-examination. The defendant may give evidence on oath, in which case he would be subject to cross-examination. At this stage the prosecution cannot call further evidence, unless the judge exercises his discretion to permit it, in order to rebut defence evidence which could not have been foreseen by the prosecution.

(f) *The closing speeches.* Counsel for the prosecution and defence then sum up their cases, with the defence having the right to the last word.

(g) *The summing up.* The judge then sums up the case to the jury, pointing out that the burden of proof is always on the prosecution (4:2(c)), directing them on points of law, possibly advising them on the weight of evidence, asking them definite questions of fact, and drawing their attention to any evidence that establishes a defence (even though defending counsel may not have done this).

(h) *The verdict.* The jury may then retire to consider their verdict and thereafter they must not separate (though an individual may withdraw for urgent reasons). During their retirement, they may have further assistance from the judge — in open court or by written note (which must be read out in open court). The first delivery of the verdict is not final, as the judge may direct the jury to reconsider it. The Criminal Justice Act 1967, s. 13, provides for majority verdicts of at least ten to two, where there are the normal 12 jurors. If the jury is reduced to 11 or 10, there may be one dissentient but, if there are only nine, the verdict must be unanimous. The court may not accept a majority verdict unless the jury has deliberated for at least two hours. If the jury cannot reach even a majority verdict, the judge may discharge them, so that the case could be retried before another jury.

(i)   *The judgment.* In order to decide upon the appropriate sentence for a defendant found guilty, the court may hear evidence of previous convictions (limited by the Rehabilitation of Offenders Act 1974), pleas in mitigation, evidence of character, etc. The convicted person may also request the court to take into consideration other offences. Common sentences are described in 7:1.

The procedures of the High Court

2.   The pre-trial procedure of a High Court action

In order to bring a civil action in the Queen's Bench Division, the following procedure must first take place:

(a)   *The plaintiff serves the writ.* The necessary form may be obtained from the Central Office of the Supreme Court in London, or from a District Registry. The plaintiff's claim is outlined in the most general terms but the remedy sought must be stated. After the writ has been completed, the next step is to *issue* it (i.e. make it an official document emanating from the court). For this purpose, the plaintiff or his solicitor must take two copies to the Central Office or District Registry, sign one and pay a fee. The signed copy is stamped and filed, whilst the other is sealed and returned; it then becomes *the writ in action.* It is necessary to *serve* the writ on the defendant, by giving him a sealed copy — though often his solicitor agrees to accept service. A writ may be served at any time of the day or night, excluding Sundays.

(b) *The defendant acknowledges service.* This entails returning a form of acknowledgement to the court office from which the writ was issued. Thus the defendant submits to the jurisdiction of the court.

(c) *The parties deliver the pleadings to each other.* The pleadings, which are generally drafted by counsel, must state facts and not law, cover material facts only and not include the evidence by which the facts are to be proved; the pleadings are delivered in three stages. In the first place, the *statement of claim* is delivered by the plaintiff to the defendant and it sets out his cause of action, giving all necessary details concerning his injuries and losses. At the trial the plaintiff will not be permitted to make any allegation of which the defendant has not been given notice. Secondly, the *defence* is delivered by the defendant to the plaintiff and it must deal with each of the allegations in the statement of claim. A general denial is inadmissible and any allegation not denied will be deemed by the court to be admitted. Thirdly, there is the *reply*; this is not essential but it enables the plaintiff to deal with any new facts raised by the defence. If a party has worded his pleading so vaguely that the line of attack or defence cannot be determined, his opponent should apply for *further and better particulars*. Furthermore, if a party refers to any document in his pleadings, his opponent can give notice that he wishes to see and copy it. This is known as *discovery of documents* — and it must be emphasised that 'discovery' relates to evidence, whereas 'particulars' concern allegations.

(d) *The plaintiff takes out a summons for directions.* This causes the parties' solicitors to appear before a Queen's Bench Master, to whom any party may apply for directions concerning the future conduct of the action. The Master has power to decide whether there shall be further pleadings, whether there is to be a jury, whether to order *general discovery of documents* (requiring a party to swear an affidavit (written statement on oath) disclosing all relevant documents in his possession), and whether to administer *interrogatories* (whereby a party is required to answer certain questions on oath before the trial), etc. Should the plaintiff fail to take out a summons for directions, the defendant may apply to have the action dismissed 'for want of prosecution'.

(e) *The plaintiff sets down the action for trial.* If the plaintiff fails to *set down* the action at the Central Office, the defendant may do it himself or apply to have the action dismissed. Eventually the case appears in the *Day's List* and the parties must attend in court.

3. The trial procedure of a High Court action

The trial procedure of a civil action in the Queen's Bench Division is as follows:

(a) *The swearing of the jury (if there is one).* The plaintiff's junior counsel then 'opens the pleadings', briefly outlining their nature but not stating the amount of damages claimed. In trials before a judge alone, this is omitted.

(b) *The case for the plaintiff.* The plaintiff's leading counsel 'opens his case', explaining the matter in dispute, reading the pleadings, outlining the plaintiff's argument, indicating the supporting evidence and possibly discounting defences, in anticipation. He calls his witnesses, who are examined-in-chief (and possibly cross-examined by the defendant's counsel) and puts in all material documents.

(c) *The case for the defendant.* If the defendant's counsel states that he does not intend to call witnesses or put in documents, the plaintiff's counsel then addresses the court. If, however, there are witnesses or documents, the defendant's counsel addresses the court. He then calls any witnesses, who are examined-in-chief (and may be cross-examined by the plaintiff's counsel), he also puts in any documents upon which he relies. Sometimes at the close of the defendant's case, the plaintiff may call 'rebutting' evidence, in answer to any affirmative case raised by the defendant.

(d) *The addresses by counsel.* These are made to the jury (if there is one) or to the judge. Counsel for the defendant makes his speech, followed by counsel for the plaintiff. During these speeches, the judge may indicate to each counsel the weak points of his case.

(e) *The summing up by the judge.* This is made to the jury, if there is one, and the judge directs them on points of law, outlines the questions of fact that they must decide and reminds them of the evidence. When the jury returns its verdict, the judge *enters judgment.* In non-jury cases, he delivers judgment at the conclusion of counsels' speeches, stating his reasons. If, however, important legal questions are raised, the judge may *reserve judgment,* for 'further consideration'. The counsel for the successful party then asks for costs (**7:4**) and, if he thinks of appealing, the counsel for the unsuccessful party should seek a *stay of execution* (suspension of the operation of the judgment). Common civil remedies are outlined **7:2**.

The procedure of the county court

4. The procedure of a county court action
The jurisdiction of a county court has been outlined at **4:7** and the procedure therein is as follows:

(a) *The request for a summons.* The plaintiff must first complete a *request* form, obtainable from the county court office, in order to obtain a *summons*. The completed request is returned to the office together with two copies of a written *particulars of claim* (outlining the facts in support of the claim) and a fee. The court prepares the summons and the plaintiff is given a *plaint note* (showing the plaint number of the action). A copy of the summons, particulars of claim and a *form of admission, defence and counter-claim* are then served on the defendant.

(b) *The filing of a defence.* If the defendant wishes to contest the action, he must complete the defence section of the form of admission, defence and counter-claim, and return it to the court office within 14 days. A simple denial of liability is not sufficient. At the same time, the defendant can file a counter-claim, which is a separate claim against the plaintiff.

(c) *The pre-trial review.* On a fixed date both parties appear before the district judge, who gives all necessary directions for securing the just, expeditious and economical disposal of the action. He endeavours to obtain all reasonable admissions and agreements, and fixes a date for the trial.

(d) *The trial.* The normal sequence of events is: plaintiff's opening speech; plaintiff's witnesses; defendant's witnesses; defendant's speech; plaintiff's speech in reply; judgment.

From this chapter it can be seen that, in both criminal and civil cases, the procedure is *accusatorial*, i.e. the courts are neutral and hear arguments by both sides. Some other countries, however, follow *inquisitorial* procedure, whereby the court produces the evidence.

Progress test 6

1. Describe the various stages of a criminal trial in the Crown Court. **(1)**

2. Outline the steps necessary before a civil action is tried in the High Court. **(2)**

3. Explain the trial procedure of a civil action in the High Court. **(3)**

4. Without the aid of a solicitor, how would you personally pursue a 'small claim' in the county court? **(4)**

7

The decisions of the law

The judgments of the law

1. The sentences of the criminal courts

In *The English Sentencing System,* Sir Rupert Cross contends that punishment by the state can be justified only if there are two key elements in its objective — the reduction of crime and the promotion of respect for the criminal code. It can also be argued that the main purposes of punishment are possibly threefold — *deterrent* (i.e. to deter others from committing a particular offence, or the offender himself from repeating it); *protective* (i.e. to protect the public from the violence and dishonesty of others); and *reformative* (i.e. to change the outlook of offenders). There are numerous theories as to the real cause of crime, and the reasons why the incidence of criminal conduct appears to vary amongst different social groups. Before passing sentence, judges and magistrates may seek the benefit of a *social enquiry report* and must, in fact, do so before imposing a term of imprisonment on anyone who has not previously received such a punishment. The principal sanctions of the criminal courts are outlined below and limitations relating to the ages of convicted offenders are indicated:

(a) *The committal to prison (21 or over).* Unlike America, Britain has no *minimum* prison sentences — though, in the case of murder, which has the statutory *fixed* penalty of life imprisonment, the judge may recommend a minimum period to the Home Secretary, who approves eventual release. *Maximum* terms of imprisonment for most offences are prescribed by statute (e.g. rape — life, burglary — 14 years, theft — 10 years), but under the Powers of the Criminal Courts Act 1973, s. 28, *extended* sentences (i.e. greater than the usual maxima) may be imposed in the case of recidivists (perpetual offenders). Sections 18–21 of the same Act provide that anyone convicted on indictment of a statutory offence where the maximum term is not specified cannot be imprisoned for more than two years. Sections 22–27 of the Act enable any court passing a sentence of up to two years to order that it be *suspended* — so as not to take effect unless, from one to two years later, the offender commits in Great Britain another offence punishable with imprisonment and a court orders that the original sentence should take effect. If a sentence for more than six months is suspended, a *suspended sentence supervision order* may be attached, placing the offender under the supervision of a probation officer. If a person is sentenced to not less than three months, nor more than two years, the court may order that, after a part has been served, the remainder (not more than three-quarters of the term, nor less than 28 days) may be suspended. The Criminal Justice Act 1967 created the *parole* system, whereby a prisoner sentenced to a minimum of nine months may be released 'on licence', if he has been of good behaviour and has served at least one third of the sentence or six months (whichever is the longer). The Criminal Justice Act 1982 empowers the Home Secretary to alter the minimum period for eligibility, also to order the *early release* of prisoners — not more than six months before the normal date and not applying to life sentences or certain excluded offences (manslaughter, rape, etc). The deterrent effect of imprisonment upon offenders is questionable — particularly in view of the fact that, of those released, about 65 per cent are reconvicted within two years. Moreover, any reformative element could be negated by association with experienced criminals. In 1990 a report by the National Association of Probation Officers showed wide disparities amongst Crown Courts in the imposition of custodial sentences for the most serious offences — varying from 38 per cent at Mold, Clwyd to 69 per cent at Wood Green, London.

(b) *The committal to Young Offenders' Institution (15–21).* The Criminal Justice Act 1988 merged the former Youth Custody and Detention Centres into single Young Offenders' Institutions. Here, those within the age-group are detained if they have a history of failure (or are unable or unwilling) to respond to non-custodial penalties *or* if only a custodial sentence would be adequate to protect the public from serious harm *or* if their offence was so serious that a non-custodial sentence could not be justified.

For young men the maximum term of detention is the lesser of the maximum term of adult imprisonment for the offence *or* 12 months (if 15 or 16). Conviction of an offence punishable with life imprisonment for an adult can result in life custody.

(c) *The fine*. This is an order that a convicted person must forfeit a certain sum of money to the Crown; courts may fine offenders in lieu of, or in addition to, other penalties apart from probation orders. Various conditions may be imposed — such as 'attachment to earnings' (i.e. the deduction of a regular sum from one's salary). The Criminal Justice Act 1982 has provided a standard scale of fines, based on five levels, and default in payment can result in imprisonment, according to a table in the Act. In the Crown Court there is no maximum limit to a fine but magistrates cannot impose more than £2,000 — or £400 in the case of young persons (14–17) and £100 for children (under 14). Although courts should take into consideration an offender's means to pay, fines can be regressive (i.e. the lower a person's income, the higher the proportion represented by the fine). Consequently, some countries (e.g. Austria and Sweden) calculate fines by multiplying the offender's daily pay by a number representing the gravity of the offence.

(d) *The probation order (17 or over)*. This is made only in respect of offenders who agree to the sanction and they are placed under the supervision of a probation officer for one to three years (though the Home Secretary is empowered to vary the period). Specific conditions may be included — e.g. regarding residence, medical treatment, attendance at a day centre (a non-residential rehabilitation establishment) for up to 60 days, etc. If the offender fails to comply with the order, he can be brought back to the court, which may fine him up to £400 or impose an attendance centre order (*see* **(g) below**). If he commits another offence whilst on probation, he may be dealt with for both the original and the subsequent one.

(e) *The supervision order (under 17)*. This is made by juvenile courts in respect of young offenders, whose agreement is not necessary. For up to three years, supervision is exercised by the local authority social services department or (in the case of those over 14 and at the specific request of the local authority) by a probation officer. A supervision order can prescribe *intermediate treatment* by requiring the juvenile to comply with directions by the superviser — e.g. to live in a specified place, to report to a specified person or to participate in a specified activity. Breach of a requirement in the order can cause the offender to be brought back to the court, which can impose a fine of up to £100 or make an attendance centre order. In the case of offences (other than murder) for which the adult punishment would be imprisonment, the court may make a *care order* which, if not discharged, remains in force until the juvenile is 18 (19 if he or she was over 16 when the order was made). When such a step is considered desirable, the person concerned must be legally represented. The effect is that the local authority is given parental power and can accommodate the juvenile in a community home or other institution, with foster parents or with its own parents. Should anyone in care be convicted of another imprisonable offence, the court may impose a residential condition whereby, for not more than six months, the local authority may not allow the offender to stay with parents, relatives or friends.

(f) *The community service order (16 or over).* This is made in respect of those convicted of imprisonable offences and who consent to the sanction. The order requires them to carry out unpaid work of service to the community during their spare time for a minimum of 40 hours and a maximum of 240 hours (120 if under 17) within 12 months. The nature of the work and the time when it is to be done are matters for a probation officer but at least 21 of the minimum 40 hours must be spent on manual work in a 'group placement' with other offenders. A CSO can be combined with other orders (e.g. a compensation order or a disqualification from driving) but not with a probation order or a fine for the same offence. Failure to comply with a CSO could result in a fine of up to £400 or the revocation of the order and its substitution with another sentence.

(g) *The attendance centre order (under 21).* This is made in respect of those convicted of imprisonable offences, provided that they have not already served a period of imprisonment, youth custody or detention. They are required to be present at an attendance centre for a specified number of hours — not less than 12 (except for those under the age of 14), nor more than 12 (if under 14), 24 (if aged 14 to 17) or 36 (if aged 17 to 21). Divided into senior and junior categories, attendance centres are often run by the police on Saturday afternoons (thus suitable for football hooligans).

(h) *The compensation order.* This is made in order to require a convicted offender to pay compensation in respect of any personal injury, loss or damage which appears to have resulted from his offence. A magistrates' court can order up to a maximum of £1,000 compensation in connection with each offence proved but there is no limit in the Crown Court. The Criminal Justice Act 1988, s. 104, requires that a court, when sentencing, must give reasons for *not* making such an order if personal injury, loss or damage is involved. The Act also enables a compensation order to be made in favour of a deceased person's relative in connection with funeral expenses, etc. Anyone who, as a result of criminal violence, suffers personal injury of such a nature that a civil court would award damages of at least £750 may seek an *ex gratia* payment from the *Criminal Injuries Compensation Board*, which is financed from public funds. In 1990 this scheme was extended to include compensation for persons (generally train drivers) who suffer shock from trespassers' suicides on the railways, for the cohabitees of deceased persons in fatal injury cases, also for victims when children are born as a consequence of rape. In the year ending March 1989, the Board received 43,385 applications, resolved 38,830 cases and had a backlog of about 96,000.

(i) *The confiscation order.* This is made, additional to other sanctions in respect of the assets of offenders convicted of highly profitable crimes. If a defendant is convicted under the Drug Trafficking Offences Act 1986, the Crown Court is required to make a confiscation order covering the total proceeds from the offender's whole drug trafficking activities. Under the Criminal Justice Act 1988, provided that the assets are not less than £10,000, the Crown Court is empowered to make confiscation orders against the proceeds from a wide range of serious offences, including: fraud; insider dealing in shares; blackmail; robbery; prostitution; and supplying pornographic videos. As in the case of drug trafficking, the High Court can order the freezing of an alleged offender's assets as soon as there is evidence to make a charge, whilst the police and customs authorities can seize restrained assets if there is a risk of their leaving the country. Assets subject to confiscation may include houses and property held by convicted offenders in other countries; moreover, refusal to surrender known assets would make the offenders liable to substantial terms of imprisonment in addition to any imposed for the original offences.

(j) *The mental health order.* This is made by a court, under the Mental Health Act 1983, when it is satisfied that the suitable course of action is to commit a person convicted of an imprisonable offence to a special hospital, provided that an appropriate certificate has been obtained from two doctors (one of whom must be a psychiatrist) and that a place can be found within 28 days. Applications for discharge from such a hospital can be made to a *Mental Health Review Tribunal*, comprising a lawyer (president), a doctor and a lay member. If it is considered necessary for the protection of the public, the Crown Court may make a *restriction order* (or magistrates may commit the offender to the Crown Court for such an order), whereby the person becomes subject only to powers exercisable by the Home Secretary and no application can be made to a Review Tribunal. By warrant, the Home Secretary may direct that any person be detained in a specified hospital 'during Her Majesty's pleasure'; this has the effect of a mental health order, together with a restriction order, without limitation of time.

(k) *The discharge.* When a court thinks that it is inexpedient to inflict punishment and that a probation order is inappropriate, it may grant an absolute or conditional discharge. An *absolute discharge* may express the court's disagreement with the decision to prosecute and no action is taken. A *conditional discharge* means that no action will be taken provided that the person concerned does not commit any offence during a period not exceeding three years. If the condition is breached, the offender may be brought back to court and punished in some other way. There is also a procedure known as '*binding over*' whereby anyone 'who is before the court' (i.e. not only the defendant) may be asked to agree to *enter in recognisances* (or find a surety) to pay a sum of money if he fails to carry out stipulated conditions (e.g. to keep the peace), generally for one year.

2.   The remedies of the civil courts

In general, the purpose of civil remedies is to redress harm and to restore injured parties to their former position. The principal examples are:

(a) *The award of damages.* As shown in 16:8(b), genuine pre-estimates of expenses that could arise from breaches of contracts are known as *liquidated damages*. Other forms of monetary compensation awarded for breaches of contracts and torts can therefore be called *unliquidated damages*. Historically, damages are of common law origin and have always been awarded to a successful plaintiff *as of right*. They can consequently be encountered in four main categories: *contemptuous damages* (e.g. one penny, awarded as a sign of the court's displeasure to unmeritorious plaintiffs who are nevertheless entitled to succeed); *nominal damages* (a small token award when there has been a minor tort or breach of contract, involving no actual loss); *substantial damages* (pecuniary compensation, intended to put the plaintiff in a position that he would have enjoyed before a tort, or if a contract had been performed); and *aggravated or exemplary damages* (in excess of the actual pecuniary loss where an injury has been made worse by the defendant's conduct or motives — and it is desired to include a punitive or deterrent element — *see* 19:1(a)–(b)).

(b) *The granting of an injunction*. This is an equitable remedy in the form of an order granted *at the court's discretion* (*see* 1:6(c)), provided that it can be effectively enforced by the court, that pecuniary damages would not be adequate compensation and that, in the case of a contract, the defendant is doing something that he agreed *not* to do. Dependent upon their purposes, injunctions may be classified in various categories. Of a temporary nature is the *interlocutory or interim injunction*, which is most commonly granted to preserve the status quo, pending a main trial, at the conclusion of which a *perpetual injunction* might be granted. In its turn, this is most likely to be either a *prohibitory injunction* (restraining someone from continuing a course of action — e.g. trespass) or a *mandatory injunction* (requiring someone to preserve or restore the status quo — e.g. re-accommodate a wrongfully-evicted tenant). There is also a *quia timet injunction*, whereby a person can be restrained from undertaking an *anticipated* course of action which is justifiably believed to be imminent (e.g. wrongful eviction), whilst the relatively recently developed *Mareva injunction* has been outlined in 1:5(a). Failure to comply with an injunction is punishable as contempt of court.

(c) *The decree of specific performance*. This is an equitable (and therefore discretionary) remedy for certain breaches of contract and it is more fully explained in 16:8(e).

(d) *The delivery of a declaratory judgment.* Without awarding any of the above remedies, a court (generally of the Queen's Bench Division) may, at its discretion, make a *declaration* on a question of law or rights. The scope for such judgments is very wide and examples have been given 1:**7(a)**, 3:**3(b)** and 5:**(b)**(*vi*). Failure to comply with a declaration does not constitute contempt of court.

(e) *The remedy of judicial review.* The manner of obtaining an injunction or a declaration differs according to whether it relates to:

(*i*) *Private law.* This covers *the infringement of one's rights by individuals or bodies which do NOT exercise statutory powers* (e.g. clubs and societies), also *torts and breaches of contract by individuals or bodies which DO exercise statutory powers* (e.g. government departments, local authorities, etc). In such circumstances an injunction or declaration must be sought by way of an *ordinary civil action* —

R v. *Derbyshire County Council, ex parte Noble* (1990): After N had been informally employed as a deputy police surgeon for five years, DCC decided to regularise the situation and not to use his services. He was granted leave to apply for judicial review (below) but, dismissing the application, the Divisional Court held that there was insufficient statutory underpinning of N's engagement to provide the necessary public law element for judicial review to be appropriate. This was upheld by the Court of Appeal.

(*ii*) *Public law.* This covers *the infringement of one's rights by individuals or bodies which exercise statutory powers* and, in these circumstances, redress must be sought by way of an *application for judicial review.* This is a procedure whereby several remedies can be sought, either solely or together, and it is more fully explained in 8:**10** —

O'Reilly v. *Mackman* (1983): Penalised by the Board of Visitors, on account of disciplinary offences, four inmates of Hull Prison brought High Court actions, seeking a declaration that the Board's findings were void through contravening the prison rules and the rules of natural justice (8:**12**). The House of Lords held that a plaintiff complaining of a public authority's infringement of his public law rights could not seek redress by ordinary action; the correct procedure was an application for judicial review.

(f) *The prerogative writ of habeas corpus.* If any person (except a prisoner of war or interned enemy alien) is confined without legal justification, he may secure his release by the prerogative writ of *habeas corpus.* This necessitates the submission of an affidavit to a Divisional Court of the Queen's Bench Division (or, in vacation, to a judge in chambers) by the prisoner or by any person acting on his behalf . If the need is urgent and a case is made out, the court may make an *order absolute* for the issue of the writ, which affords immediate release. Alternatively, an *order nisi* may be granted, to give the other side a chance to oppose. Where there is opposition, the case is argued and, if good cause for detention is not shown, the order is made absolute. The writ must be issued unconditionally or not at all, and appeal by either side lies to the House of Lords, by leave of the Divisional Court or of the House, but it is not necessary to show that a point of law of general public importance is involved. The use of the writ has been illustrated in *Sirros* v. *Moore* (1974) (5:**2(c)**) and a successful application does not preclude an action for the tort of false imprisonment (19:**6(c)**).

The reliefs of the law

3. The granting of bail

Bail is the process in criminal proceedings whereby a person suspected or accused of a crime is released from pre-trial detention by the police or a court, on the condition that he presents himself at an appointed time and place. With regard to police bail, and in the case of arrests under a warrant, the document itself states whether bail is to be granted. If the person has been arrested without a warrant, there must be compliance with PACE (the Police and Criminal Evidence Act 1984 — *see* 8:**2(g)**). Bail may also be granted by the magistrates' court, Crown Court, High Court or Court of Appeal — but then it is subject to the Bail Act 1976. Recognisances (undertakings to forfeit a sum of money) may be required of one or more persons known as *sureties* and, if it appears that he is unlikely to remain in Great Britain, the bailed person may have to provide a security. Where necessary, further conditions may be imposed — e.g. the surrendering of passports, reporting to the police, etc. Failure to surrender to bail is an imprisonable offence. On an appeal from the Crown Court to the Court of Appeal, bail will be granted only in exceptional circumstances (e.g. a *prima facie* likelihood of success or the risk that the sentence will have been served by the time the appeal is heard). In the magistrates' courts, with the exceptions outlined below, there is a general right to bail and, if it is refused, reasons must be given (in writing to those not legally represented). Furthermore, there is a right to apply to a High Court judge in chambers or to the Crown Court for release from custody or for review of unduly onerous bail conditions. Schedule 1 to the 1976 Act draws a distinction between:

(a) *The persons accused or convicted of imprisonable offences.* These may (but not must) be refused bail if there are substantial grounds for believing that they would fail to surrender, commit an offence, interfere with witnesses or otherwise obstruct the course of justice; *or* if the court is satisfied that they should be kept in custody for their own protection (or welfare, if juveniles); *or* if they are in custody as a result of a court sentence or that of a service authority; *or* if it has not been practicable to obtain sufficient information for the necessary decisions; *or* if they have been released on bail and have then absconded or broken conditions; *or* if the case is adjourned for inquiries or a report which it would be impossible to complete without custody.

(b) *The persons accused or convicted of non-imprisonable offences.* These may (but not must) be refused bail if they have previously failed to surrender to bail in criminal proceedings and the court believes that they would again do so; *or* if the court is satisfied that they should be kept in custody for their own protection (or welfare, if juveniles); *or* if they are in custody as a result of a court sentence or that of a service authority; *or* if they have been released on bail and have then absconded or broken conditions.

Despite these provisions, bail can still be subject to significant discrepancies in magistrates' courts. In 1985, for example, it was granted in 89 per cent of the cases heard by Hampshire benches, compared with 63 per cent in Dorset. It is also argued that a relatively high proportion of those remanded in custody do not ultimately receive custodial sentences.

4. The ordering of costs

The term *costs* means the sum of money which a court may, at its discretion, order one party to pay to the other in compensation for expenses incurred in the case (e.g. fees of solicitors, counsel, expert witnesses, etc). Costs are most commonly awarded in the courts of civil jurisdiction — though, under the Costs in Criminal Cases Act 1973, an acquitted defendant may seek an order for costs against the prosecution or out of central funds, whereas the prosecution may apply for such an order against a convicted person. In civil cases, the unsuccessful party generally has to pay the other's costs but procedures vary in the different courts:

(a) *The High Court.* In the normal course of events, a successful plaintiff who has recovered more than nominal damages should have an order for costs made in his favour. Generally his solicitor then puts in a bill and, if this is disputed by the other side, it becomes subject to *taxation* (i.e. examination and possible reduction) by a *Taxing Master*. Introduced in 1986, *Order 62* of the Rules of the Supreme Court, provides a 'standard basis' which enables the awarded party to recover 'a reasonable amount in respect of all costs reasonably incurred'. It is also possible to claim 'indemnity costs' — i.e. all costs incurred 'except in so far as they are of an unreasonable amount or have been unreasonably incurred'. Under the Litigants in Person (Costs and Expenses) Act 1975, even a party who has not been legally represented may be reimbursed for work done and expenses incurred in connection with the proceedings. If the unsuccessful party has paid money into court and the other fails to recover more than that sum, he cannot claim costs incurred after the date of payment. Interest on costs runs from the date of the award (not the date of taxation) and, if the plaintiff accepts a payment into court, he is entitled to his costs but not interest — as there was no judgment to give rise to it. In lieu of taxed costs, judges have the discretion to award a gross sum.

(b) *The County Court.* Here taxation is carried out by the district judge, with a right of appeal to the circuit judge, and there is a scheme of five scales of itemised costs, varying with the amount of the judgment (if the plaintiff wins) or claim (if he loses). In admitted or undefended cases, counsel's fees are not allowed and the court must certify whether small defended cases are 'fit for counsel'.

(c) *The magistrates' court.* Under the Magistrates' Courts Act 1980, s. 64, this may order 'just and reasonable' costs.

(d) *The appellate courts.* A winning party in the Court of Appeal is generally awarded the costs of the trial and the appeal but, if permitted to adduce new evidence or fresh arguments, he or she may be refused costs. If a new trial is ordered, the costs of all hearings are based on its result. A successful respondent may be awarded costs in all courts.

Taxed costs rarely cover the amount that a successful party has to pay to his own solicitor. The difference, which he must contribute himself, can be termed *extra costs,* and these can constitute an appreciable deterrent to litigation. As an unsuccessful party is seldom totally in the wrong, the 'loser pays all' principle is also open to criticism — particularly when a decision (notably relating to a point of law) is reversed on appeal and the loser has to meet the expenses of both the trial and the appellate proceedings. There has consequently been argument in favour of paying from a public fund the costs of such appeals.

5. The provision of legal aid

Under the Legal Aid Act 1988, people of limited means with legal problems can acquire the services of solicitors and barristers free of charge or at low cost, and at state expense. The administration of the legal aid in criminal proceedings described below is the responsibility of the Lord Chancellor whilst, under his general guidance, the provision of legal advice, assistance and aid in civil cases is administered by the *Legal Aid Board.* This operates throughout England and Wales in 13 areas, each with a Legal Aid Office and an area committee of practising barristers and solicitors. Help provided is free if an applicant's disposable income and disposable capital do not exceed specified amounts; thereafter, up to further limits, contributions are payable. *Disposable income* comprises gross income from employment, etc, less deductions for dependants, income tax, rent, pension contributions, mortgage repayments, etc. *Disposable capital* comprises all forms of savings, land and buildings other than the principal home, valuable items (e.g. antiques, jewellery, caravans, boats) but not household goods, personal clothing, tools of trade or the item at the centre of the legal dispute in question. Except where they are separated, or have conflicting interests, the means of couples who are married or living together are aggregated. Anyone unsure about being qualified for legal aid can seek a *fixed fee interview* with a solicitor, who provides up to half an hour's advice for £5 or less. There are three forms of legal aid:

(a) *The provision of legal advice and assistance.* On account of the necessary application document, this is often called the 'Green Form Scheme' and it covers a solicitor's advice, letter-writing, negotiating, obtaining a barrister's opinion, preparing a written case for a tribunal, etc. The solicitor may provide help to the value of two hours' fees (three hours' in matrimonial cases involving the preparation of a petition) but anything in excess would require the authority of the Legal Aid Office. Without having to give a reason, a solicitor could decline to provide such a service but might have to explain the refusal to the Legal Aid Office. Advice and assistance can include *assistance by way of representation*, i.e. the preparation of, and representation in, a civil case in a magistrates' court. Children below school-leaving age may obtain advice and assistance — generally on the application of a parent or guardian — but a solicitor can seek permission from the Legal Aid Office to advise a child. At many magistrates' courts a *duty solicitor* is available to provide free advice and representation at a person's first appearance. No means test applies to this — nor does it if anyone exercises a right to free legal advice when (albeit possibly not arrested) he or she is questioned by the police about an offence (*see* **8:2(h)**). Notably in underprivileged areas, *legal centres* have been established, often in the form of ordinary shops, to assist those living in the neighbourhood. Some are set up by the Law Society and operate within the framework of the above system, with means tests, etc. Others are funded by charitable organisations and provide a free service. Citizens' Advice Bureaux can give information about local solicitors and many have honorary legal advisers.

(b) *The provision of civil legal aid.* This covers the preparation of a civil case and representation in: the House of Lords; Court of Appeal; High Court; county courts (but not for judgment summonses or undefended divorce decree proceedings); magistrates' courts (for domestic proceedings — though these normally involve assistance by way of representation); the Crown Court (for appeals about affiliation orders); the Restrictive

Practices Court (for some cases); the Lands Tribunal; Employment Tribunal; and Commons Commissioners. Apart from the ones indicated, civil legal aid is *not* available for proceedings before most tribunals, in coroners' courts or in actions for defamation. Those seeking civil legal aid must make an application (preferably through a solicitor) to the Legal Aid Office, showing that they qualify financially, that they have reasonable grounds for taking or defending a court action, and also that it would be reasonable to grant legal aid in the circumstances.

If a case is urgent, *emergency legal aid* can be granted immediately and remains effective until a decision is reached on the full application. After due consideration, the Office may issue a Civil Legal Aid Certificate, reject the application or grant a limited certificate (e.g. to obtain a barrister's opinion). In the event of a rejection, there is generally a right of appeal to the area committee. Where a certificate is granted, the applicant may select a solicitor (and, if necessary, counsel) from a panel and, allowing for any contribution, the expenses are met from the Legal Aid Fund. A court may also order that the costs of a successful unaided party be paid from the fund. A successful aided party who recovers money or property may be liable for the *statutory charge*, whereby some or all of it may be used to pay the legal expenses.

(c) *The provision of criminal legal aid*. This covers the preparation of a defence, representation in court, and advice on, and preparation of, an appeal against a verdict or sentence of the magistrates' court, Crown Court or Court of Appeal. Legal aid may also be available in obtaining bail, but not for private prosecutions. Applications are made to the court which is dealing with the case and, for those under 17, a parent or guardian may apply. There is a wide variation in the willingness of different magistrates' courts to grant legal aid and, in the event of a refusal, it is possible to reapply to the court and help may be obtained from a solicitor under (a) above. If in relation to a serious case, the court decides that granting criminal legal aid would not be in the interests of justice, it may be possible to have the matter reviewed by the Criminal Legal Aid Committee of the Legal Aid Board.

Progress test 7

1. Describe the powers available to magistrates to deal with young offenders. Are they adequate? **(1)**

2. What alternatives are there to imprisoning an adult for a serious offence? **(1)**

3. Examine the award of damages, discussing any situations in which they might not be a satisfactory remedy. **(2)**

4. Explain the use of an injunction and describe how it may be obtained. **(2)**

5. How can release be obtained from pre-trial detention? **(3)**

6. Consider any weaknesses in the bail system and possible ways of reforming it. **(3)**

7. Describe the system of costs **(4)**

8. In what ways do costs act as a deterrent to litigation? Do you consider that any reforms are necessary? **(4)**

9. Examine the roles of solicitors and legal centres in helping persons of limited means. **(5)**

10. Describe the ways in which legal aid may be granted in civil and criminal cases. Could the system be simplified? **(5)**

8
The protections of the law

The nature of human rights

1. The protection of human rights

Although the 'freedoms' outlined in succeeding sections are looked upon as fundamental rights, most are nevertheless negative in nature as they are based on the tautologous principle that anything which is not unlawful will be lawful; hence they would be better classified as 'civil liberties'. Not having a written constitution, the United Kingdom lacks effective formal guarantees of human rights, but it is a signatory to the *European Convention for the Protection of Human Rights and Fundamental Freedoms*. Signed in 1950 and effective from 1953, this was drawn up within the *Council of Europe*, which was founded in 1949, comprises 25 member countries, and is quite separate from the European Community. Under the Convention, the contracting nations have agreed to submit to international control all of their actions which concern basic human rights and fundamental freedoms.

(a) *The protections of the Convention.* The most significant rights protected by the Convention (which nevertheless specifies provisos whereby they may be abridged) are: the right not to be subjected to torture or degrading treatment or punishment; the right to respect for private and family life, home and correspondence; the right to freedom of thought, conscience, religion and expression; the right to freedom of peaceful assembly and to freedom of association with others, including the right to form and join trade unions; the right to peaceful enjoyment of possessions; and the right to education in conformity with parents' religious and philosophical convictions.

(b) *The invocation of the Convention.* To ensure its observance by the signatories, the Convention created in Strasbourg a *European Commission of Human Rights* (with one member from each contracting country elected for six years) and a *European Court of Human Rights* (with one member from each country elected for nine years). After exhausting all domestic remedies, any person, non-governmental organisation or group claiming to be a victim of a violation of the above rights by a contracting state may petition the Commission. The role of the latter (performed by a sub-commission of seven) is solely that of fact-finding and conciliation, so, if a friendly solution cannot be reached, it draws up a Report, which is transmitted to the *Committee of Ministers.* Thereafter the matter may be referred (by the Commission or contracting country) to the Court — but, if this does not happen within three months, the Committee of Ministers must decide (by a two-thirds majority) whether there has been a violation. If it does so determine, it prescribes a time by which measures must be taken by the contracting state. Should the latter fail to comply, the Committee decides what effect shall be given to its decision and publishes the Report. Strasbourg decisions have resulted in the enactment of legislation by Parliament — e.g. the Interception of Communications Act 1985, which relates to telephone tapping.

(c) *The incorporation of the Convention.* Being a signatory, the United Kingdom is bound to observe the terms of the Convention but there have been frequent suggestion that its provisions should be embodied in English law — possibly in the form of a *Bill of Rights Act.* Proponents contend that such legislation would enable people to obtain redress in British courts, as opposed to Strasbourg, and that British judges (who already deal with human rights cases) would be able to interpret the Convention. As this must already be observed in Britain, there would be no further erosion of parliamentary sovereignty. Many Commonwealth countries have enacted a Bill of Rights. An innate difficulty would nevertheless be that the sovereignty of Parliament would preclude such law from being completely entrenched (i.e. made totally immune from amendment or repeal). At best it could include a provision ensuring that it was always taken into account in the construction of later Acts — but it would be unlikely for any government to introduce lightly a Bill tantamount to an announced intention of breaching the Convention. As this document is framed in broad terms, its incorporation in domestic law would transfer to judicial interpretation many matters (e.g. race relations, sex discrimination, freedom of speech, etc) that are in the province of statute or common law; resultantly, a large element of uncertainty would be introduced and judges would become more 'politicised'. Problems could also arise over remedies — as injunctions cannot be granted against the Crown and damages are not awarded to victims of maladministration.

The nature of civil liberties

2.   The freedom of the person

As shown in 7:2(f), persons confined without legal justification may secure their release with the writ of *habeas corpus*, and there is also the civil action for the tort of false imprisonment (19:6(c)). Lawful deprivation of liberty can arise from custodial sentencing, powers of arrest, etc, and of great significance is the Police and Criminal Evidence Act 1984 (PACE), important provisions of which relate to:

(a) *The nature of arrestable offences.* An arrest will be justified if supported by a warrant (4:2(a)), but it can also be made without a warrant in the case of *arrestable offences,* as defined in s. 24 of PACE. These are: offences for which the sentence is fixed by law (e.g. murder) or for which a person of 21 or over (not previously convicted) may be sentenced to five years' imprisonment; certain offences under the Official Secrets Acts and the Customs and Excise Acts (e.g. obstructing officers, impeding searches, destroying evidence, importing or exporting prohibited goods); and indecent assault on a woman, causing prostitution of women, procurement of girls under 21, taking a conveyance without authority, going equipped for stealing and corruption of members, officers or servants of a public body.

(b) *The police powers of arrest without a warrant.* Under ss. 24–25 of PACE, if a constable reasonably suspects that an arrestable offence (AO) has been committed, he may arrest anyone whom he reasonably suspects to be guilty of it. It is not necessary for an AO to have actually been committed. A police officer may likewise arrest anyone who is (or whom he reasonably suspects to be) about to commit an AO. Furthermore, if he has reasonable grounds for suspecting that *any* offence has been (or is being) committed or attempted, he may arrest anyone whom he reasonably suspects of committing or attempting it. However, this last power is exercisable *if* (and *only if*) there are specified doubts about the suspect's name and address or reasonable grounds for believing that arrest is necessary to prevent the suspect from causing physical injury to himself or another; suffering physical injury; committing an offence against public decency; causing an unlawful obstruction of the highway; harming a child or other vulnerable person. Anyone arrested by a constable must be informed as soon as practicable that he is under arrest and be given the grounds for it. This requirement is essential, even if the arrest and/or grounds are obvious because, if not complied with, the arrest is unlawful —

> *DPP* v. *Hawkins* (1988): H had been arrested for common assault on a constable but resisted and, during the struggle, he assaulted three police officers. At this time they could not inform him of the ground for the arrest and, after he had calmed down and made it practicable, they still failed to do so. Holding that the arrest was unlawful, the magistrates dismissed three charges of assaulting a police officer in the execution of his duty. Remitting the case to the justices, the Divisional Court held that, although the arrest was unlawful, the behaviour of the officers at the time was lawful and could not become retrospectively unlawful because of a later failure of duty.

(c) *The citizen's power of arrest.* Under ss. 24 and 26 of PACE, a private citizen may arrest (without a warrant) anyone who is (or whom he reasonably suspects to be) committing an AO. The arrest is thus limited in time — as it may be effected only when the person is (or is supposed to be) committing an offence. Where an AO has been committed, a citizen may arrest anyone who is (or whom he reasonably suspects to be) guilty of it. Here it is necessary for an AO to have been actually committed — though not necessarily by the person arrested. Certain statutes empower a private citizen to effect an arrest — e.g. the Theft Act 1968, s. 34, which relates to persons making off without payment.

(d) *The common law power of arrest.* In addition to the above provisions of PACE, a constable or a private citizen has a *common law* power to arrest, without a warrant, anyone committing a *breach of the peace* in his presence, or threatening to commit or renew such a breach so that he reasonably and honestly believes that it will be committed in the immediate future. A breach of the peace occurs whenever harm or violence is threatened, so as to be likely, to a person or his property, or when a person is put in fear by reason of some assault, riot or affray, provided that the conduct concerned relates to violence —

> *McConnell* v. *Chief Constable of Greater Manchester Police* (1990): Called to private business premises, police found M sitting in an office with the manager. When asked to leave, he refused and was taken outside by a constable. He then attempted to re-enter and was arrested, as the officer suspected that a breach of the peace might be occasioned. Acquitted by the magistrates, he issued a writ, claiming damages for false imprisonment and, as a preliminary point of law, the judge decided that a breach of the peace could take place on private premises, with no member of the public involved. Dismissing M's appeal, the Court of Appeal held that, in the circumstances, the constable was entitled to exercise his common law power.

(e) *The police powers of search upon arrest.* Upon an arrest, other than at a police station, a constable may search the arrested person if he has reasonable grounds for believing that he may present a danger to himself or others *or* that he has concealed on him any article that might be used to assist him to escape, or which might be evidence relating to the offence for which he has been arrested. The constable may also search any premises wherein the person was, when (or immediately before) he was arrested, for evidence relating to the offence. These powers arise only if there are reasonable grounds, which must also exist if anything found is seized (*see* 8:3(c)).

(f) *The police powers of stopping and searching.* Under ss. 1–3 of PACE, a constable may stop and search a person or vehicle (or anything in or on it), provided that he has reasonable grounds for suspecting that he will find stolen or prohibited articles. 'Prohibited articles' comprise offensive weapons and things made (or adapted) for use in burglary or theft. The power can be exercised only in a public place — i.e. any place to which the public (or any section of it) has access, with or without payment. However, it may include a garden or yard if there are reasonable grounds for suspecting that the person involved does not reside therein and is not there with express or implied permission. Those searched cannot be required to remove any clothing in public, other than outer coat, jacket and gloves — consequently articles could be concealed in hats. The search must be conducted in a reasonable time and, if the person involved is un-cooperative, reasonable force may be used. If not in uniform, the constable must produce proof of identity before commencing the search and he has a mandatory duty to give his name and police station — also the object of (and grounds for) the search. The person searched (or the owner of the vehicle) is entitled to a copy of the record of the search, if it is requested within 12 months. Failure to comply with the requirement to supply information would make a search unlawful but it does *not* apply to the search of an unattended vehicle, a vehicle or aircraft leaving an aerodrome/designated airport cargo area, or a vehicle before it leaves the goods area of a 'statutory undertaker' (i.e. the operator of railway, road, water-borne transport, etc), if searched by one of its own constables.

(g) *The police powers of detention.* Under s. 36 of PACE, every police station which is regularly used for detention must, at all times when it is open, have at least one designated *custody officer* — not below the rank of sergeant and not involved in the investigation of offences referred to him. At all other stations at least one officer must be available to perform such functions, when required. On arrival at a police station, anyone arrested without a warrant must be brought before the custody officer, who must decide whether there is sufficient evidence to charge him with the offence for which he was arrested. Thereafter the procedure is as follows:

(*i*) If the custody officer decides that there is sufficient evidence to charge the arrested person, he may be detained for as long as is necessary for the charge to be put to him. He may then be charged, or informed that he may be liable to prosecution and released without charge, on or without bail.

(*ii*) If the custody officer decides that there is not sufficient evidence to charge the arrested person, he must order his release (on or without bail) unless he has reasonable grounds for believing that detention is necessary to secure or preserve evidence relating to the offence *or* to obtain such evidence by questioning. In such circumstances the detained person must be informed of the grounds for his detention (unless he is incapable of understanding what is said to him, or he is violent or in urgent need of medical attention) and a written record of such grounds must be made in his presence. If, through drink, drugs or violence, the arrested person is not in a fit state to be charged or released without charge, he may be detained until fit to be dealt with.

(*iii*)   If the arrested person is detained (having been charged or not), reviews of his detention must be made not later than six hours after its commencement and thereafter at intervals of not more than nine hours, in order to confirm that the criteria for detention are still satisfied.

(*iv*)   If the arrested person is not charged, he may (subject to certain exceptions) not be detained for more than 24 hours. Detention beyond that time and up to 36 hours is permitted only if authorised by a superintendent (or above) who has reasonable grounds for believing that detention is necessary to secure or preserve evidence, that a serious AO is involved, and that the investigation is being conducted expeditiously. For extension beyond 36 hours the police must apply to a magistrates' court for a *warrant for further detention*; this may be granted for 36 hours and extended to not more than 96 hours from the time when detention commenced.

(*v*)   If the arrested person is charged, his release must be ordered unless the custody officer is unable to verify his name and address *or* has reasonable grounds for believing that detention is necessary for his own protection, to prevent him from causing physical injury to others or damage to property, or that he will fail to answer to bail if it is granted, or that he will interfere with witnesses or obstruct the course of justice. Once charged, the person must be brought before a court as soon as practicable, in any event not later than the first available sitting, which itself must be no later than the next day (excluding Sundays, Christmas Day and Good Friday).

(**h**)   *The police treatment of detained persons.* Section 66 of PACE empowers the Home Secretary to issue Codes of Practice on police powers and procedures; nevertheless, Part V of the Act makes specific provisions in respect of:

(i) *The searching of detained persons.* The custody officer must cause to be included in the custody record particulars of property in the possession of detained persons at the station. They may therefore be searched (by a constable of the same sex) only in so far as is necessary for this duty to be performed. The custody officer may seize and retain any property other than items subject to legal privilege (e.g. lawyer-client communications). However, he may retain clothes and personal effects only if he believes that they may be used by the detained person to cause physical injury to himself or others, to damage property, to interfere with evidence or to assist him in escape *or* if he has reasonable grounds for believing that they may be evidence relating to an offence by anyone. The person from whom the property is seized must be told the reason, unless he is incapable of understanding what is said.

(ii) *The rights of detained persons.* Before questioning an arrested person, the custody officer must explain the reason for the detention. He must also inform him (and give him written notice) of his rights to have someone informed of his arrest and location, to have access to legal advice, and to consult the codes of practice. He is also entitled to a copy of the custody record and to be formally cautioned ('You do not have to say anything unless you wish to do so, but what you do say may be given in evidence'). The exercise of the rights to have someone informed and to have legal advice may be delayed for up to 36 hours(48 hours for those detained under terrorism legislation), if the detention is for a serious AO and provided that authority is given by a superintendent (or above). The person detained must be informed of the reason — i.e. that the exercise of the rights might interfere with evidence of serious AOs, alert others suspected of having committed them or hinder the recovery of property. In normal circumstances the detainee must be supplied with writing materials, if they are requested, may speak on the telephone to one person (apart from the right to have someone informed) and, at the discretion of the custody officer, may have visitors. A 24-hour duty solicitor scheme ensures that detainees can receive free legal advice from a solicitor of their own choice or one from a list which must be provided.

3. The freedom of property

As shown in 19:1–3, entry on property possessed by another, without lawful authority, or remaining on it after authority has been withdrawn, constitutes the tort of *trespass*. Statutory right of entry is, however, enjoyed by numerous people — e.g. Customs and Excise Officers, Public Health officials, meter-readers, etc. Under s. 8 of PACE a magistrate may, on application, issue a warrant authorising a constable to enter and search premises (here meaning any place, vehicle, vessel, aircraft, hovercraft, off-shore installation, tent or movable structure) and to seize anything specified. There are also the following powers of entry, search and seizure *without a warrant*:

(a) *The police powers of entry to arrest*. Under s. 17 of PACE, and provided that he has reasonable grounds for believing that the person concerned is to be found thereon, a constable may enter and search any premises to execute an arrest warrant, to arrest a person for an AO (or for certain offences under the Public Order Act 1936 or the Criminal Law Act 1977), to recapture a person who is unlawfully at large, to save life or limb, or to prevent serious damage to property —

Kynaston v. *DPP; Heron* v. *DPP* (1988): Knowing that a robbery had been committed, police sought to arrest a known person, suspected of being on the premises of K and H, who resisted police attempts to enter. They were convicted of obstructing the police in the execution of their duty and of assaulting a constable. Dismissing their appeals, the Divisional Court held that the police had entered lawfully, as reasonable grounds were justified by the fact that they desired to arrest a known person and had communicated that intention.

(b) *The common law powers of entry*. In addition to the above statutory provisions, the police are entitled at common law to enter and remain on the premises without a warrant, in order to prevent a breach of the peace —

> *Thomas* v. *Sawkins* (1935): A meeting on private premises was advertised with the purpose of protesting against the Incitement to Disaffection Bill, and to demand the dismissal of the Chief Constable. Admission was open to the public and the police attended but were requested to leave. A constable committed a technical assault on the promoter, thinking that he was about to use force. The Divisional Court upheld the magistrates' ruling that this was not unlawful, because the police were entitled to enter and remain on the premises throughout the meeting, as they had reasonable grounds for believing that there might be incitement to violence and breaches of the peace.

A private citizen may enter premises to save life or limb, or to prevent serious damage to property — *see Cope* v. *Sharpe* (1912) (20:**2(a)**).

(c) *The police powers of entry and search after arrest.* Under s. 18 of PACE, a constable may enter and search any premises occupied or controlled by a person who is under arrest for an arrestable offence, if he has reasonable grounds for suspecting that there is evidence on the premises that relates to the offence — or to some other AO which is connected with or similar to it. Such entry and search must be authorised in writing by an inspector (or above) —

> *R* v. *Badham* (1987): His sons having been arrested, B refused police officers entry to his house and demanded to see the authority for their search. This had been orally obtained from an inspector, who had simply made an entry in his notebook. B was convicted of obstructing a police officer in the execution of his duty but his appeal was allowed, as the inspector's authority had not been given 'in writing'. In addition, officers were not entitled to enter the house to search under s. 32 (8:**2(e)**), as that section applies only to search 'upon arrest' and does not give an open-ended right to return to the premises.

(d) *The police powers of seizure.* Under s. 19 of PACE, a constable who is lawfully on any premises is empowered to seize anything if he has reasonable grounds for believing that it has been obtained through the commission of an offence, or that it is evidence in relation to an offence, and that it is necessary to seize it in order to prevent its being concealed, lost, altered or destroyed. On similar grounds, he may also require information contained in a computer to be produced in a visible and legible form which can be taken away.

4. The freedom of association

Persons may freely associate and demonstrate unless there is a specific rule to the contrary. Meetings and demonstrations may be subject to local Acts and by-laws, and prosecutions can be brought under the Highways Act 1980, s. 137, whereby an offence is committed if anyone, without lawful authority or excuse, in any way wilfully obstructs the free passage along a highway. Currently, however, the most relevant statutes are:

(a) *The Public Order Act 1936.* Passed at the time of the British Union of Fascists, this is still being applied and, under s. 1, it is an offence to wear a uniform signifying association with a political organisation (or with the promotion of a political object) in a public place or at a public meeting. More important today is s. 3, which empowers a chief officer of police to prescribe routes for processions and to prohibit entry into specified public places, if he has reasonable grounds for believing that there might be serious disorder. This has been extended, by the 1986 Act below, to include serious damage to property, serious disruption of the life of the community and coercion or intimidation of others. Should the police believe that the conditions which they could impose would not prevent serious disorder, etc, they can apply to the local council for a ban prohibiting the procession, and this requires the Home Secretary's consent.

(b) *The Public Order Act 1986.* This was passed to combat the growth of violence in demonstrations, etc, and relevant provisions are contained in:

(i) *Part I.* This abolished four common law offences, replacing them with:

Riot (s. 1). This is committed when 12 or more persons, who are present together, use or threaten unlawful violence for a common purpose. Guilt attaches only to the actual use of violence and the maximum penalty is 10 years' imprisonment and/or a fine.

Violent disorder (s. 2). This is committed when three or more persons use or threaten unlawful violence. It is triable on indictment in the Crown Court (maximum five years' imprisonment and/or a fine) or summarily by magistrates (six months' imprisonment and/or a fine).

Affray (s. 3). This is committed when one or more persons use or threaten unlawful violence towards another. It could be a suitable charge for fights outside public houses, etc, and it is triable on indictment (up to three years' imprisonment and/or a fine) or summarily (up to six months' imprisonment and/or a fine). Riot, violent disorder and affray (which can all take place in private, as well as public, places) can be committed only if there has been behaviour such as to cause a person of reasonable firmness to fear for his or her personal safety.

(*ii*) *Part II.* This supplements the 1936 Act in providing a legal framework for the holding of:

Marches and processions (s. 11). The organisers of marches must give seven days' notice to the police, but this requirement may be relaxed for marches called at short notice because of some emergency and it does not apply to funeral and commonly-held religious or other processions.

Static demonstrations and assemblies (s. 14). Static demonstrations and assemblies of at least three people in a public place, wholly or partly open to the air, do not require advance notice to the police. Subject to judicial review, however, the police are empowered to impose conditions to prevent serious disorder, serious damage, serious disruption or intimidation. The conditions may not alter the date and time of an assembly but they can limit its size, location and duration —

Police v. *Reid (Lorna)* (1987): R was charged with failure to comply with a condition imposed upon an assembly outside South Africa House, by a senior officer, who defined 'intimidation' as 'putting people in fear or discomfort'. The question was whether the demonstrators intended to 'compel' visitors not to enter the building, or merely to cause them discomfort, in order to make them reconsider conditions in South Africa. Causing discomfort was not intimidation, also the officer had not shown that he believed the intention to be that of compelling. Consequently, Bow Street Magistrates' Court held that he had no ground for imposing the condition and R had thus not committed any offence in failing to comply with it.

5. The accountability of the police

A complaint in respect of police conduct should be made to the chief constable of the force concerned (the commissioner, in the case of the Metropolitan and City of London forces) who, under Part IX of PACE must then determine:

(a) *The procedure for an investigation.* On receiving a complaint, the chief constable must decide which of the following methods is appropriate for dealing with the matter:

(*i*) *The informal resolution.* This is possible only if the complainant consents, and the conduct complained of would not justify a criminal or disciplinary charge. In such circumstances, an officer may be appointed to assist in seeking the informal resolution. Statements made therein may not be used in any subsequent criminal, civil or disciplinary proceedings.

(*ii*) *The formal investigation.* If an informal resolution is not either suitable or possible, the chief constable must appoint a chief inspector (or above, at least equal in rank to the officer complained of, and possibly from another force) to investigate the matter and submit a report.

(*iii*) *The referral to the Police Complaints Authority.* Constituted by PACE, this comprises a chairman appointed by the Monarch and at least eight other members (who may not be current or former policemen), appointed by the Home Secretary. Members serve for a maximum of three years at a time and the Authority is not a servant or agent of the Crown. Any complaint alleging conduct resulting in death or serious injury *must* be referred to this body, whilst other complaints *may* be so referred. The Authority may then supervise an investigation, in which case it approves the investigating officer, who must then make a report.

(b) *The procedure following an investigation.* If, on receiving a report, the chief constable decides that it indicates:

(*i*) That a criminal offence may have been committed and that it is too serious for him to deal with, by preferring disciplinary charges, he must send a copy to the Director of Public Prosecutions. After the latter has settled the question of criminal proceedings, the chief constable must send a memorandum to the Authority, stating whether he has preferred disciplinary charges and, if not, why not.

(*ii*) That a criminal offence may have been committed but that it is not too serious for him to deal with, by way of disciplinary charges, he must send a memorandum to the Authority, stating whether he has preferred such charges and, if not, why not. If the Authority considers that the report indicates a serious criminal offence, it may direct the chief constable to send a copy to the DPP.

(*iii*) That a criminal offence has not been committed, he must send a memorandum to the Authority, stating whether he has preferred disciplinary charges and, if not, why not. This would not, however, be necessary if charges have been preferred and the accused has admitted them. If the Authority considers that the report indicates a serious criminal offence, it may direct the chief constable to send a copy to the DPP.

When a memorandum states that a chief constable has not preferred (or does not propose to prefer) disciplinary charges, the Authority may recommend (and ultimately direct) him to do so. If a policeman is convicted or acquitted of a criminal offence, he may not be charged with a disciplinary offence which is substantially the same — though he may be charged with having been found guilty of a crime. Whatever the outcome of his complaint, a citizen always has the right to bring a civil action (e.g. for false imprisonment, trespass, etc) against the police.

6. The freedom of expression

As shown in 1:2(c), an important function of the law is the balancing of interests and this is of particular significance when it comes to a question of restricting an individual's freedom to communicate information or opinions on any matter. A common law inhibition exists in the action for defamation (21:1–4), which supports a person's interest in preserving his reputation. Statutory limitations have, in the main, been imposed in order to protect:

(a) *The security of the state.* For 78 years there existed an extremely unsatisfactory and all-embracing provision in the Official Secrets Act 1911, s. 2, whereby it was unlawful to retain without permission *any information* obtained in Crown employment, to communicate it to an unauthorised person, or *for anyone to receive it.* This was abolished by the Official Secrets Act 1989, which defines categories of information protected by the criminal law against unauthorised disclosure (mostly by Crown servants or government contractors). The different classes include security and intelligence (covering also former members of the relevant services), defence (if prejudicial to the capability of the Armed Forces), international relations (if jeopardising British interests abroad), crime and its investigation (if impeding prevention or detection), also confidential information between states and international organisations (if likely to cause harm). There also exists a Defence Press and Broadcasting Committee, containing representatives of the media. This approves the issue of 'D' Notices — i.e. confidential letters by government departments to editors, requesting that certain information should not be published. Disregard of these is not unlawful, unless it constitutes a breach of the Official Secrets Act.

(b) *The preservation of law and order.* Under the Public Order Act 1936, s. 5, as amended by the Public Order Act 1986, it is an offence, in a public or private place, to use threatening, abusive or insulting words or behaviour intended, or likely to cause another person to fear violence, or to provoke the use of violence by another person —

> *G* v. *Chief Superintendent of Police, Stroud* (1988): On the swings in a children's playground, G had become abusive when asked to leave. By the time the police arrived, G's mother was present in an agitated state, with several other people, and the officers noted 'a very ugly confrontation'. On being told to go home, G walked off swearing and making gestures at the police. He refused to stop doing so

and, when arrested under s. 5 of the 1936 Act, he punched and threatened to stab an officer. The Divisional Court held that the arrest (on the basis that a breach of the peace was likely) was lawful.

Under the Police Act 1964, s. 53, it is also an offence to do any act calculated to cause disaffection in a police force, or to induce a police officer to commit a breach of discipline.

(c) *The administration of justice.* It has already been shown that restrictions on the publication of information by the media exist in respect of committal proceedings (4:4(b)), juvenile offenders (4:4(c)), and contempt of court (5:2(c)) —

> *Att-Gen* v. *News Group Newspapers* (1988): After the county prosecuting solicitor had decided that there was insufficient evidence to prosecute a doctor who had allegedly raped an eight-year-old girl, the *Sun* newspaper published details of the allegations and arranged financial assistance for a private prosecution. The doctor was acquitted and the Attorney-General applied for the newspaper to be fined for contempt of court. The Divisional Court held that there had been contempt — because of the encouragement to prosecute, together with an intention to prejudice a fair trial by publishing material which would be inadmissible in evidence but could influence potential jurors.

(d) *The maintenance of racial harmony.* Provisions of the Race Relations Act 1976 are outlined in 8:7(b). More recently, the Public Order Act 1986, s. 18, has made it unlawful for any person to use threatening, abusive or insulting words or behaviour (or to display material which is threatening, abusive or insulting) if he intends thereby to stir up racial hatred, or if racial hatred is likely to be stirred up thereby. The offence may be committed in a public or private place (other than a dwelling where the words or material are not heard or seen except by other persons therein). *See also* sex discrimination — 8:7(a).

(e) *The interests of public welfare.* Various statutes proscribe the dissemination of material that might deprave or corrupt people. The Obscene Publications Acts 1959–1964 make it unlawful to publish obscene matter, or to possess an obscene article for publication for gain. The test of obscenity is whether the effect of an article, or any one of its items, taken as a whole, is such as to tend to deprave and corrupt persons likely to read, see or hear it. It is a defence that publication is justified as being for the public good in the interests of science, literature, art, learning, etc. Other statutory offences concerning obscenity relate to transmission by postal packet, photography of children, public displays, video recordings and cable programme services. Under the Children and Young Persons (Harmful Publications) Act 1955, s. 1, it is unlawful to disseminate publications consisting wholly or mainly of stories told in pictures (with or without written matter) portraying the commission of crimes, acts of violence, cruelty or incidents of a repulsive or horrible nature, in such a way that the work as a whole would tend to corrupt a child or young person into whose hands it might fall. There still exists the common law offence of *blasphemy* (the denial of Christianity, the Bible, the Book of Common Prayer and the existence of God) but a prosecution is instituted only if (written or spoken) publication might lead to a breach of the peace.

> *R* v. *Skirving; R* v. *Grossman* (1985): S and G were book distributors and had copies of a publication which described in detail how to prepare cocaine for smoking as the best form of ingestion. They were convicted under the Obscene Publications Act 1959 and their appeal was dismissed.

> *R* v. *Lemon; R* v. *Gay News* (1979): Having published a magazine containing an offensive drawing with an accompanying poem describing promiscuous homosexual practices by Christ, L and GN were convicted of blasphemous libel and the House of Lords dismissed their appeal.

7.   The freedom from discrimination

Unlike the civil liberties already outlined, freedom from discrimination in respect of sex or race is positively enforced, with the following conduct being statutorily proscribed:

(a) *Sexual discrimination.* Under the Equal Pay Act 1970, a woman's pay must be the same as that of a man (the 'male comparator') if their work is 'of equal value' (but not if there is a 'material difference') *or* if an official job evaluation study rates the work as equivalent; moreover, any collective bargaining agreement, between an employer and a trade union, which provides different rates of pay for men and women can be annulled. In addition to basic pay, the provisions cover overtime, bonuses, sick pay, holidays and fringe benefits. Claims regarding alleged breaches of the Act are made to an industrial tribunal, with appeals lying to the *Employment Appeals Tribunal (EAT)*. The Sex Discrimination Acts 1975–1986 prohibit much wider spheres of discrimination by way of: treating a woman less favourably than a man; treating a man less favourably than a woman; treating a married person less favourably than one who is single; or victimising anyone for invoking the above Acts. Most aspects of employment are covered — e.g. recruitment policy, training, promotion, redundancy and dismissal, etc. Thus, although there are obvious exceptions (e.g. in relation to actors, lavatory attendants, etc), it is normally unlawful for employment advertisements to indicate any discrimination — even if only 'constructive' (i.e. where unnecessary requirements indirectly place one sex or a married person at a disadvantage). Discrimination is likewise prohibited in the admissions policies or facilities of educational establishments (other than single-sex institutions), the disposal of premises, and 'the provision of goods, facilities and services' (e.g. by insurance and hire purchase companies, banks, restaurants, bars, etc). Complaints regarding alleged discrimination in employment are made to an industrial tribunal, but in other cases they lie to the county court. The 1975 Act also established the *Equal Opportunities Commission (EOC)* of 14 members and with three main functions: to work towards the elimination of discrimination; to promote equality of opportunity between men and women generally; and to keep under review the working of the above statutes. The EOC can conduct formal investigations into any unlawful discrimination (requiring, if necessary, the giving of evidence and production of documents), serve non-discrimination notices and apply injunctions. *See also* 2:5(c).

(b) *Racial discrimination.* Under the Race Relations Act 1976 it is unlawful to treat someone less favourably than others on account of colour, race, nationality or ethnic origin. Here again, most aspects of employment are covered and discrimination can be 'constructive' (e.g. needlessly prohibiting the wearing of headgear — which would, of course, include turbans). Similarly prohibited are discriminatory advertisements (e.g. regarding jobs or house vacancies), even if published outside the United Kingdom. Discrimination must not be practised in educational establishments or in 'the provision of goods, facilities and services' (e.g. by hotels, bars, insurance companies, banks, doctors, estate agents, clubs of 25 or more members, etc). Complaints regarding alleged discrimination in employment are made to an industrial tribunal; if, however, they relate to education, they must first be made to the Secretary of State for Education and Science, who then has two months in which to act. This apart, all complaints in respect of housing, education and the provision of goods, facilities and services lie to the county court, which can grant an injunction and award damages (even for injured feelings). The 1976 Act also established the *Commission for Racial Equality (CRE)*, which is appointed by the Home Secretary and has up to 15 members, including representatives of racial minorities. Its powers are similar to those of the EOC but the onus of making a complaint normally rests on the aggrieved person, and not the CRE. A complainant is not entitled to legal aid but, in certain circumstances (e.g. significant or complex cases), the CRE may give assistance, including arranging for legal advice and assistance, and representation.

The parliamentary review of administration

8.   The investigation of maladministration

The rights and duties of the state, and the limits of its powers in relationship with the individual, constitute what can be termed *administrative law*. In some countries this is a completely separate system — with the French, for example, having a *droit administratif*, whereby any grievance about administration can be submitted to a special *tribunal administratif*. Appeals therefrom lie to a powerful *Conseil d'Etat* and this has built up a body of case law, establishing a code of fundamental principles. In Britain, however, nothing similar exists and administrative law comprises simply the piecemeal development of rules and principles relating to the numerous governmental organisations (e.g. ministries, agencies, local authorities, commissions, boards, etc) which implement government policy. Of crucial importance to the individual is the limitation of their powers and this is supervised by both Parliament and the courts. In 1:7(a), it has already been shown that the government itself is subject to the ordinary law in the ordinary courts; furthermore, many disputes relating to the administration of policy are determined by administrative tribunals (4:**12**). Supervision of delegated legislation is primarily the responsibility of Parliament (3:**3(a)**), which also provides a system for investigating alleged injustices from the way in which government departments, health authorities and local councils handle matters concerning individuals. The following three types of independent officials (often referred to by the name of a Scandinavian counterpart, the *Ombudsman*) have been statutorily established to investigate such grievances:

(a) *The Parliamentary Commissioner for Administration (PCA).* This official investigates *maladministration* by *government departments* — and examples include: failure to reply adequately and promptly to letters; general inattention or slowness; giving misleading or inaccurate advice; rudeness, bias, discrimination or inconsistency; and failure to have (or to follow properly) administrative rules and procedures. It can thus be seen that the PCA cannot question a properly taken decision (even if it appears unfair) — as there must be some injustice caused by the way in which it was handled. His investigations are further subject to the following provisions:

    (i) *The exclusions.* The PCA will not consider complaints if alternative remedies exist through the courts of law or administrative tribunals, unless it is unreasonable to expect the complainant to resort to these. Matters not subject to his investigation include: the nationalised industries; relations or dealings with other governments or international organisations; actions taken by Crown officials outside the United Kingdom; the administration of the governments of the dependencies; extradition proceedings; the investigation of crime and the security of the state (including action relating to passports); the commencement or conduct of civil or criminal proceedings (also proceedings in military or international courts); contractual or commercial transactions by government departments (other than those relating to the compulsory purchase of land, or disposal of such land); the conditions of service in the Armed Forces or Civil Service; and the granting of honours, awards and royal charters.

(*ii*) *The procedure*. Complaints by an individual or an organisation (other than a local authority, nationalised industry or other public body) must first be made in writing to an MP, within a year of the time when the complainant first knew of the matters alleged. Complainants must be resident in the United Kingdom, *or* must have been in the United Kingdom when the action concerned took place, *or* their complaints must relate to rights or obligations which arose in the United Kingdom. If the aggrieved party dies or is unable to act for himself, a complaint may be made by his personal representatives, family or some other suitable person. On receiving a complaint through an MP, the PCA must first decide whether it falls within his jurisdiction. If it does, an investigation is conducted in private (initially by the PCA's staff) and the head of the department (and any official) concerned must have the opportunity of commenting on the allegations. The PCA has full powers to examine departmental documents (but not Cabinet papers) and to take written or oral evidence from anyone (including ministers and civil servants). Wilful obstruction of his investigations is punishable as if it were contempt of court. The PCA reports the results of his investigations to the MPs who referred the matters to him and to the heads of the departments concerned. He requests departments to remedy anything which has caused injustice but he has no power to rescind or alter administrative decisions. He submits to Parliament an annual report on his work and also draws attention to cases where it seems to him that an injustice has not been, and will not be, remedied. Such matters are then considered by a House of Commons select committee.

(b) *The Health Service Commissioner*. This official investigates complaints that a health authority has caused someone injustice or hardship by failing to provide a service which should have been provided, by failure in a service provided, or by some other maladministration. Examples are similar to those above but, additionally, the Commissioner can look into matters such as: inadequate consultation about planning (e.g. concerning the closure of hospitals, etc); ineffective liaison between branches of the Health Services and with local services; lack of information to hospital patients and relatives; loss of patients' property; wrongful detention in psychiatric hospitals; delays in admission, etc. His investigations are subject to the following provisions:

(i) *The exclusions.* Here again, complaints will not be investigated if remedies exist through the courts of law or administrative tribunals. The following matters are also excluded from investigation: clinical decisions about the care or treatment of a patient; the service provided by family doctors, dentists, opticians or pharmacists; personnel matters (e.g. staff appointments, pay, discipline and superannuation); and contractual or other commercial transactions (except those relating to the provision of services for patients).

(ii) *The procedure.* Complaints may be made to the Commissioner (i.e. not through an MP) by any individual or organisation (e.g. a patient, a patient's relatives, a hospital visitor or voluntary body), provided that the relevant authority has previously been given the opportunity to hold an investigation and to reply. If the Commissioner decides that the complaint falls within his jurisdiction, he commences an investigation and, on its completion, he sends a report to the complainant and to the authority concerned. He also submits reports to the House of Commons select committee.

(c) *The local commissioners.* These officials investigate complaints of maladministration by any local authority (other than a parish council), joint planning board or police authority. Here 'maladministration' includes neglect or unjustified delay; failure to follow the council's agreed policies, rules or procedures; failure to have proper procedures or to review them when necessary; malice, bias or unfair discrimination; failure to take relevant matters into account; faulty methods of doing things; and failure to tell people of their rights. The commissioners' investigations are subject to the following provisions:

(i) *The exclusions.* The following matters are excluded from investigation: anything affecting all or most of the inhabitants of a council's area (e.g. the size of the community charge); the commencement or conduct of court proceedings; the investigation or prevention of crime; the conduct of a police officer; personnel matters (e.g. appointments, dismissals, pay, pensions and discipline); the internal affairs of schools and colleges; contractual and commercial transactions (other than those relating to land); and public passenger transport, docks, harbours, entertainment, industrial establishments and markets.

(ii) *The procedure.* Provided that the relevant authority has been given a prior opportunity to resolve the matter, a complaint must be made through a local councillor but, if he refuses or fails to send it on, it can be forwarded direct to the Commissioner. If the latter considers that the complaint falls within his jurisdiction, he commences an investigation. On its completion, he sends a report (not mentioning people's names) to the complainant and to the council, which must make it available to the public for at least three weeks. If injustice caused by maladministration is found, the authority must inform the Commissioner what action is taken and, if it does nothing, he may make a further report, whereat the process of publication is repeated. In a number of instances, authorities have ignored second reports with impunity.

The judicial review of administration

9. The liability of the Crown

Under the Crown Proceedings Act 1947, the Crown (in the sense of the state) can be sued for breaches of contract or torts. Proceedings (which must be brought against an 'authorised department' or, if this is in doubt, against the Attorney-General) are subject to certain limitations in respect of:

(a) *The liability in contract.* The Crown is liable for breaches of contracts entered into, on its behalf, by its agents but it is not bound by (and cannot be sued on) contracts with its own employees. Thus members of the Armed Forces are dismissible at pleasure — though, under the Employment Protection (Consolidation) Act 1978, civil servants can resist unfair dismissal.

(b) *The liability in tort.* The Crown is liable, in the same manner as a private person of full age and capacity, for most torts committed by its servants or agents in the general course of their functions. Included, therefore, is the liability of occupiers of property (18:5–6), and duties owed by employers to their employees. Actions will not, however, lie in respect of the Queen in her personal capacity, the exercise of judicial process or an *Act of State* — i.e. an act authorised or ratified by the Crown and committed on foreign territory against an alien.

(c) *The forms of redress.* Damages and costs may be awarded against the Crown, also the prerogative orders outlined in 8:10. However, decrees of specific performance or orders for the recovery of land (or delivery of property) will not be made, nor will execution be levied against Crown property. Nevertheless, in such circumstances, the courts generally give declaratory judgments and invariably the Crown complies.

(d) *The discovery of documents.* As shown in 6:2(c)–(d), this occurs in the pre-trial procedure for civil action but, under s. 28 of the 1947 Act, the Crown can refuse disclosure if it would be contrary to the public interest. Formerly it rested with the relevant minister to decide whether disclosure should be withheld but this practice ceased with —

Conway v. *Rimmer* (1968): In this action for malicious prosecution, brought by C, a dismissed probationary police constable, against R, his former superintendent, the Home Secretary claimed the right to withhold certain reports. However, the House of Lords held that the Minister's statement was not conclusive and that a court should, where appropriate, inspect the documents and decide whether to accept the claim.

10. The procedure of judicial review

As shown in 7:2(e), this is confined to public law and thus relates to an infringement of rights by an individual or body exercising statutory powers. Unlike *appeal*, which concerns the *merits* of a case, judicial review is a means of challenging the *legality* of a process — generally on the grounds that it was erroneous in law, *ultra vires* (8:11) or contravening the rules of natural justice (8:12). The procedure enables an aggrieved party to obtain from the Queen's Bench Division an injunction, a declaration or any of the three *prerogative orders* outlined below. The five remedies may be sought singly or in the alternative and, where appropriate, damages may also be awarded. Within three months from the date when the grounds arose, an application must be made to a judge in chambers *ex parte* (i.e. without a writ to the other party, who should nevertheless be informed) for *leave to apply*. If this is granted, the court later hears the case and decides whether or not to grant the relief sought. Appeal lies to the Court of Appeal and the House of Lords. The prerogative orders are:

(a) *The order of mandamus.* This is used to command a person or body to perform a mandatory (but not discretionary) public law duty, which must be specific and enforceable; furthermore, the applicant must have called for its fulfilment and have met with a refusal or non-compliance. It will not be granted if a satisfactory alternative remedy exists; moreover, though technically not available against the Crown, it may issue to compel a minister to carry out a statutory duty. Additionally, the order lies to compel inferior courts and tribunals to exercise their jurisdiction, to compel the delivery of public documents or to compel the restoration of a person to a public office from which he has been wrongfully evicted. *See Re Godden* (1971) (8:**12(b)**).

(b) *The order of certiorari.* This lies only in respect of persons or bodies having judicial or quasi-judicial functions and duties, when it appears that they have acted wrongly in law, *ultra vires* or in contravention of the rules of natural justice. On granting *certiorari*, the court may quash a decision, vary a sentence, or remit the matter to the inferior body for reconsideration in accordance with its finding. *See R* v. *Secretary of State for Transport, ex parte GLC* (1985) (1:**7(a)**), *R* v. *Great Yarmouth BC, ex parte Botton Bros* (1988) (8:**12(a)**).

(c) *The order of prohibition.* This lies to tribunals and all inferior courts with limited jurisdiction (civil, criminal, ecclesiastical, military, etc). It forbids the *commencement or continuance* of proceedings if they are (or are likely to be) wrongful in law, *ultra vires* or in contravention of the rules of natural justice. It is immaterial whether an alternative remedy (e.g. an injunction) or a right of appeal is available. *See Re Godden* (1971) (8:**12(b)**).

11. The scope of the *ultra vires* doctrine

If an individual or body with statutory powers exercises them in excess of what is authorised, the use is said to be *ultra vires* ('beyond the powers') and resultantly invalid. The application of this principle to delegated legislation has been illustrated in 3:3(b). Acting *in excess of* powers has now been extended to cover *abuse of* powers; thus the doctrine may be invoked if an individual or body exercises its powers:

(a) *For an improper purpose.* This has been illustrated in —

> *R* v. *Derbyshire County Council, ex parte The Times Supplements* (1990): After the *Sunday Times* had published two articles accusing it of improper and legally doubtful behaviour, DCC withdrew all advertising for educational appointments from News International publications. The Divisional Court held that, being motivated by bad faith or vindictiveness, this decision was *ultra vires* and costs were awarded to Times Newspapers.

(b) *In an improper or unreasonable manner.* This has been illustrated in *R* v. *Secretary of State for Transport, ex parte GLC* (1985) (1:7(a)).
(c) *By delegated authority.* Sometimes a statute may expressly or impliedly authorise delegation of functions but, apart from this, *delegatus non potest delegare* ('a delegate cannot delegate'), as illustrated in —

> *R* v. *Secretary of State for the Environment, ex parte Hillingdon London Borough Council* (1986): The council's standing orders delegated to the chairman of the planning committee the function of authorising the service of enforcement notices (which relate to breaches of planning control). A company in receipt of such a notice appealed to the Secretary of State who ruled that a council could not delegate its functions to a committee with only one member. Refusing the council judicial review, the Divisional Court held that, in its modern meaning, a committee is a body of more than one member — and this was upheld by the Court of Appeal.

12. The rules of natural justice

It was in *R* v. *Sussex Justices, ex parte McCarthy* (1924) that Lord Hewart, CJ pronounced his much-quoted dictum — 'It is of fundamental importance that justice should not only be done, but should manifestly and undoubtedly be seen to be done'. To this end, the common law imposes on courts, tribunals and individuals who 'act judicially' an obligation to apply the *rules of natural justice*, and these are:

(a) *Audi alteram partem ('Hear the other side')*. This means that nobody shall be penalised by a judicial decision unless given prior notice of all relevant information which will be used against him, adequate time to prepare his case and the opportunity (orally or in writing) to state it. Application of the rule may sometimes be impractical — if, e.g., there are justifiable grounds for confidentiality, but natural justice — or fairness — must be observed in the reaching of any decision seriously affecting individual interests — notably livelihood, status, right to property, etc —

> *R* v. *Great Yarmouth Borough Council, ex parte Botton Brothers' Arcades* (1988): GYBC planning committee having recommended the granting of planning permission for an amusement arcade, sea-front traders wrote asking for the decision to be delayed while they presented objections. The full council voted not to defer the decision and to accept the recommendation. The traders sought judicial review and it was held that, although there was no duty to hear the objectors, fairness required that they be heard and *certiorari* would issue to quash the decision.

(b) *Nemo iudex in causa sua ('No one a judge in his own cause')*. This means that no one may act judicially *if he has a pecuniary interest in the proceedings or is subject to a reasonable suspicion (or real likelihood) of bias*. Any pecuniary interest, however small, would disqualify an adjudicator unless the parties were made aware of it and waived their objection, or unless all available adjudicators were affected by a disqualifying interest. There is no need to prove *actual* bias, because only a 'reasonable suspicion' or 'real likelihood' is necessary — and this may accrue on numerous grounds — e.g. kinship, prejudice, a professional relationship, a personal friendship or animosity, membership of a particular organisation, etc —

> *Dimes* v. *Grand Junction Canal Proprietors* (1852): Over a period of 12 years, in a dispute about land, decrees made by

the Vice-Chancellor in favour of GJCP were affirmed by
Lord Chancellor Cottenham. It was then discovered that the
latter owned several thousands of pounds worth of shares in
GJCP and, on appeal to the House of Lords, the decrees
were set aside.

Re Godden (1971): Accusations against his superior made by
G, a chief inspector of the Kent police, were not upheld in a
report by a chief constable of another force. Erotic
documents had also been found in G's desk and, having
seen the report, Dr Crosbie Brown, chief medical officer of
the Kent force, certified G unfit for duty, on account of
mental disorder. G's own consultant psychiatrist was not
allowed to see the report and certified him 'completely
normal'. In order compulsorily to retire G, the Police
Authority nominated Dr Brown to determine whether he
was 'permanently disabled', under the Police Pensions
Regulations 1971. Reversing the decision of the Divisional
Court, the Court of Appeal held that an *order of prohibition*
should issue, to disqualify Dr Brown from determining the
matter as, having already committed himself to a view, he
could not bring an impartial judgment to bear in
performing a quasi-judicial function. An *order of mandamus*
was also granted to compel the Police Authority to disclose
the report to G's medical advisers.

Progress test 8

1. How relevant in England are the decisions of courts on the
continent of Europe? **(1)**

2. Consider whether the enactment of a Bill of Rights would be
desirable. **(1)**

3. Walking down Bumblecombe High Street, Andrew saw a
fight break out and turned away. At that moment several police
cars arrived and suddenly Andrew was seized by the neck. He
attempted to free himself and was told he was under arrest for
obstructing a constable in the execution of his duty. In the
process of being searched, he was compelled to remove his

jersey and shirt, then he was taken to the police station and has now been released on bail, without being charged. Advise Andrew.   **(2)**

4.   Brian was holding a party at his flat and, unknown to him, one of the guests had brought along a friend who had just absconded from a Young Offenders' Institution. Suddenly, and without a warrant, four police officers forcibly entered the flat. Without giving any reason, they arrested Brian and the escapee, then searched the premises and took away an expensive watch and a camera, which Brian had received as birthday presents. In police custody, Brian now seeks your advice.   **(2–3)**

5.   Caroline wishes to organise an anti-blood sports march through Bumblecombe, and the Bumbleshire Constabulary is concerned that there might be a counter-demonstration. Advise Caroline and the police as to their rights.   **(4)**

6.   Is the procedure for dealing with complaints about police conduct satisfactory?   **(5)**

7.   Has legislation imposed unreasonable constraints upon freedom of expression?   **(6)**

8.   Do the statutory commissions adequately protect people from discrimination?   **(7)**

9.   Britain now has several statutorily-appointed 'ombudsmen'. Examine their functions and the adequacy of their powers.   **(8)**

10. Wrongly suspected of theft from a pavilion, David has had his membership of the Bumblecombe Cricket Club abruptly terminated and he has also been summarily dismissed from the Bumbleshire police force. In neither instance did he have adequate opportunity to defend himself. Advise David.   **(10–12)**

Part two

The law of contract

9

The elements of a simple contract

The forms of contracts

1. The nature of a contract

There are numerous circumstances wherein two or more persons make agreements, many of which (e.g. arranging social engagements) are not in any way legally binding. However, *an agreement which the law will enforce* constitutes a *contract* and there are two principal ways in which this is created. In the first place, there is the *deed* — an instrument (i.e. a formal legal document) described in 9:6(a). The vast majority of legal obligations are, however, informally created by way of a *simple contract*. Found in numerous everyday situations (e.g. making a purchase, travelling on public transport, etc), this is formed whenever four essential elements exist:

(a) *An offer*. This is an undertaking by the *offeror* (i.e. the party making the offer) to be contractually bound in the event of a proper acceptance by the *offeree* (the party to whom the offer is made). *See* 9:2.

(b) *An acceptance*. This occurs when the offeree accepts the offer, provided that he has not previously rejected it; also that it has not lapsed or been revoked. *See* 9:3.

(c) *Consideration*. This is some *act or forbearance* (or the promise thereof) by the offeree, in return for the promise of the offeror. Consequently, unless it is made by way of a deed, a gratuitous offer to do something for someone cannot be enforced at law. Consideration involves not only the payment of money but also forms of positive conduct (e.g. agreements to carry out tasks) or undertakings to refrain therefrom. *See* 9:**4**.

(**d**) *An intention to create legal relations.* In the majority of transactions, this is presumed to exist but it can be negated (thus precluding the creation of a contract) by an express provision in the agreement between the parties or by implication (e.g. where the agreement is purely social or domestic). *See* 9:**5**.

The essentials of simple contracts

2.   The requirements of an offer

It is possible for an offer and an acceptance to be effected without any words at all being used — thus, if a man habitually visits a particular shop, throwing down a sum of money on the counter and receiving a packet of cigarettes tossed across in return, without the exchange of any pleasantries, a simple contract will nevertheless exist. Normally, however, for an offer to be valid:

(**a**) *It must be firm in form.* An offer exists when the offeror makes a firm promise to be bound, provided that certain conditions are fulfilled. An offer will *not* be constituted by a mere statement of price or by an *invitation to treat* (i.e. an attempt to induce an offer). This is found, e.g., when goods are advertised in the media or displayed in shop windows, or when an auctioneer makes requests for bids. In such circumstances the offer is actually made by the prospective purchaser. However, certain advertisements (e.g. offering rewards for lost possessions) constitute an effective offer in what is sometimes called a 'unilateral contract' — *see* 9:**3**(**c**):

> *Partridge* v. *Crittenden* (1968): In a journal, P inserted a classified advertisement 'Bramblefinch cocks and hens 25 shillings (£1.25) each' and, having sent 25s, a customer received a bramblefinch hen. Under the Protection of Birds Act 1954, P was convicted of offering wild birds for sale but the Divisional Court quashed the conviction on the ground that he had made no offer for sale — but merely an invitation to treat.

> *Courtney & Fairburn* v. *Tolaini Bros (Hotels)* (1975): TB had agreed to instruct their quantity surveyor to negotiate terms for three building projects by C&F, if the latter could

make satisfactory financial arrangements. The Court of Appeal held that TB were not bound by the agreement, as the law did not recognise a 'contract to negotiate' any more than it would acknowledge 'a contract to enter into a contract'.

(b) *It must be definite in substance.* The terms of an offer must be certain — though sometimes an uncertainty may be cured by reference to the previous course of dealing between the parties, a special provision for resolving the uncertainty, a trade custom or a statute; meaningless terms can be ignored and the contract will operate without them —

> *Scammell & Nephew Ltd* v. *Ouston* (1941): O ordered a van from S&N 'on the understanding that the balance of the purchase price can be had on hire-purchase terms over a period of two years'. The House of Lords held that no contract existed because the offer (i.e. the order) was so vague that it had no definite meaning without further negotiations.

> *Foley* v. *Classique Coaches Ltd* (1934): F agreed to supply CC with petrol 'at a price to be agreed by the parties in writing from time to time' and, in the event of a dispute, reference should be made to arbitration under the Arbitration Act 1889. It was held that a valid contract existed because the arbitration provision resolved the uncertainty.

(c) *It must be communicated to the offeree.* An offer may be made in any manner whatsoever (e.g. orally, in writing or by implication from conduct); furthermore, it may be made to a particular person (*see Duff's Executors' Case* (1886) (9:**2(e)**)), a group of persons or to the world at large (*see Carlill* v. *Carbolic Smoke Ball Co* (1893)(9:**3(c)**)). However, it has no validity until it is communicated to the offeree — thus it appears that anyone returning a lost or stolen article cannot claim a reward unless he knew that it had been offered —

> *Taylor* v. *Laird* (1856): During a voyage, T gave up command of L's ship but helped to work it home and claimed payment for this. It was held that there was no contract as he had not communicated his offer to do the work.

(d) *It may be revoked at any time before acceptance.* Revocation is not effective until communicated to the offeree, but the information may be given by words or conduct — and not necessarily by the offeror himself. A *letter of revocation* takes effect from the *time of receipt,* but a *letter of acceptance* is effective from the *time of being properly posted* in the normal manner (but not merely handed to a postman delivering letters). An *option* (i.e. an undertaking to keep an offer open for a stipulated period) is not binding unless embodied in a second *(collateral)* contract with its own consideration. *See* 14:5**(d)** and 15:3**(b)** —

> *Dickinson* v. *Dodds* (1876): On 10th June the defendant offered to sell the plaintiff a house and it was agreed that the offer should remain open until 9 am on 12th June. On 11th June the plaintiff heard from one Berry that the defendant had agreed to sell the house to one Allen; he nevertheless handed over an acceptance of the offer just before 9 am on 12th June. It was held that no contract existed because the revocation was effective, albeit communicated by a third party.

> *Henthorn* v. *Frazer* (1892): On 7th July F offered H some houses for sale. At 12.30 pm on 8th July he wrote revoking the offer; at 3.30 pm that day H posted a letter of acceptance and at 5 pm he received the letter of revocation. It was held that a valid contract existed from 3.30 pm.

(e) *It remains open until accepted, rejected, revoked or lapsed.* An offer lapses on the death of either party or after a stipulated period (or reasonable time, if no period is stipulated) —

> *Duff's Executors' Case* (1886): Having been offered shares in exchange for others, D died and his executors purported to accept the offer. It was held that the offer had lapsed on D's death.

> *Ramsgate Victoria Hotel* v. *Montefiore* (1866): On 8th June M made an offer to take shares in the hotel and this was accepted on 23rd November. It was held that the interval was unreasonable and the offer had lapsed.

(f) *It may be constituted by a tender.* If it relates to *a single transaction,* a tender constitutes a *definite offer* (which may be accepted to form a binding contract). However, if it is for the supply of goods or services *as and when demanded*, then it becomes a *standing offer*. In the latter case there is a separate acceptance (and contract) each time an order is placed, and a standing offer can be revoked at any time (except in respect of goods or services actually ordered) unless there is a *binding* undertaking to keep it open for a stipulated period —

> *Great Northern Railway* v. *Witham* (1873): GNR accepted W's tender to supply for 12 months goods 'in such quantities as the Company may order from time to time'. Several orders were carried out but, before the year had elapsed, W refused to execute one. It was held that there was a standing offer to be converted into a series of contracts by the subsequent acts of GNR, who succeeded in their action for breach.

> *Percival Ltd* v. *London County Council* (1918): P submitted a tender for the supply of certain goods in such quantities and at such times as LCC should, from time to time, require. The tender was accepted but orders were placed elsewhere. It was held that there was no contract and therefore no breach.

3. The validity of an acceptance

Many negotiations are so complex that it is difficult to define easily the stages at which there was an offer and then an acceptance. One problem arises in the case of *cross-offers* (i.e. where two parties simultaneously communicate identical offers to each other); in such circumstances, and with no clear precedents, it would appear that there would be no acceptance and consequently no contract. Normally, however, for an acceptance to be valid:

(a) *It may be made only by the offeree.* This rule is relevant only if the offer was made to a particular person or group of persons — *see Duff's Executors' Case* (1886) (9:2(e)).

(b) *It must be unqualified.* To create a contract, an acceptance must correspond in every detail with the terms of the offer. A *counter-offer* operates as a rejection of the original offer (which therefore lapses). A *tentative assent* (e.g. an acceptance 'subject to contract') is *not* binding but this must be distinguished from a *provisional agreement* (e.g. 'this is a provisional agreement until a legal document is drawn up') which *is* binding.

Hyde v. *Wrench* (1840): W offered to sell H his farm for £1,000. H offered £950 (which W refused) and then purported to accept the offer to sell for £1,000. It was held that this had been rejected and had ceased to exist.

Stevenson v. *McLean* (1880): M offered a quantity of iron to S, who sent back a telegram asking what credit limit could be given. M then sold the iron to a third party and S sent a second telegram accepting the offer. It was held that the first was a mere request for information and not a counter-offer; there had been no revocation, therefore there was a valid contract.

Eccles v. *Bryant & Pollock* (1948): The parties agreed on the sale of certain property 'subject to contract'. The contract was drawn up and counterparts (identical forms) were provided for each party. The purchaser signed his counterpart and posted it to the vendor, who did not sign his counterpart. The Court of Appeal held that no contract existed.

Branca v. *Cobarro* (1947): B agreed to purchase the lease and goodwill of C's mushroom farm and they both signed a document which ended with the words: 'This is a provisional agreement until a fully legalised agreement, drawn up by a solicitor and embodying all the conditions herewith stated, is signed.' It was held that the words showed that the parties intended the agreement to be binding and it would therefore remain in force until its provisions were embodied in a formally drawn-up document.

Butler Machine Tool Co v. *Ex-Cell-O Corporation* (1979): BMT offered machinery for sale on condition that orders would be accepted only on the terms set out in their quotation, which contained a price variation clause. ECO placed an order on their own form (which did not include a price variation clause) with a tear-off slip, on which BMT acknowledged the order. Due to ECO's delay in accepting delivery, BMT invoked the price variation clause and the

Court of Appeal held that ECO's reply was a counter-offer which BMT had accepted by their acknowledgment.

(c) *It must generally be communicated to the offeror.* Normally an acceptance is ineffective unless and until it is communicated to the offeror. The two main exceptions to this rule arise when acceptances are made by post (in which case they are effective as soon as posted — **9:2(d)**) and also when the offeror expressly or impliedly waives communication (e.g. in a general offer, where performance constitutes acceptance) —

> *Carlill* v. *Carbolic Smoke Ball Co* (1893): CSB offered £100 to anyone who contracted influenza after using their smoke-ball thrice daily for a fortnight. C did so but caught influenza and claimed £100. It was held that the offer contained an intimation that performance was adequate acceptance and there was a valid contract

(d) *It must involve positive conduct.* Mere mental acceptance is not sufficient, nor may the offeror stipulate that he will take silence to be acceptance, and thus bind the offeree —

> *Felthouse* v. *Bindley* (1863): F was negotiating for the purchase of his nephew's horse for either £30 or 30 guineas (£31.50p) and he wrote: 'Split the difference — unless I hear from you to the contrary, the horse is mine for £30.15s (£30.75p)'. B, an auctioneer, later sold the nephew's stock, including the horse. It was held that F did not own the animal, even though there had not been any reply to his letter.

(e) *It may normally be communicated in any manner.* However, if the offeror expressly or impliedly prescribes a mandatory (but not merely directory) mode of acceptance, communication in any other manner would not suffice.

> *Yates Building Co* v. *R.J. Pulleyn & Sons* (1975): An option to purchase land was granted subject to its being exercisable by notice in writing 'sent by registered post or recorded delivery'. The intending purchaser's solicitors sent a notice by ordinary post and the Court of Appeal held that the

prescribed form of posting was directory and not mandatory; therefore the option had been validly exercised.

Domb v. *Isoz* (1980): The Court of Appeal held that, where a solicitor, acting for a vendor or purchaser, holds his client's signed part of a contract, exchange of contracts may be effected in any way recognised by law; in such circumstances, a valid contract could thus be created by a telephone conversation.

4. The existence of consideration

Consideration may be either *executed* (if carried out at the time of the agreement) or *executory* (if merely promised for some future time). For consideration to be valid:

(a) *It must be real*. Consideration must have some value, thus it cannot be constituted by an existing duty (e.g. a public duty or contractual liability); however, it may be sufficient if a party does more than he was already bound to do. It does not matter how small the value is, so long as it is worth something; therefore, inadequacy of consideration is no ground for avoiding a contract unless it is 'so gross as to amount to conclusive evidence of fraud', (*per* Lord Eldon). Nevertheless, consideration will *not* be sufficient if it is vague, incapable of performance, illegal or merely 'good' (e.g. natural love and affection) —

Stilk v. *Myrick* (1809): A ship's captain promised his crew the wages of two deserters if they would share the work of the missing men. It was held that there was no consideration by the crew, as they were already contractually bound to do any extra work to complete the voyage.

Harris v. *Sheffield United Football Club* (1987): On many occasions during the season numerous police officers had been on duty inside SUFC's ground. Contending that these were not 'special services', the Club refused to pay for them. The Court of Appeal held that the services were 'special' and they had been requested by SUFC which was financially liable for them.

(b) *It must move from the promisee*. Anyone seeking to enforce a promise must prove that *he himself* (and not a third party) has given consideration for it; the doctrine of Privity of Contract (*see* **15:1**) is merely an aspect of this rule:

> *Tweddle* v. *Atkinson* (1861): T's father and prospective father-in-law, William Guy, agreed between themselves to pay T £100 and £200 on his marriage. This took place but Guy failed to pay the £200 and later died. T sued Guy's executor for the sum and it was held that his action must fail, as he had not given any consideration.

(c) *It must not be past.* An act performed by one party prior to the other's promise cannot normally be consideration to support that promise. However, a previous act may constitute valid consideration if it was performed on the understanding that there should be some consideration and the subsequent promise simply fixed the amount —

> *Re McArdle* (1951): A bungalow was left to a widow for her lifetime and thereafter ownership was to pass to her children. A daughter-in-law, who lived there, made extensive repairs to the building and all the children then wrote to her, promising to pay her £488 'in consideration of your carrying out certain alterations and improvements'. The money was not paid and it was held that, as all the work had been finished before the promise was made, the repairs constituted past consideration and payment could not be enforced.

> *Lampleigh* v. *Brathwait* (1615): Having killed a man, B asked L to do all he could to secure a pardon from the King. L spent time and money visiting places where the King was present and B then promised him £100, but failed to pay it. It was held that there was a binding contract, as the subsequent promise fixed the sum to be paid, under an implied promise (to pay a reasonable figure) in the original request.

(d) *It must normally exist to enforce a waiver of rights.* If a party wholly or partially waives his rights under a contract, the waiver is not binding unless consideration is given for it — with the waiver thus becoming part of a collateral contract (*see D & C Builders* v. *Rees* (**16:2(c)**). Hence, if A owes B £100 and B agrees to accept £90, it would appear that he could still sue for the remaining £10, if there is no consideration for the waiver (i.e. a new element introduced at the creditor's request — e.g. payment at an earlier time than necessary, in a different place or in a different form). This rule has however been modified by the doctrine of *promissory (or equitable) estoppel*, applied in the case below. This means that if B waives his contractual rights against A, *who acts to his detriment in reliance on the waiver*, it is only fair that B should be estopped from denying that he intended the waiver to be binding. This principle is *a shield and not a sword*, i.e. it can be raised only as a defence and *not* as a cause of action (e.g. if a creditor retracts his waiver and receives payment in full, the debtor cannot later sue on the doctrine to recover the money paid) —

Central London Property Trust Ltd v. *High Trees House Ltd* (1947): In 1937 CLPT let a block of flats to HTH at a ground rent of £2,500 per annum. In 1940, on account of the War, few flats could be let; consequently HTH found difficulty in paying the ground rent and CLPT agreed in writing to reduce it to £1,250. In 1945 the whole block became full again and CLPT sued for the balance of rent at the original contract rate for the last six months of 1945, pleading that, if they had so wished, they could have claimed full rent back to 1940. It was held that CLPT were entitled to the full rent for the last six months of 1945 but, in *obiter dicta*, Denning J rejected the possibility of a claim back to 1940, thus illustrating that the effect of promissory estoppel is *suspensory* and not extinguishing.

Combe v. *Combe* (1951): After the plaintiff (wife) had obtained a decree nisi, the defendant (husband) agreed in writing to pay her an allowance of £100 per annum. He did not do so and she sued to obtain it. It was held that she was not entitled, as there was no consideration for the promise. The *High Trees* principle did not apply here, as it relates only to situations where there has been a contract in existence and where the plaintiff has made a promise with the intention that it should be acted upon, has gone back on it, and has then sought to recover from the defendant, who has acted to his detriment in reliance on the promise. Consequently, it cannot be argued that the *High Trees* principle strikes at the roots of the doctrine of Consideration.

5.   The rebuttal of a legal relationship

For a simple contract to be enforceable, it is essential that there should be an intention by the parties to enter into a legal relationship. The courts seek to give effect to the presumed intentions of the parties; thus, in commercial agreements, there is a rebuttable presumption that the parties intended to create legal relations. An intention *not* to do so (and to prevent an agreement from being binding) may be established if:

(a) *It is expressed in the agreement.* An enforceable contract will not exist if an agreement is stated to be *subject to contract* (*see* 9:**3(b)**)) or if words are used that clearly rebut the presumption of a legal relationship —

> *Jones* v. *Vernon's Pools Ltd* (1938): J sued on a football pool coupon, which he alleged he had posted and that VP had lost. It contained a condition to the effect that the sending in and acceptance, together with all associated transactions, should be 'binding in honour only' — and it was held that this was a bar to any action at law.

(b) *It is implied from the agreement.* In social or domestic agreements there is a presumption that the parties did not intend to create legal relations. This also applies to vague promises in advertising puffs, etc, and in *Carlill* v. *Carbolic Smoke Ball Co* (1893) (9:**3(c)**) the presumption was rebutted by the fact that the defendants stated that they had deposited £2,000 'to show their sincerity'; consequently, it could be concluded that they had contemplated legal liability.

> *Jones* v. *Padvatton* (1969): With the promise of a maintenance allowance, a mother persuaded her daughter to give up a secretarial post in the USA, in order to read for the Bar in England. Later it was agreed that a house should be provided instead and, when the mother claimed repossession, the Court of Appeal held her entitled to this, as the arrangement with the daughter was not intended to be legally binding. 'There is possibly a presumption that members of a family do not intend arrangements between

themselves to have the force of contract', (*per* Danckwerts LJ).

6.   The requirement of writing

Some types of contracts are required by law to be in writing and it is therefore necessary to draw a clear distinction between:

(a) *The deed.* This is a formal legal document whereby an enforceable promise may be effected without the need for consideration. The instrument must be validly executed by the promisor and it must also indicate on its face that it is intended to be a deed. Valid execution by an individual requires the document to be *signed* by him in the presence of a witness who attests the signature, also *delivered* by him — or by someone authorised to do so on his behalf. For effective delivery, it is not essential that the instrument should be handed over to the other party — as simply an act or words indicating an intention to treat it as a binding deed would be sufficient. Deeds executed by corporations must not only be signed and delivered but also *sealed* (with the corporation seal); consequently they are sometimes referred to as 'contracts under seal'. Deed are essential for certain contracts (e.g. conveyance of land) but they can be used for any promises or mutual covenants (e.g. partnership agreements).

(b) *The written contract.* Various statutes require certain simple contracts to be *in writing* — though not necessarily in the form of a deed. An important example is the Law of Property (Miscellaneous Provisions) Act 1989, s. 2, which provides that: 'A contract for the sale or other disposition of an interest in land can only be made in writing and only by incorporating all the terms which the parties have expressly agreed in one document or, where contracts are exchanged, in each.' This does not, however, apply to contracts for short leases (not exceeding three years), or made in the course of a public auction, or regulated under the Financial Services Act 1986. The essential elements to be included in such written contracts are the identities of the parties, the land affected and the consideration — or the means of agreeing it. The document(s) incorporating the terms (which may simply comprise an exchange of letters) must be signed by or on behalf of each party. The expression 'interest in land' has been held to include: rights of way; mines and minerals; machinery affixed to land;

shooting rights (including the removal of game), etc; but *not* the granting of a *licence* (e.g. a permit to enter land).

Progress test 9

1. Distinguish between an offer and an invitation to treat. **(2)**

2. Having advertised plastic gnomes for sale at a quoted price, Alan received an order for 200 from Ben and posted a reply agreeing to supply them. Half an hour later he discovered that his stock had been vandalised and could be replaced only at a large increase in cost, so he telephoned Ben with a new price. Advise Ben. **(2)**

3. Knowing that Charles wanted to buy a second-hand car, Donald wrote to him, offering one at £500. Charles replied 'I can pay only £400 but, if this is OK, don't bother to reply and I will collect the car on Saturday'. Hearing nothing further, he went to fetch the vehicle and found that it had been sold to someone else. Advise Charles. **(3)**

4. Examine the nature and scope of the doctrine of promissory estoppel. **(4)**

5. Do you consider that an intention to create legal relations is an essential element of a simple contract? **(5)**

10

The capacity of the parties

The significance of capacity

1. The capacity of minors

In its legal context, the term *capacity* means the ability to do something (e.g. to make a contract) and it can be assumed that the common law was developed to apply chiefly to the sane, sober, British adult. Special conditions therefore exist for persons differing from this norm — particularly in contract if there is *inequality of bargaining power* (*see also* 11:8, 12:3(c)–(e), 13:2(c), 13:5, 14:1(c)), and the first to be considered is the *minor* (i.e. a person under 18 years of age). A parent is not liable for his child's contracts, unless the latter was acting as his agent but, under the Minors' Contracts Act 1987, s. 2, a *guarantee* of an unenforceable or voidable contract by a minor is as valid and effective as if he were of full age. In general, most contracts made by minors with adults are enforceable against the party of full age but *unenforceable* against the minor; there are, however, the following exceptions:

(a) *The enforceable contracts for necessaries.* Under the Sale of Goods Act 1979, s. 3, a minor is under an obligation to pay *a reasonable sum* (though not necessarily the contract price) for goods or services necessary to him, according to his condition in life and requirements *at the time of sale and delivery* —

> *Chapple* v. *Cooper* (1844): The defendant (a widowed minor) attempted to avoid paying for her late husband's funeral but it was held to be a necessary for which she was liable.

> *Nash* v. *Inman* (1908): I, a Cambridge undergraduate not of

full age, was provided with proper clothes by his father but had been supplied with £145 worth of clothing (including 11 fancy waistcoats) by N, a tailor. The Court of Appeal held that these items were not necessaries and that N's action must fail.

(b) *The enforceable contracts for training.* Minors are bound by 'beneficial contracts of service' i.e. contracts of employment which are *of benefit to them in their education or training for a career* —

Chaplin v. *Leslie Frewin (Publishers) Ltd* (1966): C, a minor and the son of Charlie Chaplin, contracted to tell his life story to a 'ghost writer' in return for the royalties on the resulting book. After he had passed the text for publication, he repudiated the contract on the ground that the book was libellous. It was held that the agreement was analagous to a contract of service and binding on C, because it was for his benefit — enabling him to make a start as an author, also to support himself and his wife without relying on social security.

Mercantile Union Guarantee Corporation Ltd v. *Ball* (1937): MUGC sued B (a haulage contractor not of full age) for arrears on the hire-purchase of a lorry. It was held that this was neither a contract for necessaries nor of beneficial service; rather, it was a trading agreement which was not binding on B.

(c) *The voidable contracts of continuing obligation.* These include marriage settlements and agreements to rent property, to form partnerships and to take up shares which are not fully paid up. Such contracts are binding on minors unless expressly repudiated by them before (or within a reasonable time of) attaining full age. Complete repudiation can be made only on coming of age, prior to which it is merely suspensive and can be cancelled at 18. The minor is responsible for any liabilities accrued at the time of avoidance and cannot recover anything paid unless there has been a total failure of consideration —

Corpe v. *Overton* (1833): C, a minor, contracted to form a partnership in the following January, paying £100 down and agreeing to put in a total of £1,000. On coming of age, he repudiated the agreement, refused to sign the partnership deed and sought to recover his £100. It was held that the money had been for a future partnership which never existed; therefore there was a total failure of consideration and C was entitled to repayment.

Steinberg v. *Scala (Leeds) Ltd* (1923): The plaintiff (a minor) applied for, and was allotted, shares in the defendant company. She paid the amount due on allotment but repudiated the contract 18 months later and sued to recover her payment. It was held that she was entitled to repudiate her obligation to pay anything further but she could not recover the money paid — as the shares had some value and there was thus no failure of consideration.

In the case of voidable contracts entered into by minors, the Minors' Contracts Act 1987, s. 3, empowers the court to order the restitution of any property unjustly or unfairly acquired. In certain circumstances s. 15(1) of the Theft Act 1968 (26:6) might also apply.

2.   The capacity of insane or drunken persons

Contracts made by insane persons whose property is subject to the control of the court (under the Mental Health Act 1983) are *void*, because otherwise they would interfere with the court's right of control. Apart from this, a contract is *voidable* at the option of a party who can prove that he was, through drunkenness or insanity, incapable of understanding its nature — unless the other party can establish one of the following points:

(a) *It was ratified during a sober or lucid moment*, even though the disability may have been known to the other party —

Matthews v. *Baxter* (1873): B bought a house from M while drunk but ratified the agreement when sober. It was held that there was a valid contract.

(b) *It relates to the acquisition of necessaries*. When necessaries are sold to a person who, by means of mental incapacity or drunkenness, is incompetent to contract, he is bound to pay a reasonable price, — regardless of whether or not the disability was known to the other party.

(c) *It was entered into by the other party in ignorance of the disability.* The onus lies on the person seeking to avoid the contract to show his state of mind at the time of the agreement and *also the other party's knowledge of it —*

> *Imperial Loan Co* v. *Stone* (1892): S pleaded that he was insane when he made a promissory note but he was unable to convince the jury that ILC knew this. It was held that the defence could not succeed unless S was able to establish both issues.

3. The capacity of corporations

The contractual capacity of corporations (5:**7(a)**) depends on the manner in which they are created:

(a) *The chartered corporation.* The ability of a chartered corporation to enter into a contract is not subject to any legal limits; consequently an agreement which is *ultra vires* (beyond the powers granted in) the charter is nevertheless valid.

(b) *The statutory corporation.* The contractual capacity of a statutory corporation is defined, expressly or impliedly, in the creating statute. Any contract which is *ultra vires* the statute is *void*; consequently anyone who has supplied goods or services to a statutory corporation under an *ultra vires* contract cannot succeed in an action to recover the cost — but, if the goods can be traced and identified, he may seek to recover them.

(c) *The registered corporation.* The contractual capacity of a limited company is defined by the *objects clause* which must be included in its Memorandum of Association. Formerly any contract which exceeded the powers thus set out was held to be void; however, the Companies Act 1989, s. 108, provides that, if a person is dealing with a company in good faith, any transaction decided upon by the directors is deemed to be within its capacity.

4. The capacity of unincorporated associations

If any member of a partnership enters into a contract concerning the firm's usual business (even if he had no authority to do so), all partners will be liable unless the other party was aware of a lack of authority or did not think that he was contracting with a partnership. Should the contract be apparently unconnected with the firm's usual business, only the partner who entered into it would be liable (unless his action was authorised by the other partners). A trade union can sue and be sued in contract but a club or society is not a competent contracting party and, if a contract is made on its behalf, recourse lies only against the person who actually made it (and any other members who authorised him to do so) —

> *Rowntrees of London (Builders)* v. *Screen Writers Club* (1953): Three members of a club committee had been held personally liable in the county court for payment for work done on the club premises. Dismissing their appeal, the Court of Appeal held that, in the absence of any other evidence, the judge was entitled to infer that the work had been ordered by the committee and that the members before him were liable.

Progress test 10

1. Sam, a talented guitarist aged 16, wanted to become a pop star and entered into a two-year contract with Grasping, an agent, who agreed to pay him £60 a week for the exclusive use of his services. After a year, Sam's performances are now netting Grasping about £5,000 a week and Sam seeks your advice, as he wishes to change agents.   **(1)**

2. Goodbooks Ltd supplied two GCSE texts and a £40 work on jurisprudence to Roger, aged 15, who has a vague interest in law and who told the shop to send the bill to his father. The latter is not a customer of the firm and has declined to pay anything. Advise Goodbooks.   **(1)**

3. Fred (aged 19) formed a painting and decorating partnership with Joe (aged 16), who contributed £150 at the outset. In the first six months they made a satisfactory profit, which they shared but, after a year, Joe became discontented and withdrew, seeking the refund of his £150. Advise Fred.   **(1)**

4. Under the influence of drink, O'Reilly has ordered a luxury car which he cannot afford and he seeks your advice.   **(2)**

5. Examine the contractual capacity of corporations and unincorporated associations. **(3, 4)**

11
The nature of void contracts

The types of void contracts

1. The forms of void contract

The phrase 'void contract' can be a contradiction in terms, as it generally describes an agreement which has no legal effect whatsoever and is deemed never to have existed at all. Contracts may be rendered void as a result of:

(a) *The existence of operative mistake.* The general common law rule is that any mistake made by either or both parties does not affect the validity of a contract. However, if a mistake of *fact* (but *not* law) is *so fundamental as to destroy the basis of the agreement*, it is termed an *operative mistake* and it will cause the contract to be void *ab initio* (i.e. it never existed, right from the beginning). It may be found in three main forms: the *common* mistake (where the same error is made by both parties — *see* 11:2); the *mutual* mistake (where there is a misunderstanding between the parties which neither realises — *see* 11:3); and the *unilateral* mistake (where only one party is mistaken and the other realises the fact — *see* 11:4). At common law, contracts which may involve an operative mistake are either totally void or completely valid; however, as shown in 11:5, there may be forms of equitable relief available.

(b) *The contravention of the law.* Agreements which fulfil all the requirements of a valid contract may nevertheless conflict with legal rules laid down by statute or common law. Some contracts are absolutely prohibited and are then termed *illegal* (*see* 12:1–2); others may merely be denied their full validity and they are said to be *void*. In the main, statutory provisions relate to contracts which are contrary to the public interest (e.g. restrictive trading agreements — 11:6), whilst the common law principally concerns those that contravene public policy. In both cases, contracts do not necessarily become totally void, but only in so far as they conflict with the public interest or policy. Thus, if *severance* (i.e. the deletion of the void part without in effect creating a new contract) can be effected, the rest of the agreement may remain valid.

The existence of operative mistake

2. The forms of common mistake
The same error may be made by both parties generally in relation to:

(a) *The existence of the subject-matter.* If, at the time of making a contract, both parties are wrong in believing that the subject-matter exists, then the agreement will be void (as it relates to *res extincta*). However, if a seller is deemed to have warranted the existence of the goods concerned, he is probably liable to the purchaser for breach of contract. From 16:4 it will be seen that a close relationship exists between mistake and frustration.

> *Couturier* v. *Hastie* (1856): A contract was made for the
> sale of a cargo of corn which, unknown to the parties, had
> already been sold (having been damaged at sea). The House
> of Lords held that no contract existed. The Sale of Goods
> Act 1979, s. 6, now provides that 'where there is a contract
> for the sale of specific goods and the goods, without the
> knowledge of the seller, have perished at the time when the
> contract is made, the contract is void'.

(b) *The quality of the subject-matter.* Common mistake concerning the quality of the subject-matter is *not* operative at common law and therefore does not invalidate a contract —

> *Leaf* v. *International Galleries* (1950): L bought a painting of
> Salisbury Cathedral from IG, both parties believing it to be
> by Constable. Five years' later L discovered that it was not
> painted by that artist and claimed rescission of the contract.
> The Court of Appeal held that his claim must fail as it had
> not been brought within a reasonable time and, in *obiter*

dicta, Denning LJ said: 'There was a mistake about the quality of the subject-matter . . . . such a mistake, however, does not avoid a contract.'

3.   The forms of mutual mistake

In these circumstances both parties are at cross purposes — one believing one fact and the other believing another — generally in relation to:

(a) *The identity of the subject-matter.* No contract will exist if the parties are not *ad idem* (of the same mind) concerning what constitutes the subject-matter —

> *Raffles* v. *Wichelhaus* (1864): A contract was made for the sale of cargo to arrive 'Ex *Peerless* from Bombay'. Two ships of the same name left Bombay and W thought that the agreement referred to the one sailing in October, whereas R thought that it was the one in December. It was held that there was no contract.

> *Scriven Bros & Co* v. *Hindley & Co* (1913): SB's auctioneer sold hemp and tow. Samples of each were on view before the sale but the catalogue did not explain which lots were which, and the sacks were identical. The tow was knocked down to H, who thought that they had been bidding for hemp. On realising their mistake, they refused to pay. It was held that SB's action must fail, as there was no agreement between the parties.

(b) *The quality of the subject-matter.* Here again mistake concerning the value or quality of the subject-matter will generally *not* affect the validity of an agreement (but see *terms* at 14:1) —

> *Smith* v. *Hughes* (1871): A farmer offered to sell oats to a racehorse trainer's manager, who retained samples for 24 hours and then accepted the offer. He later refused delivery because new oats arrived and he thought he had been buying old ones. It was held that the manager's mistake (which was not induced by the farmer's conduct) would not invalidate the contract.

(c) *The terms of the contract.* Mutual mistake concerning the terms of a contract will generally *not* affect its validity —

Wood v. *Scarth* (1858): W accepted S's written offer of the lease of a public house for £63 per annum. S incorrectly thought that his clerk had told W that there was also a premium of £500 and refused to grant the lease without this. It was held that the contract without the premium was valid.

4. The forms of unilateral mistake

Mistakes made by one party only, and recognised by the other, are generally in relation to:

(a) *The identity of the other party.* Mistake concerning the identity of the person with whom a contract is made will nullify the agreement *only if the identity is of material importance* and *if the other person realises that it is not intended that he should become a party to the contract* —

Cundy v. *Lindsay* (1878): One Blenkarn ordered goods from L, signing the order to give the impression that it came from the reputable firm of Blenkiron & Co. He did not pay for them and sold them to C. It was held that the contract between L and Blenkarn was void for mistake; consequently, the property in the goods still resided in L, who was entitled to recover them from C.

King's Norton Metal Co v. *Edridge, Merrett & Co Ltd* (1897): One Wallis set up the sham business of Hallam & Co, with impressive letterheadings. Using these, he obtained from KNM, without payment, goods which were subsequently purchased from him in good faith by EM. It was held that, as KNM had previously traded with Wallis, and as he had signed the order, they could not argue that they had intended to trade with Hallam & Co, and not with him. Consequently the contract was *not* void for mistake and KNM could not recover from EM.

Lewis v. *Averay* (1973): Posing as Richard Green, a well-known actor, and identifying himself with a Pinewood Studio pass, a fraudster acquired L's car with a worthless cheque and then sold it to A. L sued A to recover the vehicle but the Court of Appeal held that L had intended to contract with the person present in front of him, whoever he was, thus the contract was *not* void and A had a good title to the car. However, Lord Denning observed that the agreement might have been voidable at the instance of L, if he had acted before A acquired a right in good faith.

(b) *The expression of intention.* If the offeror makes a material mistake in expressing his intention and the other party knows (or is deemed to know) of the error, the agreement will be void —

> *Hartog* v. *Colin & Shields* (1939): C&S offered hare skins for sale at a price 'per pound', in mistake for 'per piece'. H accepted the offer but could not reasonably have supposed that it expressed C&S's real intention. It was held that the contract was void, as H must have known that it was made under a mistake.

> *Centrovincial Estates plc* v. *Merchant Investors Assurance Co* (1983): CE leased property to MIA at a rent of £68,320 per annum, subject to review, and their solicitors wrote inviting MIA to agree to the figure of £65,000, as appropriate at the review date. MIA accepted this by letter and, five days' later, the solicitors telephoned to say that the figure should have been £126,000. The Court of Appeal upheld the agreement for £65,000, as an unambiguous offer had been accepted and MIA had given consideration (by depriving themselves of the right to suggest any other figure).

(c) *The nature of a document signed.* In general, a person is bound by the terms of any document which he signs, even though he did not read it, or did not understand its contents. However, the old common law plea of *non est factum* (it is not his deed) may be used to make an agreement void if a person can show that, *through blindness, senility, illiteracy, trick or fraudulent misrepresentation,* he signed a document which was *radically, fundamentally or totally different from what he believed it to be* and that *he had not been careless* in failing to discover its true nature —

> *Lloyds Bank* v. *Waterhouse* (1990): Relying on LB's misrepresentations about the nature of the document, W signed a bank guarantee, without reading it or informing LB that he was illiterate. The Court of Appeal held that he was entitled to rely on the defence of *non est factum* as well as on the bank's negligent misrepresentation.

Saunders v. *Anglia Building Society* (1971): A Mrs Gallie, aged 78, was induced by her nephew and his business colleague, L, to sign a document which she thought would enable the two men to raise money on the security of her house, by assigning it to the nephew as a gift, on condition that she could live there for the rest of her life. Having broken her glasses, Mrs Gallie could not read the document and did not ask for it to be read to her. It was, in fact, an assignment to L for £3,000 and he mortgaged the house to ABS but did not pay anything to Mrs Gallie. He defaulted on the mortgage payments and the Society sought possession of the house. S (Mrs Gallie's executrix) sought a declaration that the assignment was void because of *non est factum* but the House of Lords held that the plea must fail as the requirements had not been fulfilled.

5. The forms of equitable relief

The common law rules outlined above render a contract either totally void or completely valid, even though neither solution may be entirely just. However, if a person has entered into a contract under a misapprehension that does not constitute an operative mistake, he may nevertheless be able to obtain one of the following forms of *equitable* relief:

(a) *The rescission on terms.* If one party, who is not at fault, can show that it would be unjust for the other to take full advantage of his contractual rights, the court has the power to attach terms to an order rescinding the contract. This means that the original rights and obligations are dissolved and replaced by fresh ones which the court considers fair and just —

Grist v. *Bailey* (1966): B agreed in writing to sell G a house for £850 and, through no fault of either party, both believed it to be occupied by a statutory tenant, who had in fact died. With vacant possession the dwelling was worth about £2,250 and B refused to complete the sale. G sought specific performance (*see* 16:8(e)) and B counter-claimed for rescission. It was held that there was a common mistake such as to entitle B to equitable relief; specific performance was refused and the contract was rescinded on terms that B should enter a fresh contract with G at a proper vacant possession price.

(b) *The refusal of specific performance.* Specific performance is a discretionary remedy, which will not be enforced if a mistake was caused by the plaintiff's misrepresentation or if the plaintiff knew of the defendant's mistake. However, where specific performance is refused, the defendant may still be liable in damages for breach of contract —

> *Webster* v. *Cecil* (1861): W offered C £2,000 for certain land but it was rejected. C then wrote offering the land for £1,250 (really intending to write £2,250) and W accepted, subsequently seeking specific performance. It was held that W must have known of the mistake and specific performance was refused.

(c) *The rectification of a written contract.* If a written contract does not accurately express the agreement actually reached between the parties, the court will rectify the document so as to bring it into conformity. It is necessary, however, for the party seeking rectification to show that *an agreement on all points* had existed between the parties and *had continued unchanged* up to the time when it was expressed in a written document, *which failed to express the agreement* (but not merely the intention) of the parties —

> *Craddock Bros Ltd* v. *Hunt* (1923): CB agreed orally to sell H a house *exclusive of* an adjoining yard, but the written agreement and later conveyance *included* the yard. It was held that both documents should be rectified.

> *Rose (Frederick E.) (London)* v. *Pim (William H.) Jnr & Co* (1953): R received an order from Egypt for 'feveroles'. Not knowing what these were, they inquired of P, who said that they were horse-beans, which they could supply. R thereupon gave an oral order for the purchase of 'horse-beans' and the contract was later put into writing. When they ultimately reached Egypt, it was found that they were not 'feveroles'. It was held that the written contract correctly expressed the oral agreement and therefore could not be rectified.

The contravention of the law

6. The invalidity of restrictive trading agreements

Under the Restrictive Trade Practices Act 1976 (as amended by the Competition Act 1980), all agreements whereby two or more producers, suppliers or exporters restrict manufacture, supply or distribution (e.g. by fixing prices, terms of supply, quantities or descriptions of goods produced or supplied, process of manufacture, etc) are *void* unless registered with the Director General of Fair Trading (*see* 4:9(a)). The latter must submit such registered agreements to the Restrictive Practices Court and the onus lies on the parties to rebut the presumption that they are contrary to the public interest. It must be shown that the benefits arising from a restriction outweigh any detriments. If the court declares a restriction contrary to the public interest, it is rendered *void*, but the rest of the agreement may remain valid if the offending part can be severed from it —

> *Re Association of British Travel Agents Agreement* (1984): ABTA (a trade association of tour operators and travel agents) has a membership agreement which imposes restrictions on the manner of trading and provides security against loss. On a reference by the Director General of Fair Trading, the Restrictive Practices Court held that certain requirements in the agreement (e.g. relating to the lay-out of retailers' premises, the number and qualifications of staff, etc) were unnecessarily restrictive and contrary to the public interest — though provisions concerning insurance and promotional material were valid. Subsequently, ABTA applied for the court's approval of revised requirements.

7. The invalidity of contracts contravening public policy

The common law has developed the principle whereby the courts will refuse relief to parties claiming under contracts which are *contrary to public policy* (i.e. injurious to the public good) and the principal examples are:

(a) *The contracts to usurp the jurisdiction of the courts.* An agreement which purports to remove the right of either or both of the parties to submit questions of law to the courts is *void*. This does not, however, invalidate arbitration agreements where each party is free, after the arbitral award, to request the court to consider any points of law which are involved.

> *Baker* v. *Jones* (1954): The rules of the British Amateur Weightlifters' Association provided that its central council should be the only body to interpret the rules and that its decision should be final. It was held that this provision was contrary to public policy.

(b) *The contracts prejudicial to the status of marriage.* In this category, agreements which are void include marriage brokage contracts (i.e. where a reward is received for procuring marriages or introducing persons with a view to marriage); contracts to restrain persons from marrying at all (though partial restraint, e.g. from marrying a Roman Catholic, would probably be upheld); and also contracts for future separation of married persons (unless relating to a separation intended to take place immediately) —

> *Hermann* v. *Charlesworth* (1905): H entered into a contract to pay C £250 if a marriage took place following an introduction made by him. She also paid a fee of £52, of which £47 was to be returned if no engagement or marriage took place within nine months. She sued to recover the £52 after nine months had passed without an engagement. It was held that the public policy requires that unsuitable marriages should not take place and, as the incentive of a fee might well produce such marriages, contracts to arrange them are void and H was entitled to the return of her fee. It would appear, however, that agreements with 'dating' agencies (which limit their obligation to providing introductions) would not be void.

> *Lowe* v. *Peers* (1768): P covenanted not to marry anyone other than L and to pay her £1,000 if he did so. It was held that the agreement was void, because it restrained him from marrying at all if L did not marry him — and she was not bound to do so.

(c) *The contracts impeding parental duties.* A contract whereby a parent deprives himself/herself of his/her child's custody is void — though a court order to the same effect is binding.

(d) *The contracts in restraint of trade. See* 11:8 *below.*

8. The invalidity of contracts in restraint of trade

These are agreements whereby a party undertakes to suffer some restrictions as to carrying on his trade or profession. At common law such contracts are presumed to be *void* but they will be upheld if it can be shown that the restraint is *reasonable as between the parties* (i.e. no wider than is necessary to protect the proper interest of the party whom it is designed to benefit) and also *reasonable with regard to the interests of the public*. Restraint of trade may be effected between:

(a) *Purchasers and sellers of businesses.* Sometimes the vendor of the goodwill of a business is restrained from competing with the purchaser —

> *Nordenfelt* v. *Maxim Nordenfelt Co Ltd* (1894): N, a manufacturer of guns and ammunition, sold his world-wide business to MN and promised not to manufacture such products anywhere in the world for 25 years. It was held that, as the area supplied by N was practically unlimited, the restraint was reasonable and binding.

> *British Reinforced Concrete Co Ltd* v. *Schelff* (1921): In 1918 BRC purchased a small business (supplying steel reinforcements for concrete roads), the partners of which contracted not to engage in a similar business until three years after the end of the war. One partner took employment with a company, as manager of its reinforced materials department, and BRC sought an injunction to restrain this breach of the agreement. It was held that the restraint clause was wider than necessary to protect BRC's interests; therefore, the injunction was refused.

(b) *Employers and employees.* Sometimes a contract of service provides that an employee leaving the firm shall not set up (or enter the service of) another similar business within a specified area and/or for a stipulated period. Such an agreement is void unless the former employer can show that it is essential for protecting his trade secrets or business connections. Moreover, a restraint clause purporting to restrict a departing employee from using his *skill* in competition with his former employer is always void, even if the skill was acquired in that employer's service. As illustrated below, the principle embraces partners, as well as employees —

> *Littlewoods Organisation Ltd* v. *Harris* (1978): LO's mail-order business (confined to the United Kingdom) competed principally with that of Great Universal Stores (operating world-wide). Employed by LO as a divisional director, H possessed details of their biannual catalogue (crucial to the success of their business) and his contract contained a restraint clause precluding his working for GUS within 12 months of leaving LO. He attempted to do so and, granting an injunction, the Court of Appeal held that the covenant was reasonable and valid as, by the nature of their catalogue, LO possessed trade secrets which they were entitled to protect.

> *Greer* v. *Sketchley Ltd* (1979): Operating a dry-cleaning business in London and the Midlands, S employed G as a director, with a restraint clause precluding his engaging in similar business in any part of the United Kingdom within 12 months of leaving the firm. The Court of Appeal upheld a declaration that the clause was invalid, as it was unreasonably wide in its geographical application. The covenant could not be limited to London and the Midlands — though this was effectively what had been done in the *Littlewoods'* case — and the two were distinguished by the fact that the restraint in the first related to a specific competitor, rather than an area.

> *Hensman* v. *Traill* (1980): T, a general practitioner, became H's partner under an agreement which provided that, if he should leave, he would not practise within seven miles for five years. On the retirement of a third member, the partnership was dissolved and T joined another local practice. H sought an injunction which was refused on the grounds that the purported restriction offended against public policy (in preventing a doctor from caring for patients) and was also unreasonably wide.

(c) *Suppliers and traders.* Sometimes (possibly in return for a loan or lease) a trader enters into a *solus* agreement to buy only the goods of one particular supplier, but the reasonableness requirement will apply —

> *Esso Petroleum Co* v. *Harper's Garage (Stourport) Ltd* (1968): HG entered into a solus agreement with EP for two garages. In the case of the first, they received a discount on agreeing to buy all motor fuel from EP, to keep the garage open at all reasonable hours, and not to sell the garage without ensuring that the purchaser entered into a similar agreement with EP; the agreement was to operate for 53 months. The second garage was mortgaged to EP for £7,000 on terms similar to those of the first but for a period of 21 years. The first agreement was held to be reasonable and valid, but the second was not — and it was therefore void.

(d) *Users and providers of exclusive services.* Contracts *for services* (as well as contracts *of service* — i.e. employment) can be void for unreasonableness, particularly if there is inequality of bargaining power —

> *A Schroeder Music Publishing Co* v. *Macaulay* (1974): M, an unknown songwriter aged 21, contracted to supply all his compositions to S, who were to have full world copyright in return for a fixed percentage on royalties. S could terminate or assign the agreement but M could not terminate it, and could assign it only with S's consent. The contract was initially for five years and S was not bound to publish or promote any of M's compositions. It was held that the restraints could not be justified as necessary and the agreement was therefore void.

Progress test 11

1. Mary offers to sell Jane six chairs which they both believe to be genuine Chippendale. Three months' later Jane seeks your advice, as she has discovered that they are merely reproductions. **(2)**

2. James and Cyril are cousins who intensely dislike each other.

Learning that Cyril wishes to sell a valuable clock, James disguises himself as a clergyman and visits his cousin. With a cheque which is later dishonoured, he buys the clock and then sells it to Malcolm. Advise Cyril. **(4)**

3. In what circumstances will a person who has signed a contractual agreement be able to have an inaccuracy rectified? **(5)**

4. Give examples of contracts that are void at common law as being against public policy. **(7)**

5. Outline the circumstances in which a contract in restraint of trade will be enforceable. **(8)**

12

The nature of illegal contracts

The nature of illegality

1. The forms of statutory illegality

In addition to rendering certain agreements *void* (11:1(b)), statutes or delegated legislation may also make contracts *illegal* — in either their creation or performance:

(a) *The illegality of creation.* The actual promise, consideration or ultimate purpose of a contract may be illegal. One example is the Resale Prices Act 1976, which renders illegal any agreement to impose a minimum price on the resale of goods (*see* 4:9(b)). When a contract is illegal in its creation and both parties were (or should have been) aware of the fact from the outset, no action will lie (unless severance of the illegal part is possible) and neither party can claim any right or remedy (*ex turpi causa non oritur actio*), even in respect of a related transaction —

> *Fisher* v. *Bridges* (1854): F sold B some land to be used for an illegal lottery. B paid the price apart from £630 and executed a deed, promising to pay this sum. F sued on the deed and it was held that, as the original transaction was illegal, the related debt and deed were tainted with illegality and neither would be enforced.

(b) *The illegality of performance.* A contract which is legal in itself may nevertheless become illegal by reason of the way in which it is performed. For this to be the case, however, the prohibited act must lie at the centre of the agreement and not be merely incidental to it. When a contract is illegal in its performance, *a guilty party cannot claim any right or remedy*, but an innocent party has full relief —

> *St John Shipping Corporation* v. *Joseph Rank Ltd* (1957): SJSC sued for the full charge of carrying JR's cargo, despite the fact that their ship had been overloaded and the master had been fined £1,200 for a breach of the Merchant Shipping Act 1932. It was held that the illegal loading was merely incidental to the performance and SJSC was entitled to recover.

> *Ashmore, Benson, Pease & Co* v. *A.V. Dawson* (1973): D (hauliers) contracted to carry goods for ABP, whose transport manager and assistant watched the loading of vehicles to a weight in excess of that permitted by the Motor Vehicles (Construction and Use) Regulations 1966. One vehicle toppled over and its load was damaged, so ABP sued for negligence. It was held that the contract, though lawful in its inception, was illegal in its performance, to the knowledge and with the concurrence of ABP's employees; consequently damages were not recoverable.

(c) *The illegality from subsequent legislation.* The doctrine of *frustration* (*see* 16:4) covers the situation where an existing contract is rendered illegal by a change in the law. In such circumstances, the parties are excused further performance of their obligations and no action will lie for breach.

2. The forms of common law illegality

In addition to the contracts which are *void* at common law (11:7), certain others are also considered to be contrary to public policy — but of such gravity that they are held to be *illegal*. The courts will not enforce these agreements at the instance of either party and the principal examples are:

(a) *The contracts to commit crimes or torts.* Agreements to commit crimes, torts or frauds upon third parties are illegal and they include contracts to defraud the Revenue —

> *Miller* v. *Karlinsky* (1945): M was employed by K for £10 a week plus expenses (which included the income tax payable on the £10). He sought to recover ten weeks' arrears of

salary and expenses (of which £17 represented tax liability). The Court of Appeal held that the contract was illegal, as it defrauded the Revenue; consequently M could not recover even his ordinary salary.

(b) *The contracts against the interests of the state.* Any contract detrimental to the interests of the United Kingdom is illegal — and this also applies to agreements which might disturb relations between the United Kingdom and friendly states —

> *Lemenda Trading Co* v. *African Middle East Petroleum Co* (1988): AMEP agreed (but failed) to pay LT a commission for using influence to persuade the Qatar General Petroleum Co to renew a contract for the supply of crude oil. Such an agreement was unenforceable in Qatar but the parties agreed that it was governed by English law. It was held to be contrary to English public policy; consequently LT's claim failed.

(c) *The contracts prejudicial to the administration of justice.* Examples include contracts involving the concealment of an arrestable offence, promises by defendants to indemnify persons who stand bail for them, etc —

> *Keir* v. *Leeman* (1846): Having commenced a prosecution against L and others for riot and assault, K told them that he would drop the charges if they would pay off a debt owing to him. They agreed and, as no evidence was given against them, they were acquitted but failed to pay the debt. It was held that K was not entitled to recover it as the compromise was an illegal contract.

(d) *The contracts to promote corruption in public life.* Examples include contracts involving the bribery of officials and attempts to buy honours —

> *Parkinson* v. *College of Ambulance Ltd* (1925): The College Secretary fraudulently promised to obtain a knighthood for P in return for a donation. He paid £3,000 but did not receive a title and sought to recover his money. It was held that the agreement was illegal and the action must fail. Such contracts are now criminal offences under the Honours (Prevention of Abuses) Act 1925.

(e) *The contracts to promote sexual immorality.* Any contract will be invalidated if the consideration is an act of sexual immorality or if it is known by both parties that the agreement is intended to further an immoral purpose —

> *Pearce* v. *Brooks* (1886): P hired a carriage to B, knowing that she intended to use it for plying her trade as a prostitute. She fell into arrears with the hire charges and P brought an action to recover the sum due. It was held that the contract was illegal and the money could not be recovered.

The consequence of illegality

3.   The recovery of property

If one party (the *transferor*) passes money or property to the other (the *transferee*) under an illegal contract, an action for its recovery will not succeed, except in the following circumstances:

(a) *If the transferor can establish him claim without relying on the contract* —

> *Bowmakers Ltd* v. *Barnet Instruments Ltd* (1945): Having obtained machine tools from B under illegal hire-purchase agreements (which contravened wartime regulation), BI failed to pay the instalments and sold some of the tools. It was held that B's action for the tort of conversion (19:5) must succeed.

(b) *If the transferor genuinely repents*, before the illegal purpose has been substantially performed. However, he must convince the court that his repentance is real and that he is not repudiating the contract merely for convenience —

> *Bigos* v. *Bousted* (1951): In contravention of the Exchange Control Act 1947, the defendant agreed to supply the plaintiff with the equivalent of £150 in Italian lire. As security for his promise, the plaintiff deposited a share certificate with the defendant, who failed to supply the currency. The plaintiff sued for the return of the certificate, arguing that he had repented. It was held that the so-called repentance was 'but want of power to sin' because, if the lire

had been forthcoming, he would have gladly accepted them; consequently the action must fail.

(c) *If the transferor was induced to enter into the contract by force or fraud.* In such circumstances (also in those outlined in **(d)** and **(e)** *below*) the parties are not *in pari delicto* (equally to blame) —

> *Hughes* v. *Liverpool Victoria Legal Friendly Society* (1916): H was induced by the fraudulent misrepresentation of an insurance agent to enter into an illegal life assurance contract. It was held that the parties were not *in pari delicto* and the premium could be recovered.

(d) *If the transferor belongs to a class protected by statute* —

> *Barclay* v. *Pearson* (1893): A newspaper ran a missing word competition which was held to be a lottery under the Gaming Act 1802 (passed to protect lottery competitors from promoters); consequently those participating could recover their entry fees (but not prizes).

(e) *If the transferee was under a duty to protect the transferor's interests.* If the defendant is the plaintiff's trustee or agent, etc, he cannot retain property on the ground that it has come to him as proceeds of an illegal transaction.

Progress test 12

1. In relation to contract, discuss the maxim *ex turpi causa non oritur actio* ('a legal action does not arise from a base cause'). **(1–2)**

2. Sid agreed to convey Henry's furniture from London to Birmingham for £500. On arriving, Sid confessed that he had been stopped for speeding and was going to be prosecuted; whereat Henry refused to pay him. Advise Sid. **(1)**

3. Bill agreed to paint Mark's house in the evenings for £600 but said that he would accept £400 in cash, 'so that the tax man won't find out'. Mark paid the £400 but is extremely dissatisfied with the work and seeks your advice. **(2)**

4. In respect of illegal contracts, explain the position of parties not *in pari delicto*. **(3)**

5. Rich hired his private aeroplane to Rogue, knowing that it was to be used for smuggling drugs into the country on a particular date. Rogue paid £10,000 in advance but the plane developed a defect and could not be flown on the required day. Rogue wishes to recover his £10,000 and consults you. **(3)**

13

The nature of voidable contracts

The false representation of facts

1. The substance of misrepresentation

A *voidable* contract is a legally binding agreement that exists, but which can be set aside at the instigation of one party — generally on the grounds that he was induced to enter into it by *misrepresentation* or *coercion*. Many statements may be made in the negotiations leading up to a contract. Some of these may be intended to bind a party and they are then called *terms* (*see* 14), the untruth of which would give rise to an action for breach of contract. Other statements, which are made simply to induce the making of a contract and by which the parties do not intend to be bound, are called *mere representations*. If one of these is untrue, it constitutes a *misrepresentation* and the contract may become *voidable* at the option of the party to whom it was made. Misrepresentation can be defined as *an untrue statement of fact which materially induced a party to enter into a contract*, and anyone seeking relief on this ground must therefore prove that:

(a) *It was an actual statement.* Mere silence (i.e. failure to disclose a material fact) does not constitute misrepresentation except in the case of *contracts of utmost good faith* (*see* 13:2) or where there has been either *a change of circumstances* or *a half-truth* —

> *With* v. *O'Flanagan* (1936): In negotiations for the sale of his practice, Dr O'F truthfully told W that it realised £2,000 a year but, on account of his subsequent illness, the figure dropped to around £200. Having purchased the practice, W

discovered the situation and sought to rescind the contract. The Court of Appeal held that the action must succeed, as failure to disclose the changed circumstances amounted to misrepresentation.

Nottingham Patent Brick and Tile Co v. *Butler* (1866): Wishing to purchase some land from B, NPBT asked his solicitor whether it was subject to restrictive covenants (*see* 15:3(a)). He replied that he was not aware of any (simply because he had not read the deeds) and NPBT paid a deposit. On discovering that covenants did in fact exist, they sued to rescind the contract and to recover the deposit. The Court of Appeal held that, although the solicitor's statement was literally true, it was a misrepresentation and the action must succeed.

(b) *It was in respect of a fact.* The statement must relate to an existing *fact*, which may include an *intention* but cannot concern *law*. It has been held in the past that it cannot relate to *opinion* — but this needs to be considered in the light of the second case below —

Edgington v. *Fitzmaurice* (1885): E invested in F's company which had issued a prospectus inviting the purchase of debenture bonds. The stated purpose of these was to finance future expansion but the intention was really to pay off existing debts. E sued for the repayment of his money and the Court of Appeal held that his action must succeed, as the statements constituted misrepresentation.

Esso Petroleum Co v. *Mardon* (1976): In negotiations for a filling-station tenancy, EP told M that they estimated the 'throughput' of petrol to be 200,000 gallons a year by the third year. On account of the lay-out and characteristics of the site, the figure never exceeded 100,000 and EP contended that their statement was only an opinion. Nevertheless, the Court of Appeal held it to be a contractual warranty (14:4(b)) and that EP was liable in damages to M.

(c) *It was a material inducement.* The statement must be made *by one party to the other during the course of the negotiations*, as anything said after an agreement has been reached cannot constitute misrepresentation. Furthermore, a party cannot avoid a contract on the ground of misrepresentation if it can be proved that he was aware of the untruth, ignorant of its existence or made independent investigations into it —

> *Cooper* v. *Tamms* (1988): Negotiating for the purchase of a flat from T, C obtained a surveyor's report indicating that there was slight wet rot and that a specialist should be consulted, as a full investigation had not been possible. Reducing the price by £500, T stated that, to her knowledge, the property had not been subject to wet rot; however, after completion of the contract, extensive existence of it was discovered. C's action for misrepresentation failed, as it was held that reliance had been placed on the survey report, rather than the pre-contract statement.

2. The principle of uberrima fides

It was shown in 13:1(a) that failure to disclose a material fact does not constitute misrepresentation, except in the case of changed circumstances or half-truth. Additionally, however, there are six main types of contract which are said to be subject to the principle of *uberrima fides* (utmost good faith). In such agreements disclosure of all material information must be made and failure to do so renders the contract *voidable* at the option of the other party. The principal examples are:

(a) *The contracts of insurance.* The insured must disclose all material facts that would influence a prudent insurer's decision whether to decline the risk or to increase the premium. Non-disclosure would enable the insurer to avoid the contract —

> *Patten* v. *Grayston* (1977): P insured his car with G, stating on the proposal form that it was kept in a lock-up garage at a private address. When stolen, it was in fact being kept in a public house car park two miles away and G repudiated liability. Judgment was given for G, as it was held that the location of garaging was material.

(b) *The contracts for family arrangements.* For example, the settlement of property, etc —

Gordon v. *Gordon* (1821): Two brothers agreed to divide the family estates as the elder thought that he was illegitimate — although the younger knew this to be untrue. Nineteen years' later the elder learnt the truth and it was held that the agreement should be set aside.

(c) *The contracts within a confidential or fiduciary relationship.* This is deemed to exist between persons connected by certain recognised ties (e.g. parent and child, doctor and patient, solicitor and client, guardian and ward, trustee and beneficiary, but *not* husband and wife). In such cases the person in whom confidence is reposed cannot hold the other to a contract unless he can show that it is advantageous to the other party and that he has disclosed all material facts (*see also* 13:5(b)) —

English v. *Dedham Vale Properties* (1978): During negotiations to purchase his house and land, DVP made a planning application in E's name and without his consent. He was also not informed that permission to build was granted and completion of the contract took place. It was held that a fiduciary relationship had arisen and that DVP was under a duty to account to E for the resultant profits.

(d) *The contracts of suretyship and partnership.* Contracts of suretyship (guarantee) and partnership do not require *uberrima fides* at their formation but, once made, they impose a duty on the parties to disclose all material facts in their dealings with each other.

(e) *The contracts for the sale of land.* The vendor must disclose any defects in title (right of ownership) but the duty does not extend to the physical qualities of the property —

Walker v. *Boyle* (1982): In negotiations for the sale of his property to W, B stated that there were no boundary disputes. After contracts had been exchanged, W discovered that such a dispute existed and sought rescission. As the true facts were within B's knowledge, judgment was given for W, who had been induced by the misrepresentation to enter into the contract.

(f) *The prospectuses of companies.* Under the Companies Act 1985, s. 67, directors or promoters of a company must make full disclosure of all material facts in any prospectus inviting the public to subscribe for shares. Failure to do so makes the contract voidable and the director or promoter liable for damages. *See Edgington* v. *Fitzmaurice* (1885) (13:**1(b)**).

3. The redress of misrepresentation

Misrepresentation may be *innocent* — whereby a false statement is made with an honest (albeit groundless) belief in its truth. Alternatively, misrepresentation may be *fraudulent* — in which case a false statement is made 'knowingly or without belief in its truth, or recklessly, careless whether it be true or false' (*per* Lord Herschell in *Derry* v. *Peek* (1889). Under the Misrepresentation Act 1967 s. 3 (as amended by the Unfair Contract Terms Act 1977, s. 8), exemption clauses (*see* 14:**5–6**) which purport to protect a party from liability for misrepresentation (or to exclude or restrict any remedy available to the other party) are of no effect, except in so far as they are reasonable — and the burden of proving reasonableness lies on the party seeking to invoke the clause. Both innocent and fraudulent misrepresentation make a contract *voidable* and the misled party has recourse to the following forms of relief:

(a) *The passive repudiation.* The misled party may simply do nothing at all (and raise the misrepresentation as a defence, if sued for breach). Preferably, he should give notice by words or conduct (if possible, but not essentially, to the other party) that he refuses to be bound by the contract. The significance of this can be found in 13:**4(c)** —

> *South Western General Property Co* v. *Marton* (1983): M purchased land from SWGP at an auction, the catalogue of which stated that planning consent for the erection of a house had been refused because the proposed building was out of character with the existing development. The planning authority had in fact stated that it was unlikely that consent would ever be given and M refused to complete the purchase on the grounds of misrepresentation. Relying on disclaimer clauses in the catalogue, SWGP sued M for losses incurred in the resale. It was held that, although innocent, the representations were false and that the disclaimer clauses were not fair and reasonable; consequently M was entitled to rescind the contract.

(b) *The action for rescission*. Rescission is an equitable (therefore discretionary) remedy and its purpose is to restore the parties to their pre-contract position; consequently, each must return to the other all property, etc, transferred. Under the Misrepresentation Act 1967, s. 1, a contract may be rescinded even if the misrepresentation has become a term, or if the contract has been performed. There are certain circumstances in which the right to rescission does not exist and these are outlined in 13:4.

(c) *The action for damages*. At common law, a party misled by *fraudulent* misrepresentation may not only avoid the contract but also sue in tort ('deceit') for damages. This does not extend to innocent misrepresentation but, under the Misrepresentation Act 1967, s. 2(1), damages may be recovered for negligent (i.e. innocent but careless) misrepresentation. Furthermore, s. 2(2) provides that, in cases of innocent misrepresentation, the court may declare a contract subsisting and award damages in lieu of rescission, if it would be equitable to do so. It is thus possible for a plaintiff to seek redress under either contract or tort but he cannot duplicate his claim —

> *Archer* v. *Brown* (1984): With £30,000 borrowed from a bank, A purchased the share capital of a company from B, who had already sold the shares elsewhere. A had also entered into an agreement to be joint managing director at a salary of £16,750 per annum and, on discovering the fraud, he claimed the return of the £30,000 and damages for deceit or breach of contract. It was held that, as the misrepresentation was fraudulent, A was entitled to damages as well as rescission.

> *Gosling* v. *Anderson* (1972): In negotiations to purchase a flat from A, G said that she would buy it only if she could have a garage. Honestly believing it to be true, A's agent told her that planning consent for garages had been granted, although this was not in fact the case. It was held that G should be awarded damages in lieu of rescission.

4.   The loss of the right to rescission
A right to rescind a contract which has been entered into as a consequence of misrepresentation will *not* exist in the event of:

(a) *The affirmation of the agreement.* Rescission is not available to a misled party who has expressly or impliedly affirmed the contract after becoming aware of innocent misrepresentation —

> *Long* v. *Lloyd* (1958): The plaintiff purchased a lorry from the defendant who described it as 'in exceptional condition', capable of 40 mph and 11 miles to the gallon. Two days after the purchase, defects became obvious and eight gallons of fuel were consumed in 40 miles. An expert declared the vehicle unroadworthy and the plaintiff sought rescission of the contract. The Court of Appeal held that any right to rescind was barred once delivery had taken place and the plaintiff had accepted the lorry. (He should have sued for breach, rather than rescission.)

(b) *The impossibility of restitution.* Under the doctrine of *restitutio in integrum*, a contract that cannot be *totally* rescinded cannot be rescinded at all —

> *Vigers* v. *Pike* (1842): Having been granted a lease of certain mines for £165,000, V's company worked them and paid part of the money. When P (the lessor's executor) sued for the balance, V pleaded that there had been misrepresentation prior to the lease. The House of Lords held that V was liable for the balance, as the agreement could not be set aside because the mines had been substantially worked and the parties could not therefore be restored to their original positions.

(c) *The prejudice of third parties.* The right to rescission is lost if a third party acquires an interest in the subject-matter in good faith and for value — and this he can do up to the time of avoidance, but not thereafter. *See Lewis* v. *Averay* (1973) (11:4(a)).

(d) *The interposing of unreasonable delay.* The right to rescission is lost if, in the case of innocent misrepresentation, the misled party has delayed unreasonably in giving notice or in bringing an action. *See Leaf* v. *International Galleries* (1950) (11:2(a)).

(e) *The substitution of damages.* As shown in 13:3(c), the court may award damages in lieu of granting rescission, in the case of innocent misrepresentation.

The exercise of coercion

5.   The vitiating forms of coercion

A contract may be vitiated (i.e. made invalid) if a party is coerced into it by:

(a) *The exercise of duress*. In this context, duress means actual or threatened violence to (or false imprisonment of) a person, his/her spouse, children or parents. A contract induced by this means is voidable at common law at the option of the party coerced, provided that he endeavours to set it aside within a reasonable period of the cessation of the duress —

> *Friedeberg-Seeley* v. *Klass* (1957): Having entered FS's flat, K and others refused to leave until she had signed a receipt (for a £90 cheque, later found on a table); they then took away a jewel case and its contents. It was held that the transaction should be set aside, with damages awarded for trespass to goods and assault.

(b) *The exercise of undue influence*. As duress can be exercised only against persons (but not goods), it is rarely pleaded; however, equity has extended the principle by recognising *undue influence*. This means pressure on a party, not amounting to duress, whereby he is precluded from exercising free and independent judgment. At the option of the coerced party, a contract induced by undue influence is *voidable in equity* — therefore, the remedy is only discretionary and it may *not* be granted if the coerced party's conduct was devious; if he delayed unreasonably in seeking relief; if he affirmed the transaction after the influence had ceased; if he did not suffer manifest disadvantage; or if a third party acquired rights from the transaction in good faith and for value. Where it is possible, parties seeking to avoid a contract for coercion should therefore plead duress (with its common law remedy as of right) together with undue influence in the alternative. Normally the coerced party must prove that undue influence existed and was exerted; however, exertion may be presumed where there is a *confidential or fiduciary relationship* (*see* 13:2(c)). Nevertheless, this presumption may be rebutted by showing that there was a full disclosure of material facts, that consideration was adequate or that the weaker party was in receipt of independent legal advice —

> *Lancashire Loans Ltd* v. *Black* (1934): After attaining her majority, and at her extravagant mother's request, Mrs B signed a promissory note guaranteeing the repayment of loans made by LL to the mother. The only advice she received was from the mother's solicitor, and the Court of Appeal held that the transaction should be set aside, as undue influence could be presumed — even though Mrs B was of full age and married.

> *National Westminster Bank* v. *Morgan* (1985): When the mortgage repayments on Mr and Mrs M's house fell into arrears, NWB agreed to a bridging loan, subject to a legal charge. After this was signed by M, the manager visited the house to obtain the signature of Mrs M, who did not receive independent advice. When the loan was not repaid, NWB sought possession of the house and Mrs M claimed that the manager had subjected her to undue influence. The House of Lords held that the transaction should not be set aside, as it was not to the manifest disadvantage of the person subjected to the influence; by itself, a confidential relationship would not necessarily give rise to a presumption of undue influence.

(c) *The exercise of economic duress.* A relatively recent extension of undue influence has been the development of *economic duress* — generally where a party to a contract is coerced into renegotiating the terms by the threat of breach — even though there may be consideration for the resulting agreement. In such circumstances, apparent consent may be vitiated, and additional money paid as a result of the coercion may be recovered. It is necessary, however, for the coerced party to establish that the apparent consent resulted from the coercive act, that the transaction was entered into unwillingly, with no real alternative but to submit to the demand; also that it was repudiated as soon as the pressure was relaxed. Once one party has made out a *prima facie* case of economic duress, the onus is on the other to show it did not amount to a major consideration in the mind of the coerced. Economic duress, exerted upon employers by organised labour is subject to prevailing trade union legislation (*see* 14:5(e)) —

> *Atlas Express* v. *Kafco (Importers and Distributors)* (1989): K imported basketware and contracted with AE for its distribution to a national chain of retailers. The first load was far smaller than anticipated and AE told K that they would accept no more consignments without a minimum payment. Unable to find another carrier, K agreed to the new terms but subsequently refused to pay the increase. It was held that there had been economic duress and that any apparent consent was vitiated.

> *North Ocean Shipping Co* v. *Hyundai Construction Co* (1978): Contracting to build a tanker for NOS, with payment by instalments, HC agreed to open a letter of credit, to provide security in the event of default. After a devaluation of the US dollar, HC threatened to break the contract if the price was not raised by 10 per cent, but they offered a corresponding increase in the letter of credit. Needing the ship and reserving their rights, NOS agreed and paid the remaining instalments at the new level. More than six months after receiving the vessel, they sought repayment of the 10 per cent with interest, alleging lack of consideration and economic duress. It was held that the increase in the letter of credit had provided consideration, that the variation had been induced by economic duress but that, having affirmed it by payment of the final instalment and delaying their claim, NOS were not entitled to recover.

Progress test 13

1. Roy offered to sell Tony his power-boat for a certain price, saying that there was nothing wrong with it. Two days' later, Tony agreed to buy it but, after taking possession, he discovered a major engine defect which Roy had noticed developing half an hour before Tony accepted the offer. Roy had not mentioned this and Tony seeks your advice. **(1)**

2. Saying that he wished to secure her future, Brown sold his shop to his daughter, Mary, for a nominal £100. Mary soon realised that outstanding debts greatly exceeded the value of the premises and stock. Advise Mary.   **(2)**

3.   What remedies are available to a person who has been induced to enter into a contract by an honest but untrue representation made by the other party?   **(3)**

4.   Peter sold David two acres of land, saying that it would produce good crops. After demolishing some old buildings on it, David sowed seed but later discovered that the high acid content of the soil made it unsuitable for crops. Advise David.   **(3, 4)**

5.   Michael joined a religious sect whose wealthy leader insisted that all members should make over their property to it. Michael did so just before he died and his widow seeks your advice.   **(5)**

14
The terms of a contract

The types of contractual terms

1. The nature of a term

It was shown in 13:1 that statements uttered simply to induce the making of a contract (and by which the parties do not intend to be bound) constitute *mere representations,* whereas those intended to bind a party are called *terms.* The significance of this distinction lies in the difference in remedies granted for misrepresentation — as opposed to breach of a term; consequently, it is important to be able to determine which category any statement falls into. Each case must be individually decided and the test is simply — 'What would a reasonable man understand to be the intention of the parties, having regard to all the circumstances?' As a rough guide, however, a representation (made by the *representor* to the *representee*) may well be held to constitute a *term* in the following circumstances:

(a) *If the representee emphasises a requirement —*

> *Porter* v. *General Guarantee Corp* (1982): Saying that he wanted a vehicle fit for use as a minicab, P bought a car from Howard Baugh & Sons, on hire-purchase financed by GGC. On account of unroadworthiness, it was not in a condition suitable for use as a minicab and it was held that this was of sufficient importance in the minds of the parties as to make it a fundamental term. Breach therefore entitled P to repudiate the contract, and GGC to be indemnified by HB.

(b) *If the representor emphasises a fact,* so that the representee is dissuaded from confirming it —

Schawel v. *Reade* (1913): S considered purchasing a horse for stud purposes from R, who said, 'You need not look for anything. The horse is perfectly sound. If there was anything the matter with the horse, I would tell you'. S terminated his examination and bought the animal, which was found to be totally unfit for stud purposes. It was held that R's words constituted a term of the contract.

Ecay v. *Godfrey* (1947): The vendor of a boat stated that it was sound but advised the purchaser to have it surveyed. It was held that the statement was not a term of the contract.

(c) *If the representor has special knowledge or skill,* not possessed by the representee. This is a further illustration of inequality of bargaining power (*see* 10:1) —

Dick Bentley Productions Ltd v. *Harold Smith (Motors) Ltd* (1965): Having asked HS for a 'well-vetted' Bentley car, DB was shown one which HS said had done only 20,000 miles since fitted with a new engine and gearbox. It had in fact run over 100,000 miles since reconditioning. It was held that the statement was a term of the contract.

Oscar Chess v. *Williams* (1957): Purchasing a car from OC, W traded in a Morris which he said was a 1948 model (as this year was shown on the registration book). OC allowed him £290 but later found that the car was a 1939 model (value £175), so sued to recover £115. It was held that W's statement was not a term of the contract.

2. The nature of express terms
A contract may contain either *express terms* (founded on statements made by the parties in speech or writing) or *implied terms* (which may be inferred by the law). Express terms are subject to the *parol evidence rule* whereby, if the parties have reduced their contract to writing, it is not generally permissible to adduce parol (i.e. oral) evidence 'to add to, vary or contradict' the written document. There are, nevertheless, exceptions to this rule and, for example, oral evidence may be admissible in the following circumstances:

(a) *If the parties are aware that the document does not express the whole agreement —*

> *Krell* v. *Henry* (1903): H agreed in writing to rent K's flat for two days for £75. The purpose (not expressed in the document) was to view Edward VII's coronation procession but this was cancelled, because of the King's illness. It was held that K could not recover the balance of the rent, as the procession was the foundation of the contract and oral evidence concerning it was admissible.

(b) *If the operation of the agreement is conditional upon some event —*

> *Pym* v. *Campbell* (1856): The parties entered into a written agreement for the sale of an invention but orally arranged that it should not operate as a contract until the invention had been approved by a third party. Approval was not forthcoming and P sought to enforce the agreement. It was held that evidence of the oral arrangement was admissible and that there was no contract.

(c) *If the document contains a latent ambiguity,* i.e. one which does not appear on the face of it. Thus oral evidence was admissible to resolve the latent ambiguity in *Raffles* v. *Wichelhaus* (1864) (11:**3(a)**).

3.   The nature of implied terms

The parties to a contract do not always express all of the terms by which they intend to be bound and sometimes *implied terms* are therefore inferred by the law. These are binding in the same way as (but cannot override) express terms and they are based principally upon:

(a) *The existence of customs.* There may be an assumption that the parties intended to be bound by a particular custom or usage — though this can, of course, be excluded from an agreement by an express term to that effect —

> *Hutton* v. *Warren* (1836): The landlord terminated the lease of a farm and, although the lease did not provide for it, the tenant claimed a reasonable sum for his tillage, sowing and cultivation. It was held that agricultural custom required such a payment, which would be implied in the lease.

(b) *The requirement of business efficacy.* Sometimes the parties may have left no doubt as to the general scope of their obligations, but have nevertheless omitted an essential provision, the absence of which would defeat their intentions. In such a case the court may supply the necessary term to implement the presumed intention and to give 'business efficacy' to the contract —

> *Bournemouth & Boscombe Athletic Football Club Co* v. *Manchester United Football Club* (1980): B&B sold a player, McD, to MU for about £200,000 and the contract contained a term that £27,777 was to be paid when McD had scored 20 goals in first team matches. After the transfer McD scored four goals in 11 games but, on the replacement of the manager, he was dropped from the first team squad. When he was subsequently transferred, he had played in 18 matches and had not scored the stipulated 20 goals. B&B claimed the extra fee and the Court of Appeal held that it was necessary, as a matter of business efficacy, to imply a term that McD should have a reasonable opportunity to score the 20 goals; by transferring him, MU had prevented any possibility of fulfilling the agreement and were therefore in breach of contract.

(c) *The previous conduct of the parties* —

> *Hillas & Co* v. *Arcos Ltd* (1932): H agreed to purchase from A 22,000 standards of softwood in 1930, with an option to buy 100,000 standards in 1931, but without particulars as to the kind or size of timber, or the manner of shipment. After the supply for 1930 had been completed, A claimed that they were not bound to deliver the 100,000 standards as the clause was vague. It was held that, as it was couched in the same language as that of the previous year, details could be inferred from the course of dealing between the parties.

(d) *The Sale of Goods Act 1979.* Incorporating the provisions of a similarly-named statute of 1893, this Act imposes the following implied terms upon the seller of goods: that he has a right to sell them and that they are free of any charges or incumbrances (s. 12); that goods sold by description will correspond with it, also that, if they are sold by sample, the bulk will correspond with the sample (s. 13); that goods sold *in the course of a business* (i.e. not privately) are *of merchantable quality* (i.e. fit for the purpose for which they are commonly bought) unless, before a contract is made, the seller draws the buyer's attention to any defects, or the buyer carries out an examination which would reveal such defects. If the purchaser expressly or impliedly makes known to the seller any particular purpose for which the goods are being bought, there is an implied condition that they are reasonably fit for that purpose, regardless of whether it is the purpose for which they are commonly supplied — unless it can be shown that the buyer does (or can) not rely on the skill or judgment of the seller (s. 14) —

> *Rowland* v. *Divall* (1923): Having bought a car from D, R used it for four months before it was seized by the police, as being stolen property. The Court of Appeal held that, not having any right to sell the vehicle, D was in breach of the (s. 12) implied term and R had received nothing from him; consequently there was a complete failure of consideration and R was entitled to recover the full purchase price.

> *MacPherson Train & Co* v. *Howard Ross & Co* (1955): A contract for the sale of 5,000 cases of canned sliced peaches contained the words 'Shipment and destination: afloat per SS Morton Bay, due London approximately June 8'. Because of the ship's late arrival on 21st June, the purchasers (whose customers would have had great difficulty in utilising the goods) rejected the whole consignment. It was held that the words in the contract were part of the description of the goods; consequently the sellers were in breach of the (s. 13) implied term and the buyer was entitled to decline acceptance.

> *Rogers* v. *Parish (Scarborough)* (1987): Having purchased a new Landrover from P, R found defects in the engine, gear-box, oil seals and bodywork. The Court of Appeal held that he was entitled to a refund of his money as P was in breach of the (s. 14) implied term of merchantable quality; this required the performance and finish of a car sold as new to be that of a model of average standard with no mileage.

(e) *The Supply of Goods and Services Act 1982.* This has extended the implied terms relating to contracts for the sale of goods (i.e.

concerning title, description, sample and fitness) to contracts for the *supply of goods* (i.e. transfer other than by sale, hire-purchase, in exchange for trading stamps, by deed or as a security) also to contracts for the *hire of goods* (other than by hire-purchase or in exchange for trading stamps). With regard to contracts for the *supply of services*, the Act imposes an implied term that a supplier acting in the course of a business will carry out the service with reasonable care and skill, also within a reasonable time (if that has not been predetermined); there is likewise an implied term that the party contracting with the supplier will pay a reasonable charge (if the consideration has not been arranged beforehand).

4. The breaches of terms

The (express or implied) terms of a contract may vary in significance — particularly with regard to whether breaches thereof would entitle the other party to terminate the agreement. It is therefore necessary to examine:

(a) *The breach of a condition. Condition* is the name that has been given to a fundamental term, the breach of which would empower the other party to terminate the contract and to recover damages in compensation for obligations already performed —

> *L Schuler AG* v. *Wickman Machine Tool Sales* (1974): S gave W the sole rights to sell S's panel presses in England, provided that 'it shall be a *condition* of this agreement' that W's representatives should visit six named firms each week to solicit orders. On a few occasions they failed to do so and S claimed the right to repudiate the contract. It was held that the clause could not be construed as a 'condition'; therefore, S was not entitled to repudiate.

(b) *The breach of a warranty. Warranty* is the name for a less fundamental term, the breach of which empowers the other party to recover damages but *not* to terminate the contract. *See Esso Petroleum Co* v. *Mardon* (1976) (13:**1(b)**).

(c) *The breach of an innominate term.* Terms have long been classified as either conditions or warranties — a distinction which is expressed in the Sale of Goods Act 1979. However, it may well be more logical to consider the effects of a breach, rather than the construction of the contract. To this end, the use of the word *innominate* (i.e. unnamed) enables the category of a term to remain undefined until the consequences of a breach become apparent. In such circumstances, the gravity of those consequences can determine whether or not the other party should be entitled to terminate the contract —

> *Cehave NV* v. *Bremer Handelgesellschaft* (1976): C agreed to purchase from B (for £100,000) a quantity of citrus pulp for use as animal feed, a term of the contract being 'shipment to be made in good condition'. On arrival, part of the cargo was damaged, C rejected all of it and B disputed this. The whole cargo was bought by an importer for £30,000 and was immediately sold for the same figure to C, who used it for animal feed. The Court of Appeal held that the breach did not go to the root of the contract and it did not justify rejection.

The limitation of liability

5. The common law invalidity of exemption clauses

Sometimes a contract contains a term purporting to exclude or limit the liability of one of the parties in certain circumstances. However, restrictions on the validity of such *exemption* (or *exclusion*) *clauses* have been imposed by the common law and also by statutes. Under what is called the *contra proferentum rule*, any ambiguity or doubt in an exemption clause must, at common law, be resolved against the party seeking to rely on it; furthermore, it has been held that such a clause will not be effective if:

(a) *It was not clearly communicated to the other party.* The party seeking to rely on an exemption clause must be able to show that the other party was aware of it or that reasonable steps had been taken to bring it to his notice; but the other party cannot plead blindness or illiteracy —

> *Thornton* v. *Shoe Lane Parking Ltd* (1971): T drove his car into SLP's multi-storey car park, not having used it before, and at the entrance a machine activated by the car gave him a ticket. This stated that it was issued subject to conditions displayed inside the garage (and not visible from the entrance). Later T was severely injured in an accident in the garage and it was held that the conditions did not protect SLP, as T had no opportunity to read the ticket.

(b) *It was communicated after the contract was made.* To be effective, an exemption clause must normally be communicated to the other party before the contract is made; however, communication can sometimes be inferred from the previous course of dealing between the parties —

> *Daly* v. *General Steam Navigation Co* (1979): In January D's husband booked a passage for the family in GSN's ship for 7th July. Subsequently tickets arrived in a folder containing a clause exempting GSN from liability for injury to passengers. Whilst the ship was unberthing in July, D was injured when a wire whiplashed and GSN was held liable, as the contract was made in January and the clause communicated later afforded no protection.

> *Kendall* v. *Lillico* (1969): Sellers sold groundnut extractions to the buyers and, on the next day, sent a 'sold note' containing an exemption clause. It was held that this was effective — as notes containing the same clause had been sent in transactions between the parties over the previous three years.

(c) *It was overridden by an oral promise or a misrepresentation* —

> *J. Evans & Son (Portsmouth)* v. *Andrea Merzario* (1976): AM (forwarding agents) imported Italian machinery for E, in crates shipped below decks. They proposed to change over to containers and their contract, which contained exemption and limitation clauses, gave them complete freedom in the means of transportation. However, they gave an oral assurance that E's containers would be shipped below decks but, as a result of an oversight, one was stowed on deck and washed overboard. It was held that E was entitled to damages, as the oral promise overrode the printed conditions.

> *Curtis* v. *Chemical Cleaning & Dyeing Co* (1951): Depositing her wedding dress with CCD for cleaning, C was asked to sign a 'receipt', stating that clothing 'is accepted on condition that the company is not liable for any damage howsoever arising'. Before signing, she was told by the assistant that the document simply excluded liability for certain risks, including damage to beads; however, when it

returned, the dress was stained. It was held that CCD was liable, as the innocent misrepresentation had robbed it of the protection of the clause.

(d) *It was subject to a collateral contract.* This is a device whereby the courts sometimes hold that an agreement involves a second contract, co-existing with the main one, provided that its four essential elements (*see* 9:1) can be shown to exist —

> *Webster* v. *Higgin* (1948): To induce H to enter into a hire-purchase agreement, W's foreman said to him: 'If you buy the Hillman, we will guarantee that it is in good condition and that you will have no trouble with it'. H then signed the agreement which expressly excluded 'any statutory or other warranty, condition, description or representation . . . . as to the state, quality, fitness or roadworthiness'. The car was a mass of dilapidated metal and H did not pay the instalments. It was held that, by signing the document, H had accepted the offer of a separate collateral agreement which, being broken, entitled him to rescind the main contract.

(e) *It would be unfair and unreasonable for it to be relied upon.* This is of particular relevance where a contract contains a *force majeure* clause, exempting liability in the event of irresistible compulsion or coercion —

> *B & S Contracts and Design* v. *Victor Green Publications* (1984): In an agreement whereby B&S would erect stands for VGP at Olympia, there was a *force majeure* clause which made the contract subject to variation or cancellation in the event of a strike. When their employees threatened such action in support of a pay demand, B&S stated that the contract would be cancelled unless VGP paid an additional £4,500. They complied but deducted the sum from the final payment and the Court of Appeal held that they were entitled to do so, because the money had been paid under economic duress and B&S had not taken reasonable steps to avert the strike by paying the small sum involved.

6. **The statutory invalidity of exemption clauses**
Provisions in a number of statutes render exemption clauses

ineffective but the most significant is the Unfair Contract Terms Act 1977. This does *not* cover contracts of insurance or those that relate to the creation, transfer or termination of interests in land, the creation or transfer of securities or rights and interests in patents, trademarks, etc, also the formation or dissolution of companies or partnerships. Provided that the transactions take place *in the course of business* (i.e. are not of an entirely private nature) the Act negates contractual terms which purport:

(a) *To exclude or restrict liability for death or personal injury*, resulting from negligence. In this context, 'negligence' means the breach of any obligation under the express or implied terms of a contract to take reasonable care or exercise reasonable skill *or* the breach of any common law duty to take reasonable care or exercise reasonable skill (but not any stricter duty) *or* the breach of the common duty of care imposed by the Occupiers' Liability Act 1957 (**18:5**) —

> *Thompson* v. *Lohan (T) (Plant Hire)* (1987): T hired plant from L, also two of L's employees as operators, with the agreement based on the Construction Plant Association's standard terms and conditions. Clause 8 of these provided that operators should be regarded as the servants of the hirer, who would be responsible for all claims arising from the operation of the plant. One operator was killed through the other's negligence and the Court of Appeal held that Clause 8 effectively passed liability from L to T, as it did not seek to exclude or restrict liability for negligence within the meaning of the 1977 Act. Its purpose was to protect the victim of negligence and it provided a means whereby L and T decided which of them should bear liability.

(b) *To exclude or restrict liability for other loss or damage*, resulting from negligence, *unless the term satisfies the requirement of reasonableness*. In determining *'reasonableness'* various factors may be relevant — e.g., the relative bargaining powers of the parties, any inducement to agree to the term, opportunity to enter into a similar contract without such a term, the party's knowledge as to the existence and extent of the term, the reasonableness of a required compliance with a condition, also whether goods were manufactured, processed or adapted to the special order of the party —

Waldron-Kelly v. *British Railways Board* (1981): BRB accepted from WK a suitcase for delivery to another station, subject to its General Conditions of Carriage. These exempted BRB from liability for loss, damage or delay unless wilful misconduct could be proved; also, in the event of non-delivery, BRB's liability was related to the weight (27lb) rather than the value (£320) of the goods. The suitcase disappeared and it was held that the burden of proving what had happened rested on BRB, that the exemption clause did not satisfy the requirement of reasonableness under the 1977 Act, and that judgment should be entered for WK in the sum of £320.

Harris v. *Wyre Forest District Council* (1989): In order to purchase a house, H sought a mortgage from WFDC, which required a valuation. The application form stated that 'no responsibility whatever is implied or accepted by the Council for the value or condition of the property by reason of such inspection or report'. Observing that some settlement had occurred, WFDC's valuer concluded that nothing further would happen and recommended a 90 per cent mortgage, impliedly representing that no structural repairs were necessary. Three years later, when H wished to sell the house, WFDC obtained a further report from the same valuer and refused to make a loan on the security of the building unless extensive and costly repairs were effected. The House of Lords held that the valuer had owed a duty of care to H and that the disclaimer was ineffective, in not having satisfied the requirement of reasonableness under the 1977 Act — particularly in the light of the parties' bargaining power.

(c) *To exclude or restrict liability for breach*, where the other party is a consumer or bound by written standard terms of business, *unless the term satisfies the requirement of reasonableness*. In the absence of this, it is also not possible to render a contractual performance substantially different from that which was reasonably expected, or to render no performance at all —

Stag Line v. *Tyne Ship Repair Group* (1984): After being repaired in TSG's yard, SL's ship suffered a major engine room breakdown. It was held that TSG's failure to use proper materials and reasonable skill and care was in breach of duty but, in this case, it was not causative. Had it been, TSG's terms and conditions, which excluded them from liability for economic loss, would not have been unfair or unreasonable.

(d) *To require a consumer to indemnify another person* (whether or not a party to the contract) in respect of liability that may be incurred by the other for negligence or breach of contract, *unless the term satisfies the requirement of reasonableness*. This would cover, e.g., a contract for servicing a car which required the customer to indemnify the garage for loss or damage to third parties, arising from negligent handling of the vehicle.

(e) *To exclude or restrict liability under the Sale of Goods Act 1979* (14:3(d)). Examples include the seller's undertaking as to title, also (in agreements with consumers) as to conformity of goods with description or sample, etc. In the latter case, and where the party is *not* a consumer, liability can be excluded or restricted *if the term satisfies the requirement of reasonableness* —

> *George Mitchell (Chesterhall)* v. *Finney Lock Seeds* (1983): Having ordered late cabbage seed from FLS, GM received totally unsuitable seed of the wrong type. FLS's conditions of sale limited their liability to the replacement or refund of the value of the seed (£207) and the loss to GM was £61,000. The House of Lords held that reliance on the conditions would not be fair and reasonable.

In addition to making provisions concerning exemption clauses, the 1977 Act also covers: subjecting liability or its enforcement to restrictive or onerous conditions; *or* excluding or restricting any right or remedy (or subjecting a person to prejudice in consequence of pursuing any right or remedy); *or* excluding or restricting rules of evidence or procedure.

Progress test 14

1. Explain the difference between express and implied terms in

a contract. Illustrate situations in which terms may be implied. **(2, 3)**

2.   Roger paid quite a high price for a car phone, supplied and installed by Autotalk Ltd. It was in fact a cheap and defective instrument which caught fire and seriously damaged the car. Advise Roger.   **(3)**

3.   If a term in an agreement has been breached by one party, how is it decided whether the other may repudiate the contract?   **(4)**

4.   Susan telephoned Gardentasks who agreed to provide a man at £5 per hour for weeding and grass cutting. Two days later, she received a confirmation form on which was printed 'Gardentasks shall not be liable for any wrongful acts by its employees'. An inexperienced man was sent and, being unable to identify weeds, he destroyed some very rare and valuable plants. Susan seeks your advice.   **(5)**

5.   Booking a trip in a hot air balloon with Superflites Ltd, Nigel signed a form which stated that 'The company shall not be liable for any loss, damage or injury incurred by passengers'. During the trip a defect developed, through lack of proper maintenance, and an emergency descent had to be made. The balloon landed in a wood, Nigel sustained a broken leg and he now seeks your advice.   **(6)**

15

The privity of contract

The acquisition of benefits and liabilities by third parties

1. The doctrine of privity

Basically, only the parties to a contract can receive rights or be bound by duties under it. This is known as the *doctrine of privity* and it is merely an aspect of (being not really distinguishable from) the rule that 'consideration must move from the promisee' (*Tweddle* v. *Atkinson* (1861) (9:4(b))). Thus a contract cannot normally confer benefits or impose liabilities on a third party; nevertheless, other principles can conflict with the doctrine and exceptions to its operation are outlined in 15:2–5 *below*. In 1937 the Law Revision Committee (*see* 3:8(b)) recommended that 'where a contract by its express terms purports to confer a benefit directly on a third party, it shall be enforceable by the third party in his own name'. Moreover, the courts have expressed increasing doubts about the privity of contract and, in *Woodar Investment Development* v. *Wimpey Construction UK* (1980), Lord Scarman said that it 'calls for review — and now — not forty years on' —

> *Beswick* v. *Beswick* (1968): Peter B sold his coal merchant's business to his nephew John, on condition that the latter would pay £6.50 a week to Peter for life and, in the event of his death, £5 a week to his widow. Peter died and, after one payment of £5, John refused anything further, as Mrs B was not a party to the contract. She claimed arrears and specific performance, both as administratrix of her late husband's estate and also in her personal capacity. The Court of Appeal held that she was entitled to enforce the contract as administratrix, but not personally.

Scruttons Ltd v. *Midland Silicones Ltd* (1962): Contracting to ship drums of chemicals from the USA to England for MS, a firm of carriers limited their liability for loss or damage to 500 US dollars a day. They also engaged S as stevedores for the unloading, during which one drum was dropped and the damage was well in excess of 500 dollars. The House of Lords held that S were not entitled to rely on the limitation clause, as they were not parties to that contract.

2. The acquisition of benefits by third parties

There are various ways in which benefits may be derived from contracts by those who are not parties to them — and the principal examples include:

(a) *The contracts of insurance.* Many insurance policies (e.g. household, car, etc) provide cover for 'public liability' or 'third party liability'. The Road Traffic Act 1972, e.g., empowers injured third parties to sue insurers direct, whilst the Married Women's Property Act 1882, s. 11 (as amended), enables spouses to effect life assurance policies in favour of each other and their children. Under the Marine Insurance Act 1906, s. 14(2), contracts concerning 'losses incident to marine adventure' may be made for the benefit of third parties; and the Law of Property Act 1925, s. 47(1), requires the vendor of any property to pay the purchaser any insurance money received in respect of the property after the sale —

Ladd v. *Jones* (1975): Mrs L having been injured in a road accident caused by J, Mr L was awarded damages for the loss of his wife's 'society and services'. In his claim against the insurers, it was held that liability under the Road Traffic Act 1972, s. 145, meant any liability which arose by virtue of common law or statute.

(b) *The creation of constructive trusts.* A *trust* is a relationship whereby property is held by one party (the *trustee*) on behalf and for the benefit of another (the *beneficiary*). In order to satisfy the demands of justice and good conscience, equity will sometimes recognise the existence of what is called a *constructive trust* — e.g., where a person makes a profit in a fiduciary position (13:2(c)). For a long time this principle enabled a third party to claim a benefit under a contract by pleading that one of the actual parties acted as his constructive trustee. Such an arrangement has, however, become virtually discarded but it cannot be regarded as completely defunct. Furthermore, the second case below illustrates a situation in which, albeit not a trustee, a person who has entered into a contract partly for the benefit of others may recover on their behalf —

> *Re Flavell* (1883): F entered into a partnership with another solicitor and it provided that, if one died, his widow should receive an annual sum from the net profits. F died insolvent and his creditors argued that the widow was not entitled to the annuity, as she was not a party to the agreement. It was held, however, that the agreement had created a trust in favour of the widow and that she was entitled to the annual sum.

> *Jackson* v. *Horizon Holidays* (1975): A four-week holiday in Ceylon, booked by J with HH for himself, his wife and his children, was ruined mainly because the hotel lacked the facilities and failed to meet the standards advertised in HH's brochure. Upholding the award of sizeable damages, the Court of Appeal held that J could recover not only for his own loss and disappointment but also for that of the others. Although they were not parties to the contract, he had entered into it partly for their benefit.

(c) *The existence of tortious liability.* Provided that a duty of care can be established, the constraints of the doctrine of privity may well be overcome by suing in negligence (*see* 18:1) —

> *Ross* v. *Caunters* (1979): Preparing a will, the testator's solicitor (C) failed to point out that it should not be attested by the husband of the residuary beneficiary (R). Consequently, the gift of residue was void and it was held that C owed the beneficiaries a duty of care, the breach of which had caused R to suffer loss. By way of damages, she could therefore recover the benefits to which she would have been entitled under the will.

(d) *The law of agency. See* 15:4 *below.*

3.   The acquisition of liabilities by third parties

Liabilities from contracts may accrue to those who are not parties in the following circumstances:

(a) *If there is a restrictive covenant.* If someone purchasing land covenants not to use it in some stipulated manner, there is said to be a *restrictive covenant*. This will bind persons who later buy the land with notice of the covenant and, in equity, the benefit may generally be enforced by an assignee of the one who imposed the restriction. The principle does not, however, extend to anything other than land —

> *Tulk* v. *Moxhay* (1848): T sold the garden in the centre of Leicester Square to one Elms, who agreed not to build upon it. Eventually M bought the garden and, despite knowledge of the restriction, he planned to erect a building. It was held that equity would not permit him to disregard the covenant and that an injunction should be granted.

(b) *If there is a collateral contract.* As explained in 14:5(d), it may be possible to show that one of the parties is bound by another contract to the third party. In such circumstances, liability (both for and against the third party) will arise on the second contract —

> *Shanklin Pier* v. *Detel Products* (1951): SP (pier owners) required their contractors to use paint manufactured by DP, who had expressly warranted to SP that it had a life of seven to 10 years. In fact it lasted only about three months and SP were put to extra expense. It was held that, although SP's main contract was with the contractors, they could nevertheless recover from DP on the collateral contract to insist on the use of the paint, in consideration for the warranty.

(c) *If 'letters of comfort' are written concerning commercial matters.* Where, e.g., a company negotiates a loan for one of its subsidiaries and provides the lender with a 'letter of comfort', accepting certain responsibilities, the document gives rise to the presumption that it intends to create legal relations —

> *Kleinwort Benson* v. *Malaysia Mining Corp* (1988): Acquiring a £10m loan facility from KB for M (its wholly-owned

subsidiary), MMC provided two 'letters of comfort'. After the collapse of the tin market in 1985, M went into liquidation, owing the whole loan. It was held that, as the letters gave rise to the presumption that they were intended to create legal relations, KB was entitled to sue on them and obtain judgment.

(d) *If there is a relationship of principal and agent. See* 15:4 *below.*

4. The law of agency

An *agent* is a person authorised to act on behalf of another (his *principal*) and the relationship may be created in various ways — e.g., by express appointment, by implication from conduct or necessity, by subsequent ratification of an act, etc. Under the maxim *qui facit per alium facit per se* ('he who acts through another is deemed to act in person'), all acts which a person can do (except those that can only be performed personally) can be done by his agent. Thus, on behalf of his principal, an agent can make or perform contracts (except those that can only be performed personally), make or receive payments and sign memoranda. However, a principal with limited contractual capacity (e.g. a minor) cannot make by an agent a contract which he is incapable of making himself. Contracts made by agents are subject to the following requirements:

(a) *If the agent discloses that he is acting as such*, the principal (but *not* the agent) can sue and be sued on the contract, regardless of whether the principal was actually named. Exceptionally, the agent may become a party to the contract if it is the express intention of the parties, if the agent puts his own name to a deed, or if there is some relevant trade usage.

(b) *If the agent does not disclose that he is acting as such*, the *doctrine of the undisclosed principal* will apply and, on discovering the principal, the other party may elect to treat either the principal or the agent as liable — but, having chosen one, he cannot then elect for the other. However, if he commences proceedings against the agent before becoming aware of the principal, he does not lose his right of choice. Either the principal or the agent can normally sue on the contract but an undisclosed principal cannot intervene if this would be inconsistent with the terms of the contract or if the third party can show that he wished to deal only with the agent —

> *Cyril Lord Carpet Sales* v. *Browne* (1966): CLCS had a county court summons served on B's agent for the price of goods sold. Discovering that the agent was in America, they then obtained judgment against B. The Court of Appeal held that the institution of proceedings against the agent was a definite election; therefore CLCS could not recover from B.

(c) *If the agent names his principal but acts without authority*, the principal can ratify the contract, so that it becomes binding as between himself and the other party. If the principal does not do so, the agent becomes liable to the other party for the breach of a separate collateral contract — with a promise that he had authority in consideration for the other party's entry into the contract —

> *Olorunkoya* v. *McCarthy* (1965): Acting as O's agent, M invested 15p a week for her in a football pool. On one occasion he showed her a winning coupon, entered in her name with £96 staked, and thereupon she paid him £150. When she sued for the £6,000 winnings, it was held that M embarked on a transaction outside the scope of his authority but that O had ratified it and was therefore entitled to the money.

> *Chitholie* v. *Nash & Co* (1973): C wished to purchase a particular house and N (the vendor's solicitors) signed and exchanged contracts without authority. When the vendor repudiated the contract, C sued N for breach of warranty of authority and it was held that he was entitled to damages.

The transfer of rights and liabilities to third parties

5. The assignment of rights to third parties

In law, the term *property* means basically anything which belongs to a person and it may be classified as *real property* (relating to land) and *personal property* (everything other than real property). One form of personal property is *chattels personal*, which comprise *choses in possession* (physical things, such as cars, books, etc) and *choses in action* (intangible things, such as debts, patents, copyright, business goodwill, etc), a right to which can be effectively asserted only by court action. A right or benefit arising under a contract is a chose in action and, in certain circumstances, it may be transferred (by the *assignor*) to a third party (the *assignee*) by a transaction known as *assignment*. It is, however, *not* possible to assign a bare right of action (e.g. solely the right to sue for a breach of contract or for a tort) or contractual rights of a personal nature (e.g. contracts for personal service). A valid assignment of a chose in action may be effected in the following ways:

(a) *The statutory assignment.* The Law of Property Act 1925, s. 136, empowers the assignment of a chose in action provided that it is *in writing, signed by the assignor, absolute* (i.e. relating to the whole chose and not merely part of it) and *communicated by express notice in writing to the party from whom the assignor was entitled to claim.* The assignee need not give the assignor any consideration and the assignment takes effect from the date when the written notice was given to the other party. The assignment transfers the full legal obligation, the right to enforce it (in the assignee's own name) and the power to give a good discharge without the consent of the assignor.

(b) *The equitable assignment.* If there has been an intent to assign a chose in action but the requirements outlined above have not been fully complied with, there may nevertheless be a valid assignment in equity. However, in the case of contractual rights, the assignee must show that he gave consideration to the assignor (unless the assignment was complete and perfect) and, in any action, he must join the assignor as co-plaintiff (or co-defendant, if he refuses). Both statutory and equitable assignments are 'subject to the equities' — in that any defence or counter-claim available to the other party at the time of the assignment is available against the assignee.

(c) *The involuntary assignment.* Choses in action are assigned automatically on the death (to the personal representatives) or the bankruptcy (to the trustee in bankruptcy) of the owner.

6. The transfer of liabilities to third parties

Contractual obligations *cannot* be assigned and may be transferred only by *novation* (i.e. the discharge of the old contract and the making of a new one — *see* 16:**2(b)**)); unlike assignment, this necessitates the consent of both contracting parties and also the third party. That does not, however, preclude the possibility of *vicarious performance* — whereby A contracts to do some work for B but transfers the task to C; in such circumstances, B cannot object, provided that the work is not of a personal nature and that performance is in accordance with the terms of the contract (with A remaining liable to B until completion).

Progress test 15

1. Explain the doctrine of privity of contract and consider any ways in which you think it should be modified.   (1)

2. Elderly Mrs Grey was friendly with her dentist, Brown, whom she asked to negotiate the sale of her car. He sold it for £30,000 to Green, who was so pleased with the purchase that he gave the dentist an additional £2,000, which Brown donated to a charity. Advise Mrs Grey.   (2)

3. Describe how liabilities from contracts may accrue to third parties.   (3)

4. Jason wished to purchase anonymously a painting from Artreasures Ltd, so Keith acquired it on his behalf but has disappeared with the money given to him by Jason. Artreasures seek your advice.   (4)

5. How may contractual rights be assigned?   (5)

The discharge of a contract

The termination of contracts

1. The discharge by performance

A contract is discharged (i.e. comes to an end) when the promisor *completely and precisely* performs his *exact* obligation. Thus, if he does something less than (or different from) what he promised, the other party may reject *the entire agreement*; furthermore, if the promisor only partially performs the contract, he has no right of action *for any reimbursement at all.* The strictness of this rule is nevertheless relaxed and the promisor can sue on a *quantum meruit* ('as much as he deserved') for *pro rata* remuneration in the following circumstances:

(a) *If the contract is severable (divisible).* If consideration is not promised in relation to an entire work and the promisor agrees to carry out a requested task by instalments, or without any definite arrangement regarding consideration, he will be able to recover —

> *Cutter* v. *Powell* (1795): P agreed to pay C 30 guineas (£31.50) for performing duties as second mate in a ship for a 10-week voyage but, after seven weeks, C died and it was held that his widow could not recover anything.

> *Roberts* v. *Havelock* (1832): R agreed to carry out repairs to a ship for a reasonable remuneration but there was no agreement for a specific sum to be paid only on completion. After doing some of the work, he sought payment and it was held that he was entitled to recover.

(b) *If the promisee accepts partial performance.* If the promisee had full freedom of choice but accepted less than complete performance, the promisor may recover reasonable remuneration, provided that it is possible to infer an implied agreement by the parties to abandon the old contract and to make a new one (*see* 16:2) —

> *Christy* v. *Row* (1808): C contracted to carry R's coal from Shields to Hamburg but the ship was prevented from reaching its destination by a state of war. At the request of the consignee, some of the coal was delivered at a different port. It was held that C was entitled to remuneration, as partial performance had been accepted.

(c) *If the promisee prevents performance.* If the promisor cannot complete the contract because of some act or omission by the promisee, he may sue either for damages or on a *quantum meruit.* In an action for breach of contract, it is a good defence for the defendant to prove *tender of performance* (i.e. that he offered to perform his part of the agreement and the plaintiff refused to accept this) —

> *Planché* v. *Colburn* (1831): P agreed to write a book to form part of a series to be published by C but, after P had completed part of it, C abandoned the project. It was held that P could recover £50.

(d) *If the promisor effects substantial performance.* If there have been only minor omissions or defects in performance, the promisor can sue on the contract, subject to a counter-claim in respect of them. The two cases below merit comparison —

> *Kiely & Sons* v. *Medcraft* (1965): As the cost of remedying defects amounted to £200, M refused to pay K, who had contracted to paint his house for £520. The Court of Appeal held that the contract had been substantially performed and that K was entitled to the balance of the price.

> *Bolton* v. *Mahadeva* (1972): B contracted to install a heating system in M's house for £560. On completion, the house was 10 per cent less warm than it should have been and there were fumes in the living rooms; the cost of remedying these defects would have been £174. The Court of Appeal

held that B had not substantially performed the contract
and therefore could not recover anything.

2. The discharge by agreement

As contracts are created by agreement between the parties,
they may consequently be discharged in a similar way. A
subsequent agreement may thus have the following effects:

(a) *The termination of an executory contract.* This means the
extinction of a contract not wholly performed on either side,
without replacement by a new agreement. It is, in effect, a simple
contract whereby each party relinquishes his rights in
consideration of a similar action by the other. An *oral* agreement
is sufficient to dissolve *all* contracts — including those which must
be in writing (*see* 9:6).

(b) *The replacement of an executory contract.* This constitutes
substitution — i.e. the extinction of an executory contract and its
replacement with a new agreement (called *novation*). The terms of
the new contract must be fundamentally different from those of
the original one — otherwise there would be merely a *variation*
(i.e. the alteration of an *existing* contract). As the *parol evidence rule*
(14:2) does not preclude the making of a new contract, substitution
may be effected orally in respect of all types of contract —

> *Berry* v. *Berry* (1929): In a deed of separation, the
> defendant (husband) covenanted to pay his wife £18 a
> month. Subsequently, in writing but not by deed, they
> agreed to change the amount to £9 a month plus 30 per
> cent of his earnings if they exceeded £350 a year. It was
> held that the wife could not recover the sum fixed by the
> deed, as it had been replaced by the simple contract.

(c) *The unilateral discharge of an executed contract.* This constitutes
waiver — i.e. an agreement whereby one party (who has executed
his part of a contract) releases the other from his obligation. To
be enforceable, such release necessitates either a deed (which does
not require consideration) or *accord and satisfaction* (i.e. agreement
and consideration) — though the doctrine of promissory estoppel
(9:**4(d)**) may nevertheless be applicable —

Elton Cop Dyeing Co v. *Broadbent & Son* (1919): Having
purchased from B machinery which proved defective, ECD
sought damages for breach of warranty. Both parties then
agreed to compromise the dispute by ECD withdrawing its
claim and B remedying the defects. Changing its mind,
ECD then sued on the original contract but it was held that
the claim must fail, as there had been true accord and
satisfaction.

D & C Builders Ltd v. *Rees* (1966): In serious financial
difficulties, D&C were owed £483 by R. She offered them
£300 in full settlement and they accepted this, to avoid
bankruptcy. It was held that there was no true accord (as
D&C had been under pressure) or consideration;
consequently D&C could recover the residue of the debt. *See
Atlas Express* v. *Kafco* (1989) (13:**5(c)**).

3.   The discharge by operation of a term
Terms providing for the discharge of a contract may be
included in the agreement and are of the following types:

(a) *The condition precedent.* This must be satisfied before any rights
come into existence — *see Pym* v. *Campbell* (1856) (14:**2(b)**).
(b) *The condition subsequent.* This provides for discharge in the
event of a specified occurrence —

Head v. *Tattersall* (1871): H bought from T a horse
'guaranteed to have hunted with the Bicester hounds', on
the understanding that, if it did not answer the description,
it could be returned by the following Wednesday. Injured
whilst possessed by (but not through any fault of) H, the
horse was found not to have hunted with the Bicester
hounds. It was held that, despite the injuries, H was entitled
to return the animal within the specified time and recover
the price.

(c) *The determination clause.* Commercial (e.g. building) and
employment contracts often include a clause enabling one party
to terminate the agreement before completion (e.g. in the event
of serious default by the other) and sometimes such a term may be
implied by the courts —

Beverley Corporation v. *Richard Hodgson & Sons* (1972): For 49 years H had made fixed annual payments for discharging waste into BC's sewage system. Although there was no provision for termination, BC served notice to terminate when the system was replaced. It was held that this was effective, there being an implied term which empowered BC to determine the agreement on giving reasonable notice.

4. The discharge by frustration

The case of *Paradine* v. *Jane* (1647) (in which J was held liable for the rent of property which he could not occupy on account of enemy invasion) established the rule that anyone binding himself by contract unconditionally to do something cannot escape liability by proving impossibility of performance. It has been argued that unforeseen contingencies should have been provided for by express stipulation; however, this rule has been mitigated by the *doctrine of frustration*, whereby a contract will be discharged if certain types of impossibility arise after it was made; e.g.:

(a) *The non-availability of the subject-matter.*

Taylor v. *Caldwell* (1863): C contracted to hire a music hall to T for a series of concerts but, before they took place, the building was destroyed by fire. It was held that the parties were discharged from their obligations.

(b) *The unavoidable non-availability of a party.*

Shepherd (FC) & Co v. *Jerrom* (1986): Two years after entering into a four-year contract of apprenticeship, J was convicted of affray and sentenced to Borstal training. When S refused to take him back, an industrial tribunal found that there had been unfair dismissal; the Employment Appeal Tribunal upheld this but the Court of Appeal held that, on the facts of the case, the custodial sentence frustrated the contract.

(c) *The complete non-occurrence of a fundamental event.* This has been illustrated in *Krell* v. *Henry* (1903) (14:**2(a)**), which merits comparison with —

Herne Bay Steamboat Co v. *Hutton* (1903): A boat was hired on

a specified date 'for the purpose of viewing the Naval
Review and for a day's cruise round the Fleet'. The review
was cancelled but the fleet remained to be seen and it was
held that there had not been sufficient change of
circumstances as to amount to frustration.

(d) *The consequence of supervening illegality.* Already mentioned in
12:**1(c)**, this is illustrated in *Avery* v. *Bowden* (1855) (16:**7(b)**).

5. The limits of frustration
The doctrine may *not* be invoked in the following
circumstances:

(a) *If the frustration was self-induced.* A party cannot sustain a claim
for frustration if he was himself responsible for it, or if he made it
impossible for the other party to perform his obligations —

> *Maritime National Fish* v. *Ocean Trawlers Ltd* (1935): MNF
> chartered from OT a trawler which was useless unless fitted
> with an otter-trawl and, to the knowledge of both parties,
> this could be used only under licence. MNF, who had four
> other ships, applied for five licences but only three were
> granted. In naming the ships to which these should apply,
> MNF excluded the trawler chartered from OT. It was held
> that MNF could not claim frustration and would therefore
> be liable for the hire charge.

(b) *If an obligation is merely made more onerous.* The impossibility
must make any attempted performance amount to something
quite different from what was originally contemplated by the
parties. It is not sufficient for an event merely to make an
obligation more onerous —

> *Davis Contractors Ltd* v. *Fareham Urban District Council* (1956):
> DC contracted to build 78 houses for FUDC at a cost of
> £85,836, the work to be completed in eight months. On
> account of weather and labour problems, the construction
> took 22 months. Receiving the contract price, DC claimed
> that, because of the delay, they were entitled to treat the
> contract as discharged and to be paid on a *quantum meruit*. It
> was held that, although the delay was greater than was to be
> expected, it was not caused by any new and unforeseeable

event. The work had merely proved more onerous than expected and this did not constitute frustration.

(c) *If the contingency was (or should have been) foreseen.* —

Walton Harvey Ltd v. *Walker & Homfrays Ltd* (1931): The defendants granted the plaintiffs the right to display an advertisement on the defendants' hotel for seven years. Within the period, the hotel was compulsorily purchased and demolished. It was held that, as the defendants had been aware of this risk, the contract was not frustrated and they were liable in damages.

6. The effects of frustration

Where frustration is established, a contract is discharged for the future but is not void *ab initio*. The Law Reform (Frustrated Contracts) Act 1943 provides that:

(a) Money paid before frustration is recoverable.

(b) Money due (but not in fact paid) before frustration ceases to be payable.

(c) A party who has incurred expenses is entitled to reimbursement up to the value of the sums paid or due to him at the time of frustration. If, however, nothing was paid or due at that moment, he could not recover.

(d) A party who has gained a valuable benefit under the contract at the time of frustration may be required to pay a just sum for it.

7. The discharge by breach

A *breach* of contract occurs if a party fails to perform one or more of his obligations, renders defective performance, repudiates his obligations or disables himself from performing them. In the last two instances, the breach may occur before the date fixed for performance; it is then called an *anticipatory breach* and it immediately entitles the other party to seek remedies, even though there is still time for the breach to be revoked. When a breach occurs, the innocent party always has a right to an action for damages but, if *both* of the following conditions are fulfilled, he may also elect to treat the contract as discharged — i.e. refuse to perform his own obligations and decline to accept further performance by the other party:

(a) *If the breach creates an option to treat the contract as discharged.* Not every breach can be regarded as a cause of discharge and the simple test is *whether it is of such a nature as to render further performance of the contract purposeless.* This situation would exist if one party *either* indicates expressly or impliedly that he no longer intends to be bound by the contract *or* breaks a stipulation which is so essential that the very foundation of the contract is destroyed —

> *Hochster* v. *De La Tour* (1853): DLT agreed to employ H as from 1st June but subsequently, in May, he stated that he would not do so. It was held that H was entitled to damages, even though DLT might have again reversed his decision before the specified date.

> *Decro-Wall International SA* v. *Practitioners in Marketing* (1971): In 1967 DW (French manufacturers) orally granted PM (English marketing company) the sole right of selling their products in the United Kingdom, it being agreed that payments should be made within 90 days of invoice. Of the 27 invoices issued over three years, 26 were paid between two and 20 days late but there was never any doubt about PM's ability to pay. In 1970 DW wrote to PM alleging that they had wrongfully repudiated the agreement by failing to pay bills on time and that the contract was therefore discharged. It was held that PM's breach did not go to the root of the contract and could result only in damages; DW's breach did not oblige PM to treat the contract as at an end.

(b) *If the innocent party exercises the option to treat the contract as discharged.* If he wishes, he may give the party in breach an opportunity to change his mind and perform his obligations. However, in such circumstances, the right to treat the contract as repudiated will be lost if the agreement is discharged in some other manner —

> *Avery* v. *Bowden* (1855): B chartered A's ship at a Russian port and agreed to load her with cargo within 45 days. Before this period had elapsed, he informed A that he could not provide a cargo but A kept the ship at the port, hoping that B would carry out his obligation. During the 45 days the Crimean War broke out, making it illegal for B to load

a cargo at a hostile port. It was held that, as A had not exercised his option to treat the contract as discharged, the supervening illegality provided B with a good defence to an action for breach.

The forms of redress

8. The remedies for breach
Depending on the type of breach, the innocent party may initiate the legal proceedings outlined below. However, under the Limitation Act 1980, actions in respect of *simple contracts* must be brought within *six years*, while those for agreements by deed must be commenced within *12 years*. The limiting periods begin as from the date on which the cause accrued — but, if the plaintiff is suffering from a legal disability (e.g. is a minor) on that date, it will be postponed until the removal of the disability. Similarly, if the action is based on fraud (or is for relief from the consequences of mistake), the period commences when the injured party discovers (or should have discovered) the fraud, etc. As a result of a breach of contract, the innocent party has recourse to the following proceedings — the first three of which are at common law, while the last two are in equity (hence discretionary):

(a) *The action for unliquidated damages.* The meaning of 'unliquidated' is explained in 7:2(a). In assessing damages, the question of *remoteness* must be considered and the rule in respect of contract was stated in *Hadley* v. *Baxendale (below)*, though it was refined in later cases. It is to the effect that: the party in default will be liable for *such damage as a reasonable man would have foreseen as a likely result of the breach, and in the light of the actual or implied knowledge which he had at the time of the contract.* However, the aggrieved party must take all reasonable and prudent steps to mitigate the loss and he cannot obtain compensation for any damage arising from his neglect to do so (but he can claim for expenses reasonably incurred in mitigation); the onus of proving such neglect rests on the party in default —

Hadley v. *Baxendale* (1854): H (a miller) sent a broken crankshaft by B (a carrier) to an engineer, as a pattern for a new one. On account of B's delay, there was a longer stoppage of work than would otherwise have been the case and, claiming loss of profits, H sued for breach of contract. It was held that B was not liable as he had no actual or implied knowledge that the breach would cause the long stoppage.

Koufos v. *Czarnikow* (1967): Appellant shipowners contracted to carry respondent sugar merchants' cargo from Constanza to Basrah. They were aware that there was a sugar market at Basrah but they did not know that the respondents intended to sell the cargo immediately upon arrival. In breach of contract, the ship deviated and arrived nine days late, during which time the price at Basrah fell sharply and the respondents lost £4,000 profits. The House of Lords held that the respondents were entitled to recover the £4,000, because the appellants were aware of the sugar market and it was *not unlikely* that the cargo would be sold at market price on arrival; furthermore, they must be held to have known that market prices fluctuate.

Brace v. *Calder* (1895): B had been employed by four partners, two of whom died. The remaining pair wished to continue the business and gave B notice, terminating his employment by the four but offering immediate re-employment by the surviving two. Resenting the technical dismissal, B refused the offer of re-employment and sought damages from the original four for wrongful dismissal. It was held that only nominal damages should be awarded, as B could have mitigated the breach by accepting the reasonable offer of fresh employment.

Hoffberger v. *Ascot International Bloodstock Bureau* (1976): After AIBB had broken their contract to buy his horse, H incurred considerable expense in keeping the animal, in the hope of selling advantageously; eventually, however, it was sold for a much reduced figure. The Court of Appeal held that H had acted reasonably and was entitled, as part of his damages, to the expenses of attempting to mitigate his loss, even though his final claim exceeded the original sale price.

(b) *The action for liquidated damages.* Liquidated damages constitute *a specific sum, agreed between the parties beforehand, as a pre-estimate of* *possible damage arising from a breach.* They may be recovered in full but they must not be confused with a *penalty* (i.e. a threat to be held over the other party *in terrorem*). In the latter case, the plaintiff may recover only for the actual damage suffered (which may be more or less than the penalty). It was held in *Dunlop Pneumatic Tyre Co* v. *New Garage & Motor Co* (1915) that the use of the words 'penalty' or 'liquidated damages' in a contract is relevant but not decisive; furthermore, a sum may be presumed to constitute a *penalty* if it is an excessive figure in relation to the greatest possible damage *or* if it is an increased amount for failing to pay a smaller sum *or* if it is a single figure relating to breaches of differing gravity —

> *Cellulose Acetate Silk Co* v. *Widnes Foundry (1925) Ltd* (1933): A contract by WF with CAS contained a *penalty* of £20 for each week's delay but, after a 30-week delay caused a loss far in excess of £600, CAS sued for the full deficit. It was held that CAS was entitled only to the stipulated figure — which comprised liquidated damages and *not* a penalty.

> *Forrest* v. *Davies* (1971): The parties negotiated for the sale of a house with a poor water supply and the contract provided for a better one to be established at the vendor's cost. This proved more difficult than anticipated and it was then agreed that the vendor should pay the purchaser £800 if a supply was not installed within six months. The Court of Appeal held that the sum was a penalty and should not be forfeited.

(c) *The action on a quantum meruit.* Instead of suing for damages for breach of contract, a plaintiff may seek remuneration *for work actually done* if his performance was on the understanding that there should be some consideration, although it was not fixed at the time of the agreement (*Lampleigh* v. *Brathwait* (1615) (9:**4(c)**)); *or* if performance was incomplete but circumstances as in 16:**1** existed; *or* if the plaintiff discovered that he was a party to a void contract (*see* 11).

(d) *The action for an injunction.* This remedy has been outlined in 7:**2(b)** and it will *not* be granted in contract if the effect would be to grant a decree of specific performance in circumstances where it would not be given (*see* 16:**9**). However, it *will* be granted with contracts of personal service — but only to enforce a negative stipulation (i.e. where someone is doing something which he promised *not* to do); it is also a suitable remedy to enforce the negative element of restraint of trade clauses (*see* 11:8) —

> *Evening Standard Co* v. *Henderson* (1987): ES's contract with H, its production manager, was terminable by either party giving one year's previous notice in writing. There was also a term which prohibited H from working for anyone else, whilst in ES's employ. Intending to join the 'London Daily News', H gave two months' notice and the Court of Appeal held that an interlocutory injunction should be granted.

> *Page One Records Ltd* v. *Britton* (1968): POR (pop group managers) sought to restrain The Troggs from seeking alternative management. It was held that an injunction could not be granted, as it would amount to ordering specific performance of the contract to compel The Troggs to employ POR as their managers.

(e) *The action for a decree of specific performance.* By this means a person can be compelled to carry out a promise that he has made. It is an appropriate remedy in cases of breach of contract for the sale or lease of land, or the sale of something not available on the open market.

9. The refusal of specific performance

Specific performance will *not* be granted in the case of void or voidable contracts, simple contracts lacking any of the requirements outlined in 9:1, certain situations involving non-operative mistake, and also in the following circumstances:

(a) *If damages provide an adequate remedy.* Specific performance will not be decreed in, e.g., agreements relating to the loan of money or the sale of mass-produced items —

> *Cohen* v. *Roche* (1927): C sued for the delivery of eight Hepplewhite chairs which he claimed to have bought at R's auction. It was held that C was entitled to damages for breach of contract but not specific performance, as the chairs were 'ordinary articles of commerce'.

> *Verrall* v. *Great Yarmouth Borough Council* (1980): The Conservative-controlled council granted the National Front

a licence to hold an annual conference at their hall for
£6,000. After the local government elections, the council
became Labour-controlled and purported to cancel the
agreement, offering to refund the money. Unable to find
alternative accommodation, the National Front sought
specific performance. The decree was granted and an
appeal by the council was dismissed by the Court of Appeal.

(b) *If the contract is unfair or imposes hardship.* Specific performance
may, however, be decreed if the hardship could have been
anticipated by foresight and the party concerned apparently
decided to take the risk. Mere inadequacy of consideration (9:4(a))
cannot normally constitute hardship.

(c) *If there is a lack of mutuality.* Specific performance will not be
decreed against one party if it is not available against the other
(e.g. on account of incapacity) —

Lumley v. *Ravenscroft* (1895): Through an agent, R (a minor)
agreed to grant a lease to L but broke the agreement and L
sought specific performance. It was held that an action for
specific performance cannot be maintained against a minor;
consequently, a minor cannot maintain such an action
against anyone else.

(d) *If the contract concerns personal services or performance requiring
supervision.* Specific performance will not be decreed in respect of
agreements concerning personal services (but *see* **16:8(d)**), nor
where the performance involves continuous successive acts
necessitating constant superintendence.

(e) *If there has been undue lapse of time.* 'Delay defeats the equities'
and undue delay, sufficient to cause the court to withhold an
equitable remedy, is known as *laches*.

10. The alternatives to contractual remedies

Quite apart from the law of contract, the consumer also has
recourse to:

(a) *The law of tort.* From 15:2(c) it can be seen that, in certain
contractual situations, it may be possible to make a claim in
negligence. For such an action to succeed, it is normally necessary
(as shown in 18:1) to establish three requirements: that the
defendant owed the plaintiff a duty of care; that the defendant

broke that duty; and that the plaintiff suffered damage in consequence of the breach. Though a duty of care may be established, it can be more difficult to prove a breach thereof — as was demonstrated when the Distillers Company marketed a drug containing thalidomide for pregnant mothers and it caused gross deformities in their children. This reinforced demands for the statutory creation of *product liability,* whereby manufacturers become strictly liable for injury caused by their products to anyone (not only contractual purchasers). The resultant Consumer Protection Act 1987 is outlined in 17:6.

(b) *The criminal law.* The Trade Descriptions Act 1968 makes it a criminal offence (with prosecutions brought by local authorities) to apply a false trade description to any goods, or to supply (or offer to supply) any goods to which a false trade description has been applied. Trade descriptions include descriptions as to: quantity and size; method, place and date of manufacture; other history; composition; other physical characteristics; fitness for purpose; behaviour or accuracy; testing or approval. It is also an offence to make a statement known to be false (or recklessly to make a false statement) regarding the provision (in the course of trade or business) of services, accommodation or facilities —

> *Dixons* v. *Barnett* (1989): An Astral 500 telescope was sold, being described as capable of '455x magnification'. Though, scientifically, 455 could be achieved, the maximum useful magnification was 120. The Divisional Court upheld a conviction under the Trade Descriptions Act 1968 as, although not false, the statement was likely to mislead.

Progress test 16

1. Alfred, a skilled carpenter, agreed to make six chairs for Bob but, after three had been completed, Bob said that he had decided to emigrate and would not require the chairs. Advise Alfred. **(1)**

2. Having completed the chairs, Alfred agreed to sell them to Colin, who paid him the quoted price of £300 but, before they were delivered, they suffered severe damage through a flood. At no extra charge, Alfred therefore offered Colin a £400 table in lieu of the chairs and Colin agreed to take it. As his wife does not like the table, Colin has returned it and is seeking performance of the original agreement. Alfred seeks your advice. **(2)**

3. Reading that a well-known TV personality liked to stay at the Grand Hotel, Muddysea, Elsie inquired when he would be there and booked a room for the same period, as she wished to meet him. It was later reported that the personality would have to forgo his holiday, on account of overseas filming, and Elsie cancelled her booking, claiming that the contract had been frustrated. Advise the Grand Hotel. **(4)**

4. Awaiting the delivery of a medicinal drug that they had purchased in bulk in the Far East, Importco contracted to sell the whole consignment to Magicures. A week later, the latter purported to cancel the agreement and Importco took no immediate action. It was then discovered that the drug had harmful side effects and its sale was banned in the United Kingdom. Importico seek your advice. **(7)**

5. Having agreed to buy Frank's car for £2,000, Keith arranged a continental tour and booked a passage on a car ferry for £80. Frank then decided to keep the vehicle and Keith tried to find a similar model elsewhere. Eventually he obtained one for £2,300 but by now the date of the ferry passage had passed. Advise Keith. **(8)**

Part three

The law of torts

17

The principles of tortious liability

The breaches of duties

1. The law of torts

Just as people require safeguards against criminal offences and breaches of contract, so do they have a further variety of interests which need protection from the activities of others. Examples include: negligence causing harm; trespass interfering with the occupation of property; wrongful detention effecting loss of freedom; defamation damaging reputation, etc. It is the law of torts which determines whether one should be protected from such experiences — by rendering actionable the *breach of a legal duty* not to indulge in certain acts or omissions. It has long been debated whether there is a *law of tort* (whereby, unless it is justified by the law, any harm caused to another creates liability) or a *law of torts* (whereby specific rules prohibit particular kinds of harmful activity). The examples above are all, in fact, actionable and it can be seen that several totally different forms of conduct are involved — with separate legal principles developing independently in respect of each. As a result of this piecemeal evolution, liability normally exists only in certain areas and there appears to be no general right to compensation. The law of torts is therefore not a comprehensive compensatory system — but, as shown in 18:4, it is also not immutable and its ambit is constantly being broadened by judicial decisions. As duties connote corresponding rights, authorities have maintained that tortious liability is based on *injuria* (the violation of a right recognised by law) and it is not always necessary to prove *damnum* (actual harm caused); consequently a distinction has been drawn between:

(a) *Injuria sine damno* (the violation of a legal right without any harm being caused). In the case of torts such as negligence, nuisance, etc, an action will not succeed unless the plaintiff can show that some actual harm accrued. However, there are others (e.g. trespass and libel) where the plaintiff enjoys an *absolute right* and, if the defendant infringes this, he is legally liable — even though he may not have caused any real harm. Such torts are said to be actionable *per se*.

(b) *Damnum sine injuria* (harm caused without any legal right being violated). Not all unjustifiable harm (e.g. invasion of privacy) is actionable and a plaintiff cannot normally obtain redress if no legal right has been violated. The strictness of this rule has been thrown into question by the decision in the first case below, but it was applied in the subsequent second one —

> *Stephens* v. *Avery* (1988): Being very close friends, S and A discussed personal matters on the basis of confidentiality and secrecy. When A passed details of S's sexual conduct to a newspaper, S claimed damages on the ground that publication was in breach of A's duty of confidence. A applied to strike out the claim as disclosing no cause of action but the master refused. Dismissing the appeal, Sir Nicholas Browne-Wilkinson, Vice-Chancellor, held that, although the courts would not enforce a duty of confidence relating to matters of grossly immoral nature, information concerning sexual conduct could be the subject of a legally enforceable duty of confidence, if it would be unconscionable for someone who had received it, as expressly confidential, to reveal it to another. The defendants had not shown that there was no legal basis for S's claim.

> *Kaye* v. *Robertson* (1990): Whilst recovering from brain surgery and not being in full control of his faculties, K (a TV celebrity) was photographed and interviewed. He sued for breach of privacy but the Court of Appeal held that there was no cause of action. However, as the draft article implied consent, which was impossible in the circumstances,

the elements of malicious falsehood existed and an injunction to restrain publication was granted. *See also Bradford Corporation* v. *Pickles* (1895) (20:3(a)).

2. The nature of torts

As shown above, tortious liability affords protection to the individual additional to that in respect of:

(a) *Criminal offences.* As outlined in 4:1(a), crimes are offences against *society*, giving rise to prosecutions (in the magistrates' court or Crown Court), with a view to *punishment*, in order to protect the interests of *the public*. A tort is a wrong against a person and gives rise to civil action, to obtain *redress*. In a number of instances, one single act or omission (e.g. causing injury by reckless driving) may constitute both a crime and a tort.

(b) *Breaches of contract.* As in the case of contract, actions for tort are heard in the county court or High Court, which may grant redress to a successful plaintiff — generally by way of damages and/or an injunction (*see* 7:2(a)–(b)). However, in tort the duty not to violate a legal right is imposed by *the law* — whereas contractual liability stems from an agreement between *the parties*. Furthermore, as shown in 15:1, anyone who is not party to a contract cannot normally sue for its breach — whereas anyone suffering a violation of a legal right can sue in tort.

3. The capacity of the parties

In general, anyone may sue in tort — including convicted criminals, (non-enemy) aliens and minors (though an adult usually represents them as 'next friend'). Under the Law Reform (Husband and Wife) Act 1962, husbands and wives may sue each other for torts, even if committed after the marriage. Under the Law Reform (Miscellaneous Provisions) Act 1934, all causes of action (except defamation) vesting in (or subsisting against) a person survive his death and vest in (or subsist against) his estate. Under the Fatal Accidents Act 1976, executors or administrators may bring an auction on behalf of a deceased person's dependants (wife, husband, parent, grandparent, children, grandchildren, brother, sister, uncle, aunt), who may sue if death was caused by an accident which would have entitled the deceased to maintain an action. With regard to tortious liability, special consideration needs to be given to:

(a) *The liability of the Crown.* This is outlined in 8:9(b).

(b) *The liability of corporations.* A corporation (*see* 5:7(a)) is fully liable for torts, except those (e.g. assault) which it could not possibly commit, and the liability of company directors has been enunciated in —

> *Evans (C) & Sons* v. *Spriteband* (1985): Seeking damages from S for breach of copyright, E claimed similar relief from a director of S for authorising, directing and procuring the acts complained of. There was no allegation that he knew (or was reckless as to the fact) that the acts were tortious but the Court of Appeal held him liable, in circumstances where knowledge was not an essential ingredient.

(c) *The liability of partnerships.* All members of a partnership are liable for any tort committed in the ordinary course of the firm's business, or with the authority of all the partners —

> *Hamlyn* v. *Houston & Co* (1903): A partner bribed a rival's clerk to betray his employer's secrets and all the partners were held liable, as the act — though wrongful — was performed in the ordinary course of the business, part of which was to obtain information concerning competitors.

(d) *The liability of clubs and societies.* Theoretically all members of a club or society should be joined as co-plaintiffs or co-defendants in any action for tort. Where, however, all the members have an *identical interest* in defending an action, application can be made to the court for a *representation order* against certain members, who are sued as representing the members as a whole. Where such an action succeeds, judgment can be enforced against the association property and also that of any individual member —

> *Campbell* v. *Thompson* (1953): C sought to sue a members' club (which employed her as a cleaner) for injury sustained on the stairs of the premises. As all the 2,500 members had a common interest in resisting her claim, an order was made that the Honorary Secretary and Chairman of the House Committee be appointed to represent all the persons who were members on the relevant date.

(e) *The liability of trade unions.* Under the Employment Act 1982, trade unions are liable in tort — though liability for acts such as inducing breach of contract, intimidation or conspiracy will exist only if the conduct was authorised by a senior person in the union. There are also financial limits upon some forms of tortious liability —but these are subject to ballots (Trade Unions Act 1984) and individual members' rights of challenge (Employment Act 1988).

(f) *The liability of minors.* Minors are fully liable for their torts — but, where it is necessary to prove *malice* or *intention,* a minor defendant may be held to be too young to have evinced it. Similarly, when *lack of reasonable care* must be shown, the standard expected of a minor will be that commensurate with his age and understanding. (*See also* 17:**13**).

(g) *The liability of mentally disordered or drunken persons.* Insanity is, in itself, no defence in tort, unless it is so extreme as to make the defendant's act involuntary, or to prevent the defendant from evincing malice or intention (where this is a necessary element), or to preclude the defendant from possessing the necessary knowledge (in negligence) —

> *Morriss* v. *Marsden* (1952): To all appearances a normal person, the defendant violently attacked the plaintiff, was charged with criminal assault, found unfit to plead and detained at Broadmoor; nevertheless the plaintiff's action against him succeeded.

(h) *The liability of joint tortfeasors.* If two or more persons commit the same wrongful act and cause the same harm, then liability is *joint and several* — i.e. the plaintiff may sue all of them jointly in one action, or any one of them for the full damages (in which case, each is bound to contribute a fair share).

4. The relevance of motive

In most actions for tort, the defendant's motive is entirely irrelevant. Thus the absence of malicious intent will not make an unlawful act lawful; likewise, the presence of malice will not make an otherwise lawful act unlawful (*Bradford Corporation* v. *Pickles* (1895) (20:**3(a)**)). Nevertheless, in certain actions, the existence of malice may be:

(a) *An essential element of the tort.* In torts such as malicious prosecution, the plaintiff must prove the defendant's malice, in the sense of an improper motive.

(b) *A reinforcement of the tort.* There are other torts (e.g. nuisance, conspiracy and injurious falsehood) in which malice is not an essential element but where the plaintiff will succeed if he proves that the defendant acted maliciously. Thus an act which is not otherwise a nuisance may become one if malice makes the defendant's conduct unreasonable (*see Christie* v. *Davey* (1893) (20:**1(a)**).

(c) *A factor affecting the quantum of damages.* As shown in 7:**2(a)**, damages in excess of actual pecuniary loss may be awarded if an injury has been aggravated by motive or conduct — *see Loudon* v. *Ryder* (1953) (19:**1(a)**)) and *Merest* v. *Harvey* (1814) (19:**1(b)**)).

(d) *A detriment to a defence.* In actions for defamation, the defences of qualified privilege or fair comment will fail if the plaintiff proves malice on the part of the defendant — *see Thomas* v. *Bradbury Agnew* (1906) (21:**6(a)**)).

The instances of strict liability

5. The strict liability for animals
Liability in tort is generally dependent upon fault, and the defendant must be shown to have committed some breach of a legal duty, either deliberately or negligently. However, in a number of instances, the duty imposed on the defendant is such that liability for breach exists without there being any element of fault, in the sense of intention or negligence. In such circumstances, the liability is said to be *strict* (*see also* 22:**4**) but it cannot be described as *absolute* (i.e. totally unavoidable), in view of possible defences which exist. Cases of vicarious liability and certain statutory liabilities (17:**10–14**) can be described as 'strict' but the principal examples relate to animals, defective products and things which escape from one's land (17:**6–9**). In the case of animals, the Animals Act 1971 defines the liability of a *keeper* — i.e. a person who owns an animal, has it in his possession or is head of a household wherein a member under the age of 16 owns or possesses it. If an animal ceases to be owned or possessed by its keeper, he remains liable until someone else owns or possesses it. Taking possession of an animal to prevent it causing damage, or to return it to its owner, does not make anyone a keeper. Liability exists in respect of:

(a) *Animals of a dangerous species.* This is a species which is not commonly domesticated in the British Islands and whose fully grown animals are likely to cause severe damage, unless restrained. The keeper of such an animal is liable for any damage it may cause (not limited solely to human injury but relating also to property or the spreading of disease, etc) *unless* it was wholly due to the fault of the person suffering it *or* unless that person was a trespasser and the animal was not there for the purpose of protection (or, if it was so there, the keeping for that purpose was not unreasonable). Under the Dangerous Wild Animals Act 1976, it is an offence to keep such an animal without a licence.

(b) *Animals of a non-dangerous species.* In this case, and with the exceptions given above, liability will exist for damage which the animal was likely to cause, unless restrained, or which was likely to be severe, *and* the likelihood of the damage (or of its being severe) was due to characteristics not normally found in such animals (or found only at particular times or in particular circumstances) *and* the keeper was aware of those characteristics. In addition to these provisions, keepers of non-dangerous animals have a duty to take reasonable care to avoid damage to persons or property, and would be liable in negligence for any breach thereof —

> *Cummings* v. *Grainger* (1975): Without permission and late at night C entered G's scrapyard where she knew there was a fierce alsatian, left to guard old cars. The dog savaged her and the Court of Appeal held that, by trespassing, C had voluntarily accepted the risk of injury, also the keeping of the dog was reasonable — so the action failed.

> *Kite* v. *Napp* (1982): Having been bitten by a dog which attacked people carrying bags, K was awarded damages, as the characteristics were known to the owner and the injury was of a kind likely to be severe.

(c) *Livestock.* Anyone in possession of livestock is liable if it strays on to the land of another and causes damage to the land or to any property thereon *also* for any expenses reasonably incurred by the other person in keeping the livestock while it cannot be restored to its owner. If the plaintiff wishes to recover for personal injuries, he must either claim under (b) *above* or establish negligence. An occupier of land has a duty to prevent his animals from straying on to the highway but there is no breach of this duty if they are rightfully placed on common land. The keeper of a dog is liable if it kills or injures livestock — unless the livestock had strayed on to land and the dog belonged to (or its presence was authorised by) the occupier. The Dogs Act 1871 grants powers to courts in respect of complaints concerning dogs not under proper control and these were extended by the Dangerous Dogs Act 1989.

6. The strict liability for defective products

Where damage is caused wholly or partly by a defect in a product, the Consumer Protection Act 1987 imposes strict liability on the producer, any person holding himself out to be the producer (e.g. by brand name, trade mark, etc), any person who has imported the product into the European Community in order to supply it to another, or the supplier — if, having been requested, he fails within a reasonable time to give the name of a person in the foregoing categories to the sufferer of the damage. This liability is additional to that for breach of contract or negligence and its essential elements are:

(a) *The meaning of 'product'.* This generally implies goods but includes services (e.g. water, gas, electricity), also components and raw materials. Excluded are buildings, primary agricultural products and printed matter (except when it is an instruction or warning for a product).

(b) *The meaning of 'producer'.* This is usually the manufacturer or, in the case of a raw material, the person who mined or otherwise obtained it. The term includes canners (of fruits, vegetables, etc) but not those who simply package goods, unless the packaging alters essential characteristics of the product. If a final product contains a defective component, then the manufacturers of both the product and the component would be liable.

(c) *The meaning of 'defective'.* A product is defined as defective if its safety is not such as persons are generally entitled to expect. In assessing this, courts may take into account the manner in which the product is marketed, any instructions given with it, what might reasonably be expected to be done with it, also the time when the producer supplied it (important in relation to the ageing of goods and improvements in safety standards).

(d) *The meaning of 'damage'.* This includes death, personal injury and damage exceeding £275 to a person's private property (including land). Excluded is damage to the product itself — which would necessitate an action in contract.

7. The defences to actions for defectives products

The extent of liability would be affected by any contributory negligence (18:8) on the part of the plaintiff and the 1987 Act provides the following defences to an action:

(a) *The compliance with the law.* The plaintiff cannot recover if the defect was attributable to compliance with any statutory or European Community requirement.

(b) *The absence of supply.* The plaintiff cannot recover if the defendant did not at any time supply the product to another (e.g. where it was stolen and supplied by the thief).

(c) *The absence of commercial motive.* The plaintiff cannot recover if the supplier was not acting by way of business or with a view to profit (e.g. sales of second-hand goods by private individuals, sales of home-made articles at charity fetes, etc).

(d) *The absence of defect at the time of supply.* The plaintiff cannot recover if the defendant is a producer, own brander or Community importer and can prove that the product was not defective at the time when he supplied it to another. If, however, the defendant is a retailer or supplier, the time of supply is when the product was supplied to him. Consequently, if a product is rendered defective by a retailer, neither he nor the manufacturer would be liable under the Act — though an action might succeed against the retailer for breach of contract or negligence.

(e) *The absence of technical knowledge at the time of supply.* The plaintiff cannot recover if the defendant is a producer who can prove that the state of scientific and technical knowledge ('the state of the art') at the time of supply was not such that he might have been expected to discover the defect. The critical time is that of *supply* (not *manufacture*) — thus a producer must keep up to date with new developments until he actually supplies the product.

(f) *The defective design or specifications for a subsequent product.* The plaintiff cannot recover if the defendant is the supplier of a defective component and can prove that the defect was due *either* to the design of the complete product *or* to specifications received from the producer of the complete product.

8.   The strict liability of *Rylands* v. *Fletcher*

In the case of *Rylands* v. *Fletcher* (1868), heard originally in 1866 *sub nom Fletcher* v. *Rylands*, the defendant had employed a contractor to construct a reservoir on his land but did not know of (and could not reasonably have discovered) the existence of disused mineshafts on the site. As a result, the plaintiff's adjoining coal mine was flooded and the defendant was held liable. It had not been possible to prove negligence, trespass or nuisance but Blackburn J established the rule that: *The person who, for his own purposes, brings on his land and collects and keeps there anything likely to do mischief if it escapes, must keep it in at his peril and, if he does not do so, is prima facie answerable for all the damage which is the natural consequence of its escape.* This was upheld in the House of Lords when the case was concluded in 1868 and liability covers damage to property or persons. The essential elements of the liability are:

(a) *The meaning of 'brings and keeps'.* There must be an *artificial* accumulation — thus the rule does not apply to the land itself or to things naturally upon it — e.g. natural (as opposed to artificial) lakes, wild animals or weeds —

> *Giles* v. *Walker* (1890): W had ploughed waste land, thereby causing thistles to grow on adjacent land, but he was held not liable.

(b) *The meaning of 'anything'.* Examples include: water, electricity, gas, sewage, beasts, projecting poisonous trees and even persons —

> *Att.-Gen.* v. *Corke* (1933): C allowed caravan dwellers to camp on his land and, when they 'escaped' and committed nuisances on adjacent property, he was held liable.

(c) *The meaning of 'likely to do mischief'.* Whether a 'thing' is likely to do mischief is a question of fact; consequently, a particular 'thing' may come within the rule in one case but not in another. In general, it will give rise to liability if it is potentially dangerous and will cause damage if it escapes — even though it may be harmless while confined. There must be some foreseeability of the risk (though not the likelihood) of the thing escaping — and, as it is a matter of strict (as opposed to negligence) liability, it would not be a defence to claim that all reasonable precautions had been taken to prevent the escape.

(d) *The meaning of 'if it escapes'*. There must be 'an escape from a place where the defendant has occupation of (or control over) land to a place which is outside his occupation or control' — *per* Lord Simon in —

> *Read* v. *J. Lyons & Co Ltd* (1946): While on L's premises, a munitions inspector was injured by the explosion of a shell in process of manufacture. As there had not been any escape from the premises, the rule did not apply.

9. The defences to actions in *Rylands* v. *Fletcher*

The following defences are available to a defendant in an action under the rule:

(a) *The consent of the plaintiff*. The plaintiff cannot recover if he · expressly or impliedly consented to the defendant's bringing and keeping the dangerous thing on his premises and, in such circumstances, the defendant might be liable only in negligence —

> *Peters* v. *Prince of Wales Theatre (Birmingham) Ltd* (1943): P leased a shop in POWT's theatre premises, which contained a rehearsal room fitted with fire sprinklers. On account of heavy frost, and no default by POWT, the sprinklers burst and water percolated into the shop. As P had taken the premises as he found them (and therefore impliedly consented to the installation of the sprinklers), it was held that he could not recover.

(b) *The default of the plaintiff*. The plaintiff cannot recover if he caused the injury himself, or if his property was abnormally sensitive —

> *Eastern & South African Telegraph Co Ltd* v. *Cape Town Tramways Co* (1902): CTT were held not liable when a very small escape of electricity disturbed the operation of ESAT's sensitive submarine cables.

(c) *The act of a stranger.* The plaintiff cannot recover if the escape of the dangerous thing occasioned by the act of a stranger, over whom the defendant had no control —

> *Rickards* v. *Lothian* (1913): Leasing offices on the second floor of a building occupied by L, R had his property damaged by water from a fourth floor lavatory which had been blocked by an unknown third party. L was held not liable.

(d) *The statutory authority.* The plaintiff cannot recover if the defendant can successfully plead that he is exempt from liability by statutory authority —

> *Dunne* v. *North Western Gas Board* (1963): Injured by explosions caused by gas escaping from a main which had been damaged by the bursting of water pipes, D claimed damages from NWGB and the water authority. The Court of Appeal held that, as they supplied services under statute, they were not liable in the absence of negligence.

The instances of vicarious liability

10. The vicarious liability for employees

Under the maxim *qui facit per alium facit per se* ('he who acts through another acts in person'), anyone who authorises another to commit a tort is liable as fully as if he himself had committed it. This indirect form of liability is termed *vicarious* and it arises where special relationships exist — e.g. in respect of acts or omissions by employees, independent contractors, agents and children. An employer (who should insure against public liability) is liable for all torts committed by his employees (i.e. persons under a contract *of service*) in the course of their employment — that is to say when they do improperly what they are employed to do properly — even if the employer had expressly forbidden the wrongful act. Furthermore, if an employee is loaned to someone else, the original employer is still liable for his torts, unless he can prove that responsibility has been transferred to the temporary employer, to direct the manner in which the work is done —

> *Rose* v. *Plenty* (1976): Contrary to an express prohibition by his employers (the Co-op), P (a milkman) arranged for R (a

13-year-old boy) to help him on his round, and gave him a lift on his vehicle. Due to P's negligent driving, R was injured and the Court of Appeal held the Co-op liable.

Iqbal v. *London Transport Executive* (1973): Employed by LTE, a bus conductor, who had been frequently prohibited from driving buses, injured a fellow employee when attempting to drive a bus at the depot. He was assisting in getting his own bus on the road but the Court of Appeal held that he was not driving in the course of his employment; consequently, LTE were not liable.

McConkey v. *Amec plc and Others* (1990): G.W. Sparrow & Sons plc hired a crawler crane and driver to William Press Production Ltd (a subsidiary of A) for use in a yard occupied by A. The contract stated that the driver should be competent and under the direction of the hirer. Due to the driver's incompetence, McC, a scaffolder employed by another company, was seriously injured when metal plates were being lifted by (and fell from) the crane. The Court of Appeal held Sparrows to be vicariously liable. *See also* 14:6(a).

11. The vicarious liability for independent contractors
An independent contractor (who has a contract *for services*) is a person who is under the control of an employer as to what he must do, but is free to select the method of doing it. Generally, an employer is not liable for the torts of his independent contractors, unless he employed them:

(a) *To do something unlawful* —

Ellis v. *Sheffield Gas Consumers' Co* (1853): Without legal authority, SGC's contractors opened trenches in the streets and, falling over a pile of stones which they had left, E sustained injury. It was held that SGC were liable.

(b) *To do something 'extra hazardous'.* For this to apply, there must be an inherent danger which subsists, however much care is taken —

Honeywill & Stein Ltd v. *Larkin Bros Ltd* (1934): Having employed LB to take flashlight photographs in a third party's cinema, H&S were held liable to the owners for a fire caused by LB's negligence.

(c) *To do work on a highway* —

Holliday v. *National Telephone Co* (1899): Laying telephone cables, NT were held liable for a contractor's negligence, whereby molten solder was scattered over H.
See also 18:5(c).

12. The vicarious liability for agents

As shown in 15:4, an *agent* is a person authorised to act on behalf of another (the *principal*), who can be held liable for his agent's torts. Thus, if agency could be proved, the owner of a vehicle would be liable for the negligence of someone else driving it — though mere permission to drive would not be sufficient to establish vicarious liability —

Ormrod v. *Crosville Motor Services Ltd* (1953): O was asked by his friend Murphie to drive M's Austin Healey to Monte Carlo, so that they could use it for a joint holiday. On the way, he collided with CMS's bus and the Court of Appeal held that M was liable, as O was his agent — because the car was being used at the time partly for M's purposes.

Morgans v. *Launchbury* (1973): L owned a car which her husband regularly used and she asked him not to drive when he had been drinking. One evening he was not sober and requested a friend to drive him home. Proceeding at 90 mph in the wrong direction, the car collided with a bus; the husband and friend were killed and other injured people sued L. Reversing the decision of the Court of Appeal, the House of Lords held that she was not vicariously liable as the friend was not her agent.

13. The vicarious liability for children

Generally a parent is not liable for the torts of his/her children unless he/she authorised the tort, employed the child (*see* 17:10) or was negligent in affording the opportunity for the tort. The following cases merit comparison —

Donaldson v. *McNiven* (1952): D, a five-year-old child, lost the sight of an eye, on account of a pellet fired from an air rifle by a 13-year-old boy in a populous alley way. He had been ordered by his father not to fire it outside the house and it was held that there was no ground for imputing negligence to the father.

Newton v. *Edgerley* (1959): A farmer allowed his son, aged 12, to buy a gun and showed him how to use it. He told him not to take the gun off the farm and not to use it when other children were present. Disobeying these instructions, the son went off shooting with four other boys and accidentally shot one of them in the heel. It was held that the farmer had been guilty of negligence because he could not ensure that his instructions were obeyed and he had not taught his son how to handle the gun when other persons were present.

The liability for breaches of statutory duties

14. The breach of statutory duty

Civil proceeding may arise from certain statutes which generally create a public duty but do not necessarily provide for tortious liability. In recent years, some (e.g. the Sex Discrimination Act 1975, the Race Relations Act 1976 — *see* 8:**7(a)**–**(b)**) do in fact state that they confer a right of action, whilst others (e.g. the Safety of Sports Grounds Act 1975, the Guard Dogs Act 1975) expressly exclude it. In the absence of any such provisions or precedents, it is the task of the court to ascertain whether the intention of Parliament was to create solely a public duty — or one owed as well to an aggrieved party; consequently it is necessary to determine:

(a) *Whether the statute confers a right of action in tort.* The question as to whether or not a civil remedy exists may well be one of policy, rather than construction; there has thus been criticism of the courts' creation of new civil duties, founded on unexpressed parliamentary intent and following no really discernible pattern. Contravention of statutory requirements has given rise to past civil proceedings for failure to supply wholesome drinking water but not for supplying infected bottled milk (but *see* 17:**6**); moreover, although actions may arise under the Health and Safety at Work

Act 1974, it is unlikely that they would under the Trade
descriptions Act 1968 (16:**10(b)**). It has been suggested that a civil
remedy may be intended when a statutory duty is prescribed but
no sanction for its breach is specified; conversely, however, the
provision of a specific sanction does not necessarily exclude a right
of action —

> *Clarke and Wife* v. *Brims* (1947): On a dark, wet night, C's
> car ran into the rear of B's car, which was stationary with
> the rear light unlit. Contending that this was a breach of a
> statutory duty under the Road Transport Lighting Act 1927,
> C claimed damages but it was held that he could not found a
> cause of action on such a breach, as the Act imposed public
> duties which were unenforceable by an individual.

> *Reffell* v. *Surrey County Council* (1964): Having sustained
> injury by putting her hand through an exceptionally thin
> glass panel in a swing door, R (a schoolgirl) successfully
> sued the Education Authority for failure to comply with the
> Standards for School Premises Regulations 1959 (which did
> not provide any sanction for breach).

(b) *Whether the statute imposes strict liability.* Many statutes (e.g. the
Health and Safety at Work Act 1974) impose a duty to take all
reasonably practical steps to avoid a particular risk. In such
circumstances, the duty of care largely equates with that of
common law negligence — and has consequently been described
as *statutory negligence* — with the statute specifying the standard of
reasonable conduct. In other cases, however, statutes have been
held to impose strict liability, with no need to prove any default
on the part of the defendant —

> *Adsett* v. *K & L Steelfounders* (1953): Having contracted
> pneumoconiosis, A sued his employers, claiming that — in
> not safeguarding him from dust — they had been negligent
> and had committed a breach of their duty under the
> Factories Act 1937. The Court of Appeal held that, having
> taken all reasonable steps, K&L were not in breach of their
> duty.

> *Galashiels Gas Co* v. *O'Donnell (or Millar)* (1949): Although no

fault could be found in the mechanism, a gas company employee, who had been injured by a lift failure, recovered damages for his employers' breach of the Factories Act 1937. The words that 'every hoist or lift shall be properly maintained in efficient working order' were held to be imperative, thus imposing an absolute obligation.

(c) *Whether the statute was intended to protect the plaintiff.* Here the basic question is whether the plaintiff is of a class of persons whom the statute was intended to protect —

> *Thornton* v. *Kirklees Metropolitan Borough Council* (1979): Being homeless and with a priority need, T sued the housing authority for failure to provide him with accommodation under the Housing (Homeless Persons) Act 1977. The county court judge ruled that a civil action did not lie, but the Court of Appeal upheld T's right to bring an action for breach of statutory duty.

> *Lonrho* v. *Shell Petroleum Co (No. 2)* (1982): Companies including SP had contracted to use a pipeline, built and operated by L, for transporting all petroleum products imported by sea and destined for a refinery in Rhodesia. When the country unilaterally declared independence, the unlicensed supply of oil to it became illegal under the Southern Rhodesia (Petroleum) Order 1965 but SP and others maintained their imports by different means. L sought damages for the consequent prolonging of the unlawful independence and the disuse of the pipeline. As the sole purpose of the Order was to undermine the illegal government, the House of Lords held that it did not give a right of action to anyone suffering loss from its breach.

(d) *Whether the statute was intended to prevent the alleged injury* —

> *Gorris* v. *Scott* (1874): Transporting G's sheep in his ship, S failed to comply with a statutory order requiring animals to be divided into pens. As a result, they were washed overboard and drowned but G's action failed because the legislation was intended solely to prevent the spread of disease.

The nature of general defences

15. The defence of consent

Some torts have special defences (*see* 19:3, 20:3, also 21:5–8) but there are also several general defences, which can be raised in answer to most claims, and the first to be considered is *consent*. Under the maxim *volenti non fit injuria* ('no wrong is done to one who consents'), a defendant who is *prima facie* liable for a tort can escape liability if he can show that the plaintiff expressly or impliedly consented to run the risk which resulted in the injury complained of. Thus in *Morris* v. *Murray* (1990) the Court of Appeal held that, by knowingly and willingly flying with a drunken pilot, the plaintiff was not entitled to damages for personal injuries. Whether consent exists is a question of fact, to be individually decided in each case, but it will be held *not* to exist in the following circumstances:

(a) *If the defendant was negligent.* Normally the defendant cannot claim that the plaintiff consented to be injured by the negligence of others — thus persons who use the highway impliedly consent to the risk of harm arising from traffic conditions — but not negligent harm. At sporting events, therefore, participants and spectators are taken to have assumed the risks involved — but are not *volenti* in respect of negligence or unusual risks not generally related to the sport — *see Condon* v. *Basi* (1985) (19:6(b)).

(b) *If the plaintiff merely knew of the risk.* Knowledge is not the same as consent (the maxim being *volenti* non fit injuria, not *scienti* non injuria); hence the defence is dependent upon the fact that the plaintiff *consented to* the risk, and it is insufficient to show that he merely *knew of* it. Moreover, the consent must be real and freely given — and not induced by threats or the pressure of duty. Thus, unless he is specifically engaged for dangerous work, an employee will rarely be held to have consented to a risk arising from his employment, even though he may be aware of its existence —

> *Burnett* v. *British Waterways Board* (1973): Employed by BWB to work on a barge as a lighterman, B was injured when a capstan rope parted, due to BWB's negligence. As he had read a notice stating that persons availed themselves of the dock facilities at their own risk, BWB contended that B had

voluntarily undertaken the risk of injury. However, the Court of Appeal held that, as he was an employee, it could not be said that he had freely and voluntarily incurred the risk of his employers' negligence.

(c) *If the plaintiff acted under a compelling legal or moral duty* — or if he went to the rescue of an endangered third party in a situation arising from the defendant's negligence —

Haynes v. *Harwood* (1935): A policeman ran from a police station and stopped runaway horses, thereby averting serious danger to women and children. It was held that he freely undertook the risk but was not *volens*, because he acted under a legal and moral duty; he could therefore recover damages from the owner of the horses.

Cutler v. *United Dairies (London) Ltd* (1933): C was injured while attempting to stop a runaway horse in the country. He had not been asked to help and there was no danger to others; consequently *volenti non fit injuria* succeeded as a defence.

16. The defence of statutory authority
A defendant can escape liability if he can show that he was authorised by a statute or delegated legislation to do the act complained of. In such circumstances compensation cannot be obtained unless it is provided for by the statute itself. The defence is of general application but is particularly relevant to nuisance, and two aspects must be considered:

(a) *The nature of absolute statutory authority.* In this case the authority confers immunity in respect of the act itself and also all necessary consequences of it. A consequence would be held to be necessary if it could not have been avoided by reasonable care and skill —

Allen v. *Gulf Oil Refining* (1981): Under a private Act of Parliament (which contained no provision for compensation), GOR acquired the right to build an oil refinery with associated jetties, railways, etc. As a test case, A (a local inhabitant) brought an action alleging nuisance; however, the House of Lords held that the Act expressly or impliedly conferred immunity from proceedings for any nuisance which was the inevitable result of constructing and operating a refinery.

> *Tate & Lyle Industries* v. *Greater London Council* (1983): Under statutory authority, GLC's predecessors had constructed two ferry terminals, thereby causing the channels and berths of T&L's jetties to silt up. If expert advice had been taken, the problem could have been avoided and the House of Lords held that GLC had been guilty of a public nuisance which had caused particular damage to T&L, thus entitling them to redress.

(b) *The nature of conditional statutory authority.* Here there is authority to do an act *only if* it does not interfere with private rights. Whether statutory authority is absolute or conditional depends on the construction of the statute. In general, if it is *imperative* it will be absolute, whereas authority which is merely *permissive* is *prima facie* conditional —

> *Metropolitan Asylum District Managers* v. *Hill* (1881): MADM had statutory authority to erect a smallpox hospital but was restrained from doing so in a place where it would have been dangerous to local inhabitants. (*See also* 20:3(e).)

17. The features of other general defences.
In addition to consent and statutory authority, defendants in tort may also plead:

(a) *The defence of effective disclaimer.* By way of notices, etc, it is possible for liability to be disclaimed; e.g., farmers can exclude liability towards ramblers, pot-holers and students on field trips. However, in particular situations, such exemptions may be prohibited by statute — thus the Public Passenger Vehicles Act 1981, s. 29, provides that liability cannot be disclaimed in respect of death or injury incurred as a passenger in a public service vehicle. *See also* 14:5–6 —

> *White* v. *Blackmore* (1972): As a member of a 'jalopy' racing club, W attended a meeting organised by B and was killed when watching an event in which he was not competing. B

had displayed notices warning the public of danger and disclaiming liability for all accidents. The Court of Appeal held that an action by W's widow must therefore fail.

(b) *The defence of mistake.* Mistake (of law or fact) will normally *not* succeed as a defence except in the case of torts requiring malice as a constituent element (17:4(a)) also false imprisonment (e.g. where a genuine mistake by a police officer effecting an arrest without a warrant would be a valid defence).

(c) *The defence of inevitable accident.* This defence will succeed only if an accident was *inevitable* — i.e. could not have been avoided by any care, precaution or forethought which a reasonable person would have taken in the circumstances of the case —

> *Stanley* v. *Powell* (1891): S was wounded by a pellet, fired in a proper manner by P (a member of the same shooting party) but which had glanced off a tree at right angles. It was held that the accident was inevitable and that P was not liable.

(d) *The Act of God.* This defence will succeed only if harm suffered was the direct result of natural causes, which no human care or forethought could have avoided, and in which there was no human intervention. The tests are: 'Was the direct and immediate cause of the injury an act of God or act of man?' also 'Could the harm have been prevented by human care?'. It might appear that Act of God would be a defence to torts of strict liability (e.g. *Rylands* v. *Fletcher*), whereas inevitable accident would probably not be adequate —

> *Nichols* v. *Marsland* (1876): A storm of exceptional violence caused properly constructed artificial pools on M's land to overflow and damage N's bridges. The defence Act of God succeeded.

(e) *The defence of necessity.* This defence may succeed in respect of damage done (possibly intentionally) by the defendant *in order to prevent a greater harm.* Thus the saving of human life should justify damage to property, whilst the protection of property could be a defence to the killing of animals —

> *Esso Petroleum Ltd* v. *Southport Corporation* (1956): As a result of a steering defect, EP's tanker ran aground in an estuary and, to refloat the vessel, part of the oil cargo was

discharged. No negligence was attributable to EP and, as the discharge was reasonably necessary to prevent loss of life on board, the House of Lords held that EP was not liable for costly damage to SC's foreshore and marine lake.

Andreae v. *Selfridge & Co Ltd* (1938): In response to A's action in nuisance for noisy building operations, S pleaded necessity — for the purpose of saving time and money — but the defence failed. (*See* 19:3(c) and 20:2(a).)

The relationship of cause and effect

18. The remoteness of damage

An action in tort will not succeed if the wrong complained of is too remote from (i.e. not sufficiently closely connected with) the harm suffered by the plaintiff. However, damage is never too remote if it was *intended* by the defendant — and a person is presumed to intend *the natural and inevitable consequences of his acts and omissions*. Remoteness of damage generally relates to negligence but it needs to be considered in respect of tortious liability as a whole:

(a) *The nexus of reasonable foreseeability.* In negligence the defendant is liable only for such harm as he should *reasonably have foreseen*, when the tort was committed.

(b) *The nexus of direct consequence.* The test of reasonable foreseeability does not apply to torts of strict liability (17:5–10), the tort of deceit or breaches of strict statutory duties (17:14 — also claims where it is simply a question as to whether the plaintiff is entitled to compensation provided for in a statute). In such circumstances the defendant is liable for all the damage which is the *direct consequence* of his tort — regardless of whether such harm was foreseeable or not.

19. The chain of causation

For any action to succeed, there must be an unbroken chain of causation, linking the defendant's tort to the harm suffered by the plaintiff. Such a chain may be broken by a *novus actus interveniens* — i.e. an intervening act committed by a third party or by the plaintiff himself. However, to break the chain, such an act must so disturb the sequence of events as to divorce the defendant's tort from the consequences suffered by the plaintiff. The defence of *novus actus interveniens* will *not* succeed in the following circumstances:

(a) *If the intervention was the natural and probable consequence of the tort.* In *Haynes* v. *Harwood* (1935) (17:15(c)), the policeman's action was held *not* to be a novus actus, as it was reasonably foreseeable.

(b) *If the intervention was that of the defendant.* The defendant remains liable if he committed the intervening act or instigated another to commit it.

(c) *If the intervention was contemporaneous with the tort.* If simultaneous but independent acts cause the same damage, one cannot be a *novus actus*, so as to negate liability for the other.

(d) *If the intervention was under a legal or moral duty,* or to minimise danger. *See Haynes* v. *Harwood* (1935) (17:15(c)).

(e) *If the intervener lacked full tortious liability.* Novus actus would not be a defence if, for example, the intervening act was that of a child or someone whom the defendant had thrown into a state of sudden alarm —

> *Scott* v. *Shepherd* (1773): The defendant threw a lighted squib on to a stall at a fair; in self-defence, the stall-keeper threw it off; it alighted on another stall and was thrown away again; finally it exploded in the plaintiff's face and blinded him. The defendant was held liable.

The effluxion of time

20. The limitation of actions

The Limitation Act 1980 (*see* 16:8) provides that an action in tort must be brought (i.e. the writ must be issued) within *six years* of the date on which the right of action accrued. In the case of torts actionable *per se*, the time commences from the date when the wrong was committed but, with those involving continuing harm (e.g. nuisance, false imprisonment), it runs from when the harm stopped. If tortious conduct is concealed by fraud, the time begins when it was (or could reasonably have been) discovered. The six-year rule is subject to the following qualifications:

(a) *The actions for personal injury.* Actions for personal injury resulting from negligence, nuisance or breach of statutory duty, must be brought within *three years* of the date at which the cause of action accrued — or the date of the plaintiff's knowledge, if later. The date of knowledge is that on which the plaintiff first knew that the injury was significant, that it was attributable to the alleged act or omission or the identity of the defendant. Under the Nuclear Installations Acts 1959 and 1965, the limitation period for injury caused by radiation is *30 years*.

(b) *The actions for death.* If an injured person dies without instituting proceedings within the three-year period, any action on behalf of his estate must be brought within three years of the date of death — or that of the personal representative's knowledge, if later. Actions under the Fatal Accidents Act 1976 must commence within *three years* of the date of death — the date of knowledge of the person for whose benefit the action is brought, if later. In respect of actions for personal injury and death, the courts are empowered to extend the time limits, if it would be equitable so to do.

(c) *The actions for latent damage.* If damage resulting from negligence and not involving personal injury is *latent* (existing but not manifest), the Latent Damage Act 1986 provides for a limit of either *six years* from the date at which the cause of action accrued or *three years* from when the plaintiff knew (or ought to have known) of significant injury, whichever is later. This applies particularly to cases involving faulty building construction, but there is an over-riding time limit of *15 years* from the date of the defendant's breach of duty.

(d) *The actions for theft.* A *bona fide* purchaser for value acquires title to stolen property *six years* from the date of the theft (but *see* 19:5(e)); however, the original owner's right to claim against the thief is *unlimited* in time.

(e) *The actions for defamation.* The Administration of Justice Act 1985, s. 57, provides a *three-year* limitation period for cases of libel and slander; nevertheless, the High Court can extend the time if facts relevant to the claim were not known to the plaintiff at the expiration of three years.

Progress test 17

1.   Define 'torts', explaining also how they differ from criminal offences and breaches of contract.   **(1, 2)**

2.   'In the law of torts, the presence or absence of malice is irrelevant.' Discuss.   **(4)**

3.   State and explain what is meant by the rule in *Rylands* v. *Fletcher*. What defences are available to anyone sued for this tort?   **(8, 9)**

4.   Distinguish between employees and independent contractors, explaining the significance of the distinction, in so far as torts are concerned.   **(10, 11)**

5.   Playing rugby one day, George was wilfully tripped up by Horace, an opposing player, in an off-the-ball incident which the referee did not see. George fell to the ground and was immediately trampled upon by Ian, a member of his own team who was running behind him and could not stop. Sustaining a broken leg, George (who was self-employed) could not work for two months. Advise all parties.   **(15, 17, 18, 19)**

18

The tort of negligence

The nature of negligence

1. The concepts of negligence

In so far as torts are concerned, the term *negligence* has two possible connotations. In the first place, it may simply be an *integral element* of a particular tort (not of strict liability) wherein there is the need to show that the defendant committed some breach of a legal duty, either deliberately or negligently. Secondly, as a *specific tort*, negligence covers many areas of activity (e.g. road accidents, incorrect professional advice, faulty construction of buildings, etc) and, for an action to succeed, it is necessary to establish three (possibly interrelated) elements:

(a) *That the defendant owed the plaintiff a duty of care.* The plaintiff must show that, in all the circumstances of the case, he has a right of action against the defendant, who owed him a duty of care, as outlined in 18:2 *below*.

(b) *That the defendant broke this duty.* The plaintiff must show that the *standard* of care exercised by the defendant fell short of that which ought to have been adopted, in all the circumstances of the case (*see* 18:3).

(c) *That the plaintiff suffered harm in consequence of the breach.* The plaintiff must show that he suffered damage which was caused by the defendant's act or omission (*see* 18:7).

The duty of care

2. The extent of the duty of care

In *Donoghue* v. *Stevenson* (1932), Lord Atkin established the general rule that a duty of care is owed to one's *neighbour*. He then posed the rhetorical question 'Who then, in law, is my neighbour?' to which he gave the answer: 'Persons who are so closely and directly affected by my act that I ought reasonably to have them in contemplation, as being so affected, when I am directing my mind to the acts or omissions which are called in question.' In *Anns* v. *London Borough of Merton* (1977), the House of Lords refined this principle and Lord Wilberforce suggested that the existence of a duty of care is dependent upon two factors. First, it is necessary to establish that there was a *sufficient relationship of proximity or neighbourhood* between the defendant and the plaintiff so that, within the reasonable contemplation of the former, carelessness on his part might be likely to cause damage to the latter. Secondly, if the first requirement is fulfilled, it is necessary to consider whether there are *any considerations which ought to negative or to reduce or limit the scope of the duty*, or the class of persons to whom it is owed, or the damages to which a breach may give rise (*see* 18:7). In a number of recent cases, however, the House of Lords has retreated from these views —

Hill v. *Chief Constable of West Yorkshire* (1988): H, the mother of the last of about 13 young women murdered by Peter Sutcliffe (the so-called 'Yorkshire Ripper') claimed that, but for the negligence of the police, he would have been apprehended before her daughter's death. Dismissing her appeal, the House of Lords held that there was no duty of care owed by the police to the public at large to apprehend an unknown criminal. Moreover, as a matter of public policy, the police were immune from allegations of negligence in crime detection.

Kirkham v. *Anderton* (1989): Though aware that a prisoner had suicidal tendencies, the police failed to pass this information to a remand centre, where he was detained. He committed suicide and damages awarded to his widow were confirmed. The Court of Appeal held that, when they had taken K into custody, the police had assumed responsibilities with regard to his well-being; moreover, affording relief in such a case would not affront the public conscience.

3.　The standard of care

This is a question of fact in each particular case and the test is: whether a reasonably prudent man would have foreseen the danger to the plaintiff in the circumstances of the case and, if so, whether he would have done (or desisted from doing) anything other than that which the defendant did, to avert the danger. 'People must guard against reasonable probabilities — not fantastic possibilities'; nevertheless, foresight is not the same as balance of probability, also foreseeability of damage is not itself sufficient to establish a duty of care. It may be unreasonable (and therefore negligent) not to guard against a rare — or even a unique — event, if the likelihood of damage is such that a reasonable man would take precautions against it. However, the plaintiff need not show that the *particular* accident or damage was foreseeable — but only that it was *of a kind* which the defendant ought reasonably to have foreseen. If this is so, the defendant will be liable notwithstanding that the *amount* of damage is larger than he could reasonably have predicted. Failure to take a precaution which is not 'the normal practice' is no defence (as 'neglect of duty does not cease by repetition to be neglect of duty'); conversely, failure to follow a usual and approved practice will be negligent only if a reasonably prudent person would have followed it. The defendant must always take his victim as he finds him as, under what is known as the *eggshell skull* rule, if harm caused to the plaintiff is aggravated because he suffers from a latent physical or psychological predisposition, the defendant will be liable for the additional, unforeseeable damage —

> *Smith* v. *Littlewoods Organisation* (1987): S's premises were severely damaged when a fire deliberately started by vandals destroyed an adjacent, disused cinema owned by LO. The House of Lords held that it was not reasonably foreseeable that vandals would set fire to the building in such a manner as would be likely to engulf it. In a case involving injury or damage by independent human agency, what the reasonable man is bound to foresee is the probable consequences of his acts or omissions. A clear basis is required to show that the injury or damage is more than a mere possibility.
>
> *Paris* v. *Stepney Borough Council* (1951): P, a mechanic employed in SBC's garage, was blind in one eye and lost the

sight of the other when working beneath a vehicle. He had
not been provided with protective goggles, nor was it
customary in the trade to supply them. However, SBC was
held to be negligent in not doing so, because they owed P a
higher duty of care, on account of his disability.

Robinson v. *Post Office* (1974): Through PO's negligence,
R suffered a cut on his left shin and a doctor injected
anti-tetanus serum, to which R was allergic. As a result, he
contracted encephalitis and the Court of Appeal held PO
liable — stating that anyone who could reasonably foresee
that the victim of his negligence might require medical
treatment is liable for its consequences — although he could
not reasonably foresee them.

NOTE: In addition to statutory requirements, safety at work is an
implied term (*see* 14:3) of all contracts of service. Furthermore, in
tort, an employer owes each employee a common duty of care, to
ensure health and safety — particularly with regard to equipment,
system of work and competence of staff.

4. The development of the duty of care

It can be argued that each of the three requirements in
negligence — duty, breach and damage — is a factor which limits
the scope of the tort, and liability therefor. In recent years there
have been significant developments in the concepts of the duty
and, where restraints (additional to the 'neighbour' test) have been
imposed, they have generally been based on grounds of *public
policy*. This has been shown in Lord Wilberforce's second
requirement in *Anns* v. *London Borough of Merton* (1977) (18:2); also
the cases summarised thereunder. Questions which might affect
the recognition of a duty have thus included: whether it would
open the floodgates to countless claims; whether it would
discourage people from undertaking socially desirable activities;
whether it would affront the public conscience; whether either of
the parties is in a stronger position (e.g. by way of insurance) to
bear the loss; or whether immunities in certain areas (e.g. the
police) are justified. In their turn, the public policy tests have been
giving way to the view that a duty should not be recognised unless
it is 'just and reasonable'. The development of the duty of care (one

instance of which is illustrated in 19:6(b)) has been of particular significance in the following areas:

(a) *The liability for economic loss.* For the past century the courts have awarded damages for *consequential economic loss* (i.e. financial loss arising from injury to the plaintiff's person or property) but it has been held that there is no duty of care to protect a person from *pure economic loss* (i.e. simple loss of profits). In the second case below the House of Lords deviated from this principle but, in the third case, it reverted to the original concept — that financial loss is recoverable only if it is consequent upon physical damage —

> *Spartan Steel & Alloys Ltd* v. *Martin & Co (Contractors)* (1973): Repairing an adjacent road, M negligently damaged an electric cable to SS's stainless steel factory and caused a 14-hour power loss. As a result, SS sought to recover £368 (the value of the metal being processed at the beginning), £400 (the profit on that metal) and £1,767 (the profit on subsequent melts). The Court of Appeal held that only £768 was recoverable, as the £1,767 was pure economic loss and too remote.

> *Junior Books Ltd* v. *Veitchi Co Ltd* (1983): As specialist sub-contractors, V laid a floor in JB's factory but had no contractual relationship with JB. Claiming that the floor was defective on account of V's negligence, JB sought to recover for loss of profits. The House of Lords held that there was sufficient proximity between V and JB to give rise to a duty of care and that JB could accordingly recover.

> *D & F Estates* v. *Church Commissioners for England* (1988): Owning flats built by Wates, CC leased one to D&FE. Due to negligence by Wates's sub-contractors, the plaster was defective and had to be replaced. D&FE sued Wates but the House of Lords held that they could not recover, as Wates owed no duty to supervise the work of their sub-contractors and the defective plaster had not caused damage to property or injury to persons.

(b) *The liability for negligent mis-statements.* The possibility of successful actions for pure (as opposed to consequential) economic loss has arisen from the first case below, wherein it was stated that liability for financial loss may accrue from negligent mis-statements. For such liability to exist, there must have been a 'special relationship' between the parties — i.e. the person who was asked for information or an opinion must have been someone on whose statement it would be reasonable to rely (e.g. an expert or professional adviser); secondly, he must (or should) have known that the inquirer intended to rely on the information or opinion; thirdly, the circumstances must have been such that the reliance was reasonable. It must have been clear that the plaintiff was seeking considered advice and the requirement of 'reasonable reliance' has been used by the courts to impose limits on the scope of liability. Provided that it is valid under the Unfair Contract Terms Act 1977 (14:6), an effective disclaimer may be an adequate defence —

Hedley Byrne & Co Ltd v. *Heller & Partners Ltd* (1964): Mentioning a possible £1 million advertising contract with Easipower, HB made an enquiry through their bank to H&P (E's bankers) about the company's financial standing. Headed 'Confidential. For your private use and without responsibility on the part of the bank or its officials', the reply stated that E was 'a respectably constituted company, considered good for its ordinary business engagements. Your figures are larger than we are accustomed to see'. Relying on this, HB incurred expenditure and lost £17,000 when E went into liquidation. The resulting action, alleging that the statement had been made carelessly and that H&P owed a duty of care, failed because of the disclaimer but, in *obiter dicta*, the House of Lords held that, in other circumstances, liability could arise for financial loss caused by negligent mis-statements.

Thomas Saunders Partnership v. *Harvey* (1990): Refitting office premises, TSP (architects) required special flooring and, offering to supply it, H (director of a flooring company) stated that it conformed to the required standard. It was, in fact, found to be inadequate and TSP sought to recover from H the loss incurred. It was held that, being a specialist with expertise, H had assumed a duty of care and, in making the statement, he was personally liable in negligence.

(c) *The liability for nervous shock.* Anguish or grief caused by a distressing event is actionable only if it leads to a positive psychiatric or physical illness — though it can affect the quantum of damages if it prolongs recovery from injuries sustained in the same event. Formerly the right of action was limited to persons who actually witnessed the event and who were related to the victim(s). However, in the first case below, the House of Lords extended liability for nervous shock to all situations where the suffering of such an injury was reasonably foreseeable; moreover, there are no limitations of time, space, distance, nature of injuries, or relationship of victim to plaintiff — though these are all factors to be considered. The event must be of a nature that would cause nervous shock to a person of ordinary fortitude and, although it appeared to be related only to physical harm, the second case below has extended the principle to property —

> *McLoughlin* v. *O'Brian* (1982): M was at home when her husband and three children suffered serious injury in a collision between their car and a negligently driven lorry. About an hour later, she received the news and went to the hospital where she saw her husband and one child cut and bleeding, heard the anguished screams of another, and was told that the third had died. As a result, she suffered severe and persisting nervous shock, for which she claimed damages. The Court of Appeal held that the shock was foreseeable but, as a matter of policy, O'B did not owe a duty of care to someone who was not at or near the scene of the accident. Over-ruling this decision, the House of Lords held that M could recover damages.

> *Attia* v. *British Gas* (1987): A engaged BG to install central heating in her house and, when she returned home one afternoon, she saw smoke pouring from the loft. She telephoned the fire brigade and it took them four hours to get the fire under control, by which time the house was extensively damaged. The Court of Appeal held that, provided the elements of liability were proved, the recovery of damages for nervous shock was possible in such circumstances.

5. The duty of occupiers (1957 Act)

The occupier of any premises has a duty of care to all persons entering thereon. In this context an *occupier* has been held to be one who has overall control of the premises — even though he may be absent, leaving someone else in charge. By definition, *premises* covers any fixed or movable structure — thus including boats, vehicles, aircraft — and even bed-sittingrooms, lifts, holes, machinery and scaffolding. Formerly, the common law classified persons entering premises in three categories (invitees, licensees and trespassers), each owed a particular standard of care. Nowadays, however, separate statutes make provision for two classes of people — visitors and 'non-visitors'. The Occupiers' Liability Act 1957 relates only to *visitors* — i.e. those who enter premises with the occupier's express or implied permission. Limits (e.g. in respect of time, place or purpose) may be placed on the permission and mere knowledge of entry is not equivalent to consent. Anyone who enters premises in the exercise of a right conferred by law (e.g. a police officer with a search warrant, an inspector with a statutory right) is treated as permitted by the occupier to enter for that purpose (but not in excess of it), irrespective of whether permission has in fact been granted. To all of these the occupier owes a *common duty of care* — i.e. a duty *to take such care as, in all the circumstances of the case, is reasonable to ensure that the visitor will be reasonably safe in using the premises for the purpose for which he is invited or permitted by the occupier to be there.* The duty covers not only injury to persons but also damage to the visitor's property; however, it relates solely to dangers arising from the condition of the premises, and not to those stemming from activities carried out thereon (as these would be treated in accordance with the ordinary principles of negligence). If the occupier attempts to draw the visitor's attention to a danger, his liability (or lack thereof) will depend upon whether the warning was 'enough to enable the visitor to be reasonably safe'. With regard to the necessary standards of care, the 1957 Act takes into consideration:

(a) *The precautions in respect of children.* Children must be accepted as being less cautious and more inquisitive than adults. Special care must therefore be taken in connection with anything on one's premises which would be attractive or alluring to them, and which contains dangers which they might not appreciate (e.g. derelict machinery). Thus an occupier who fails to observe the appropriate standard may be liable to children although, in the same circumstances, he would not be liable to adults. Furthermore, in cases involving children, the courts are more inclined to hold that the occupier has, by acquiescence, converted a trespasser into a visitor. Conversely, an occupier is entitled to take into account the habits of prudent parents, who normally do not allow young children to go out unaccompanied —

> *Simkiss* v. *Rhondda Borough Council* (1983): RBC was occupier of a mountain with a steep bluff, opposite flats in which S (aged seven) lived. Her parents took her to a picnic spot at the foot of the bluff and left her there with a friend aged 10. The children walked to the top of the mountain and then slid down the bluff on blankets; losing control, S sustained serious injury. Finding LBC not liable, the Court of Appeal held that it was under no obligation to adopt a higher standard of care than that appropriate to a reasonably prudent parent.

(b) *The precautions in respect of skilled visitors.* If a person enters premises in the exercise of his calling (e.g. an electrician), the occupier is entitled to assume that he will appreciate, and guard against, any special risks ordinarily incidental to it (so far as the occupier leaves him free to do so) —

> *Roles* v. *Nathan* (1963): Sealing up a flue, two chimney sweeps had been repeatedly told by the occupier not to do so whilst the fire was alight. Ignoring this warning, they both died of carbon monoxide poisoning. In this action by their widows, the Court of Appeal held that the warnings were enough to make the sweeps reasonably safe, also the occupier was under no duty of care, as the risk was incidental to their calling.

> *Ogwo* v. *Taylor* (1987): Using a blow-lamp on fascia boards, T negligently started a fire in his home. The fire brigade was called and, in protective clothing, O entered the roof-space and extinguished the fire, but suffered serious burn injuries from scalding steam. Finding T liable, the Court of Appeal held that O's injuries were foreseeable,

albeit the fact that their severity might not have been foreseen.

(c) *The precautions in respect of entry by contract.* If a person enters (or uses, or brings or sends goods to) any premises, in exercise of a right conferred by a contract with the occupier (e.g. visiting a cinema), the common duty of care will be an implied term (14:3); moreover, if the contract is otherwise silent, this would be the only such requirement. With regard to vehicles, ships and aircraft, it is necessary to distinguish between damage caused by careless operation (with liability in negligence) and harm suffered from structural defects (with occupier's liability). In the latter case, an implied term arises from the common law (as opposed to the 1957 Act) and the duty of care is not discharged unless *all reasonable care and skill have been used to ensure that the vehicle, ship or aircraft is safe.* This means that, unlike other situations, the occupier could be liable for negligence by independent contractors.

6. The duty of occupiers (1984 Act)

The Occupiers' Liability Act 1984 relates to persons who are not 'visitors' — i.e. those who enter land without lawful authority (e.g. trespassers — *see also* 19:1), or without permission but with lawful authority (e.g. exercising a right of way). Towards such persons the occupier's duty is as follows:

(a) *The existence of the duty.* The duty exists if the occupier is aware of a danger or has reasonable grounds to believe that it exists *also* if he knows (or has reasonable grounds to believe) that the other is in (or may come into) the vicinity of the danger *also* if the risk is one against which, in all the circumstances of the case, he may reasonably be expected to offer the other some protection. The circumstances of the case may include the age and character of the entrant, also the purpose of the entry (e.g. whether it was criminal) —

> *White* v. *St. Alban's City and District Council* (1990): Taking a short cut to a car park, W walked across the council's fenced-off property and suffered injury when he fell into a deep trench. Sustaining the rejection of his claim, the Court of Appeal held that there was no evidence that people tended to use the land as a short cut and the council had no

reason to believe that W would be in the vicinity of the trench.

(b) *The nature of the duty.* If a duty exists, it is *to take such care as is reasonable, in all the circumstances of the case, to see that the other does not suffer injury on the premises, by reason of the danger concerned.* Liability does not include damage to the other person's property.
(c) *The discharge of the duty.* The duty may be discharged by taking such steps as are reasonable, in all the circumstances of the case, to give warning of the danger concerned, or to discourage persons from incurring the risk.
(d) *The exclusion of the duty.* No duty of this nature exists in relation to the highway (irrespective of whether or not it is maintained at public expense) or with regard to risks willingly accepted by the other person (*volenti non fit injuria* — 17:15).

7. The causation of the damage

In actions for negligence, the onus is on the plaintiff to prove that damage which he suffered was caused by the defendant's breach of duty. Generally, this necessitates establishing that the harm would not have occurred but for the defendant's negligence. However, under the maxim *res ipsa loquitur* ('the fact speaks for itself'), a plaintiff may establish negligence if the cause of the harm cannot be precisely proved, but it is more likely than not that it was some act or omission by the defendant (or someone for whom he was responsible), constituting a failure to take proper care for the plaintiff. This is simply a rule of evidence and it does not shift the burden of proof to the defendant. As shown in 17:**19**, there must be an unbroken chain of causation linking the defendant's act or omission to the harm suffered by the plaintiff — and this may be broken by a *novus actus interveniens* —

Carter v. *Sheath* (1990): Driving at about 30 mph near the kerb, S collided with C, a 13-year-old boy, causing him serious injury. As there was no evidence as to C's whereabouts immediately before the accident, the Court of Appeal held that his action must fail, because the mere fact of the blow did not prove negligence.

Lloyde v. *West Midlands Gas Board* (1971): L was seriously injured in a gas explosion, resulting from disintegration of the supply system. The Court of Appeal held that he could invoke *res ipsa loquitur*, on proof of the improbability of outside interference, despite the fact that the apparatus was not under the exclusive control of WMGB.

The nature of contributory negligence

8. The effect of contributory negligence

The Law Reform (Contributory Negligence) Act 1945, s. 1, provides that 'Where any person suffers damage as the result partly of his own fault and partly of the fault of any other person', damages recoverable may 'be reduced to such extent as the court thinks just and equitable, having regard to the claimant's share in the responsibility for the damage'. In such cases, the defendant must show that the plaintiff failed to take reasonable care for his own safety, in respect of the risk to which the defendant's negligence exposed him. However, the plaintiff may be able to rebut a plea of contributory negligence by showing that, having been placed in a dilemma by the defendant's negligence, he chose the wrong alternative 'in the agony of the moment' —

Capps v. *Miller* (1989): Driving a moped and wearing a crash helmet with the chin-strap unfastened, C was injured in a traffic accident with M. The helmet came off and C suffered severe brain damage, from his head striking the road. The Court of Appeal held that there was clearly contributory negligence, and that C's damages should be reduced by 10 per cent.

Jones v. *Boyce* (1876): Seeing that a coach was in imminent danger of being overturned, through the breaking of a coupling rein, J jumped from the top and broke his leg. The coach was in fact halted safely but it was held that J could recover damages (at a time when they were precluded if there was contributory negligence).

Progress test 18

1. With regard to the tort of negligence, what tests are applied in respect of: (a) the duty of care; (b) the standard of care? **(2, 3)**

2. 'Financial loss is recoverable in tort only if it is consequent upon physical damage.' Discuss.   **(4)**

3. Examine the liability of a farmer towards: (a) his young son's 10-year-old guest; (b) an agricultural engineer repairing a tractor on the farm; (c) a stranger walking through his woods. **(5, 6)**

4. Explain the nature of contributory negligence.   **(8)**

5. Anticipating a price rise, James stored four drums of petrol in his garden shed. During a snow storm, a notorious local vagrant entered the shed for shelter and lit a cigarette. The petrol fumes immediately ignited and the vagrant escaped. Not realising that petrol was involved, James's neighbour, Ken, turned a hose on the fire, which spread to his own property and burnt down his greenhouse. Advise James and Ken.   **(2, 3, 6, 7)**

The tort of trespass

The trespass to land

1. The nature of trespass to land

Trespass is a tort which is actionable *per se* (i.e. with no need to prove any actual damage — 17:1(a)) and it is committed when there is a direct interference with the land, the goods (19:4) or the person (19:6) of another. The concept of a 'trespasser' in the criminal offence of burglary is outlined in 26:4(c). Trespass to land comprises any unlawful *incursion* on to land or into premises in the *immediate and exclusive* possession of another. In these circumstances, *possession* means *the right to exclude others* and it may exist through employees or agents. However, it must be *immediate* — thus a tenant could sue for trespass but not a landlord, unless he could show damage to his reversionary interest in the land. The fact that possession must also be *exclusive* would preclude anyone who merely has use of the land (e.g. lodgers, hotel guests, etc) from bringing an action. The incursion may be in any of the following ways:

(a) *The wrongful entry on to land.* The slightest crossing of a boundary (e.g. placing a hand through a window) is sufficient; nevertheless, the entry must be voluntary — thus, if a person is pushed on to land by another, it is the latter who would be liable —

> *Loudon* v. *Ryder* (1953): Living in a flat to which she was entitled under her late father's will, L barricaded the doors when her mother threatened to break in. Arriving with the mother, R put a ladder against a window, broke the glass and jumped into the kitchenette. After punching L about

the head and shoulders, he dragged her downstairs by her hair, but she did not suffer serious injury. The Court of Appeal upheld damages of £1,500 for trespass, £1,000 for assault (19:6(a)) and £3,000 exemplary damages (7:2(a)).

(b) *The wrongful remaining on land.* A person permitted to enter land commits a trespass if he remains there after the permission has ended. Thus a football spectator would become a trespasser if he did not leave the ground within a reasonable time of the match ending (or of being asked to leave, in the event of misbehaviour) and could suffer *ejection* (19:2(a)) —

> *Merest* v. *Harvey* (1814): M was shooting on his estate when H (an MP and magistrate) joined the party. M asked him to leave but H fired several shots, used bad language and threatened to commit M to prison. Exemplary damages of £500 were awarded for trespass.

(c) *The abuse of a right of entry.* A person who has authority to enter another's land for a particular purpose becomes a trespasser if he goes beyond that purpose. If the entry on the land is in pursuance of *a right conferred by common or statute law* (not merely by leave of the occupier), and the person entering commits *a wrongful act which is positive* (i.e. not merely an omission), his misconduct relates back so as to make his *original entry* tortious — whereby he is liable for the entry and all subsequent acts. This is known as trespass *ab initio* —

> *Hickman* v. *Maisey* (1900): H possessed the sub-soil of a highway which crossed his land, whereon race horses were trained. M, who owned a racing journal, walked up and down the highway for two hours, to observe the form of the horses. As this conduct exceeded the normal and reasonable use of a highway, it was held to constitute trespass.

(d) *The wrongful introduction of things on to land.* Trespass to land does not necessarily involve personal entry but may consist of introducing such things as animals, structures, objects, oil, gas, etc upon it. The continued presence of the offending item on the land (or failure to remove it, if it was originally there by permission and this was revoked) constitutes a *continuing trespass,* whereby a series of actions may be brought on a day-to-day basis, until it ceases. Rights and liabilities in respect of a continuing trespass pass to subsequent possessors of the land or offending item. The problem of straying livestock has been considered in 17:5(c) —

> *League Against Cruel Sports* v. *Scott* (1985): On seven occasions, hounds under the mastership of S trespassed on unfenced areas of Exmoor which LACS had purchased to create wild deer sanctuaries. An injunction was granted in respect of one area where trespass had been repeated and it was held that persistent hunting close to prohibited land, in circumstances where it was effectively impossible to prevent trespass by the hounds, could amount to evidence of an intention to trespass. The master's liability extended also to those hunt servants and followers over whom he could exercise control.

(e) *The invasion of superincumbent air.* Theoretically, proprietary rights over land are presumed to extend upwards to infinity. However, in the first case below, Griffiths J stated that, as a general principle, an occupier of land has rights in the air space above it only to such a height as is necessary for the ordinary use and enjoyment of the land and the structures upon it. Thus it is that most actions of this nature relate to projections from buildings, cranes, etc. The Civil Aviation Act 1982 (which does not apply to military aircraft) provides that no action in trespass or nuisance may lie in respect of the flight of an aircraft over any property at a reasonable height; nevertheless, the Act imposes *strict* liability for damage caused to persons or property by the taking off or landing of an aircraft, or by things or persons falling from it —

> *Bernstein* v. *Skyways & General* (1978): S&G took an aerial photograph of Lord B's country house and offered to sell it to him. It was held that B could not recover damages for trespass, as there had been no infringement of his rights in the air space above his property.

> *Anchor Brewhouse Developments* v. *Berkley House (Docklands Developments)* (1987): From time to time, tower cranes, placed on BH's land by their contractors, oversailed AB's land at a height which did not affect its normal use.

However, it was held that the invasion of AB's air space by the booms constituted trespass, and there were no special circumstances sufficient to justify the withholding of an injunction.

(f) *The invasion of subjacent strata.* Theoretically, proprietary rights over land are also presumed to include the sub-soil, tapering downwards until it reaches the centre of the earth, at a point. Nevertheless, possession of the surface may be severed from that of the sub-soil (e.g. by the granting of mining rights). Furthermore, even in the absence of such severance, it is doubtful whether a surface occupier is able to establish claims in respect of sub-soil if he cannot control, utilise or gain access to it.

2.   The remedies for trespass to land
These are as follows:

(a) *The effecting of ejection or re-entry.* If the occupier is *in possession*, he may immediately force out a trespasser who enters by force. However, if the entry is peaceable, the occupier (after requesting the trespasser to leave and allowing time for him to do so) may use reasonable force to eject him — but unreasonable force would constitute trespass to the person of the trespasser. If the occupier is *out of possession* of his dwelling, he may re-enter (by force, if necessary) and eject trespassers therein. If tenants covered by the Rent Act 1977 or Housing Act 1988 remain in possession after the expiration of a lease, they may be evicted only by means of court proceedings.

(b) *The institution of civil proceedings.* The most common forms of redress in actions for trespass to land are *damages* (compensating for any loss caused, or diminution in the value of the property) or an *injunction* (prohibiting continuance or repetition of the trespass). The court may also make an *order for possession* and thereafter, on the plaintiff's application, issue a *writ of restitution* (directing the sheriff to restore the land to rightful possession) —

> *Wiltshire County Council* v. *Frazer* (1986): Despite a possession order made in 1983 (dispossessing 66 nomadic squatters of sites around Stonehenge), trespassing nevertheless continued for another two years and WCC sought leave to issue a writ of restitution. Although only two of the original

66 were now members of the group, it was held that leave should be granted to issue the writ, as there was sufficient nexus between the order and the need to effect recovery of the land, also a close nexus between the various unlawful occupiers.

(c) *The institution of criminal proceedings.* The Criminal Law Act 1977 makes it an offence for a person: to use or threaten violence for the purpose of securing entry into any premises (s. 6); to enter and remain on premises as a trespasser once he has been requested to leave (s. 7); to enter and remain on premises as a trespasser with a weapon of offence on him (s. 8). The Public Order Act 1986, s. 39, provides that: if a senior police officer reasonably believes that two or more persons have entered land as trespassers, with the common purpose of residing there for any period, also that the occupier has taken reasonable steps to ask them to leave, and that they have caused damage to property on the land *or* used threatening, abusive or insulting words or behaviour to the occupier, *or* that they have between them brought 12 or more vehicles on to the land — then he may direct them to leave. Anyone who fails to comply as soon as reasonably practicable, or who re-enters within three months, is liable on summary conviction to three months' imprisonment and/or a fine —

> *Krumpa* v. *DPP* (1989): On 11th December, a company which owned some houses warned squatters living therein that it intended to bulldoze the site probably after Christmas. On 4th January a police officer informed the squatters that they were trespassers and directed them to leave; a company representative who was present then asked them to leave. Two days' later, all those still there were arrested and subsequently convicted of failing to leave as soon as reasonably practicable after a police direction. Allowing their appeal, the Divisional Court held that the December conversation did not constitute a request to leave — which had been made only after the officer's direction.

3. The defences to actions for trespass to land
The principal defences are:

(a) *The entry by authority.* This might include the entry of a police officer with a search warrant, in certain circumstances without a warrant, or to prevent a breach of the peace (8:3(b)), also by persons exercising a right of way.

(b) *The entry by licence.* In this context 'licence' means consent by the occupier, permitting a person to enter land but not giving him any interest in it. A *bare* licence (i.e. one made without any consideration — *see* 9:4) may be revoked at will; however, a licence created by contract may be revocable in accordance with the terms of the agreement. Remaining on land after the revocation of a licence constitutes trespass (19:1(b)) and an executed licence cannot be revoked — e.g. an occupier cannot require the removal of rubbish dumped on land in accordance with (and prior to the revocation of) a licence —

> *Snook* v. *Mannion* (1982): Following a motorist into the driveway of his house, police asked him to take a breath test. Refusing, he told them to 'f... off' and was arrested. The Divisional Court held that, like all citizens, police officers had an implied licence to proceed from a gate to a front or back door of a dwelling-house, if they had legitimate business with the occupier; also, it was for the justices to decide whether, in all the circumstances of the case, the licence had been revoked.

(c) *The entry under necessity.* An act which might otherwise be a trespass may be justified on the grounds of necessity, especially that of averting danger to life (*see* 17:17(e)) —

> *Rigby* v. *Chief Constable of Northamptonshire* (1985): To evict a dangerous psychopath, who had taken refuge in R's shop, police fired a canister of CS gas into the building, as a result of which it was set on fire and burnt out. R sued for trespass and the police defence of necessity succeeded but, as they had no fire-fighting equipment in attendance, R recovered damages for negligence.

(d) *The entry to retake goods.* It is a defence for the defendant to show that he entered the land to retake his goods which had been wrongfully placed there by the plaintiff or someone else.

(e) *The entry to abate a nuisance.* See *Cope* v. *Sharpe* (1912) (20:2(a)).

The interference with goods

4. The elements of trespass to goods

The Torts (Interference with Goods) Act 1977 has applied the term *wrongful interference with goods* to various forms of liability covering: trespass to goods; conversion of goods (19:5); also negligence; and any other torts which result in damage to goods. As a specific tort, *trespass to goods* (which, like any other form of trespass, is actionable *per se*) comprises an *intentional, direct and unlawful injury to, or interference with, goods in the possession of another*. The essential elements (inability to prove any of which would provide a defence) are therefore:

(a) *The act must be intentional.* It would be a defence to show that damage was purely accidental — though liability might then be established in negligence. A mistaken belief that the goods belonged to the defendant is no defence —

> *National Coal Board* v. *J.E.Evans & Co* (1951): Contracted to excavate a site occupied by the County Council, E damaged a high-tension electricity cable, laid by NCB's predecessors in title, without the council's permission or knowledge. The Court of Appeal held E not liable in trespass or negligence.

(b) *The act must be direct.* The conduct may involve destroying, damaging, using or simply moving goods — thus the plaintiff does not have to be dispossessed. Actual physical contact is not necessary — as wrongfully driving away cattle would constitute trespass —

> *Kirk* v. *Gregory* (1876): On the death of her brother-in-law, G moved his jewellery to another room in the house, to safeguard it from revellers. It was then stolen by some unknown person and the executor successfully sued G for trespass — but damages were nominal.

(c) *The act must be unlawful.* The proper exercise of police powers of search and seizure (*see* 8:3), also the proper levying of distress (the taking of property to compel the performance of an obligation — e.g. the payment of a debt) would, of course, be lawful. Provided that the conduct was reasonable, it is also a defence to show that a trespass was committed in order *to avert immediate danger to persons or property* —

> *Cresswell* v. *Sirl* (1948): As his ewes in lamb were being worried by C's dog, S ordered his son to shoot the animal, although no actual attack was in progress at the time. The Court of Appeal held that the killing was justified.

(d) *The goods must be in the possession of another.* Possession is the essence of the right of action, and even wrongful possession is sufficient against a person without a better title. Normally, possession involves personal, physical custody — but an employer has legal possession of goods in the custody of his employee (unless the latter has received them from a stranger and is withholding them). Likewise, an executor or administrator has possession of the deceased's goods between the time of death and the grant of probate or letters of administration —

> *Wilson* v. *Lombank* (1963): Having bought a car from someone with no title to sell it, W took it to a garage for repairs. Misled into believing that they had purchased the vehicle, L removed it from the garage but, on discovering the true situation, they delivered it to the rightful owner. However, they were held liable in trespass to W, as he had never lost possession of the car and could have demanded its return at any time. He was awarded the value of the vehicle and the cost of the repairs.

5. The tort of conversion

Conversion comprises *a wilful and wrongful interference with the goods of one entitled to the possession of them, in such a way as to deny his right to that possession, or in a manner inconsistent with such a right.* The interference must be wilful and wrongful — thus conduct which is merely negligent will not amount to conversion. Mistake is no defence and the Torts (Interference with Goods) Act 1977 provides that contributory negligence is also not a defence to proceedings founded on conversion or intentional trespass. The principal remedies are damages, injunction (ordering the defendant to stop using the goods in a manner inconsistent with the plaintiff's rights), also *recaption* (recovery with minimum necessary force —

including, if essential, peaceable entry on the other's land).
Conversion may take the form of:

(a) *The wrongful taking of goods.* Here there must be *an intention to exercise temporary or permanent dominion over the goods* —

> *Moorgate Mercantile Co* v. *Finch & Read* (1962): Having hired
> a car from MM, F was behind with his payments and MM
> was entitled to recover possession immediately. F lent the
> car to R, who used it for smuggling watches and it was
> seized by the customs authorities. As F had disappeared,
> MM sued R for conversion and the Court of Appeal held
> him liable, as the car's confiscation was a natural
> consequence of the use to which he put it.

(b) *The wrongful detention of goods.* Here there must be some *positive denial of possession* to the person entitled —

> *Howard E. Perry & Co* v. *British Railways Board* (1980):
> Fearing industrial disruption because the National Union of
> Railwaymen was in sympathy with striking steelworkers,
> BRB refused either to deliver, or to allow P to collect, a
> quantity of steel from BRB's depot. It was held that BRB
> had wrongfully converted P's goods and that the threat of
> unpleasant consequences should not dissuade the court
> from making an order requiring BRB to permit P to collect
> the steel.

(c) *The wrongful retention of goods.* If anyone finds an article, he is
under a duty to the owner to take reasonable care of it and to
return it, if possible. If the owner cannot be found, the finder has
a title to sue in conversion against all others. If it is not possible to
identify the original owner, any gold or silver coins, plate, bullion
or other valuables found hidden in the earth, or in some other
secret place, must be reported to the coroner. One of his duties is
to determine whether such items constitute *Treasure Trove*; this
belongs to the Crown, which may award the things or their value
to the finder —

> *Parker* v. *British Airways Board* (1982): Finding a gold
> bracelet on the floor of an airport lounge, occupied by BAB,
> P handed it in, requesting that it be returned to him, if
> unclaimed. As no one claimed the bracelet, BAB sold it for
> £850 and retained the proceeds. The Court of Appeal held

that P's rights could be displaced only if BAB could show, as occupiers, an obvious intention to exercise control over all articles in the lounge, such that the bracelet was in their possession before P found it. P was awarded £850 plus interest.

(d) *The wrongful destruction of goods.* Destruction constitutes conversion if someone wilfully destroys the article of another, or it ceases to exist, or changes its identity (e.g. apples made into cider). Mere damage cannot amount to conversion — though it may be trespass; moreover, the destruction must be wilful, and not merely negligent. *See Hollins* v. *Fowler* (1875) (*below*).

(e) *The wrongful disposal of goods.* Here, there must be a dealing with goods in such a way as to confer a good title to someone other than the person entitled to possession. If, for example, anyone sells a car to another and conceals the fact that it is on hire purchase then, under the Hire Purchase Act 1964, the buyer obtains a good title and the seller is liable in conversion. Acting for his employer or principal, an employee or agent may incur such liability if he knows that he is affecting title, and not merely possession —

> *Schott Sohne* v. *Radford* (1987): Subject to a clause whereby title did not pass until payment was made, SS sold gramophone records to a company which went into voluntary liquidation before a supply had been paid for. R was appointed liquidator and, although informed of the clause by SS, he sold the goods in the course of the liquidation. It was held that the rule of agency applied also to liquidators — so R was liable to SS in conversion.

(f) *The wrongful delivery of goods.* Here possession of goods is denied to the lawfully entitled person by wrongfully delivering them to another —

> *Hollins* v. *Fowler* (1875): Having purchased cotton from a third party, H (Liverpool cotton brokers) sold it to a client who made it into yarn. The cotton in fact belonged to F, who had parted with it as a result of fraud by the third party. The House of Lords held H liable to F in conversion (but nowadays protection is afforded to bona fide purchasers in certain circumstances).

NOTE: The Public Order Act 1986, s. 38, makes it criminally unlawful to contaminate or interfere with goods, with the intention of causing alarm, injury or economic loss; it is also an offence for anyone to threaten to do this, or to claim that he has done so.

The trespass to the person

6. The nature of trespass to the person
Trespass to the person exists in three main forms:

(a) *The tort of assault.* This consists of *intentionally putting another person in reasonable fear of immediate violence* (e.g. pointing a gun at him). Fear is the essence of the tort — so it could not exist if a threat comprised mere words, *or* was unknown to the other (e.g. pointing a gun at his back), *or* could not reasonably be effected (e.g. shaking a fist from a distance), *or* was qualified in such a way as to negate grounds for fear —

> *Stephens* v. *Myers* (1830): As chairman of a parish meeting, S was sitting not far from M, who started shouting. The meeting resolved that M should be expelled and, approaching S with a clenched fist, he was restrained by the churchwarden — but he was nevertheless held liable for assault (*see also* 19:1(a)).

(b) *The tort of battery.* This is commonly combined in an action for assault and it comprises *intentionally causing contact with the person of another, without consent or lawful authority.* Thus striking, spitting or throwing something could all constitute battery, and it is not necessary to prove the use of force or any resulting harm. Moreover, the other person need not even be aware of a battery — which, unlike assault, could occur during his sleep. However, the act must be *direct* and it therefore could not consist of 'spiking' another's drink. In the absence of consent, a surgical operation would constitute battery — and *implied consent* would be a defence in a number of everyday situations — such as a haircut, a passionate embrace, presence in a crowd or participation in games. In such circumstances, and as shown in 17:**15(a)**, consent does not extend to negligent harm —

> *Condon* v. *Basi* (1985): in a football match, C suffered a broken leg from a late and dangerous tackle by B, who was

sent off by the referee. The Court of Appeal held that C was entitled to damages in negligence, as B had breached the duty of care reasonably to be expected of those participating in the game.

T v. *T* (1988): When a severely mentally-handicapped 19-year-old female became pregnant, doctors recommended termination of pregnancy and sterilisation. As she was unable to give consent, a declaration authorising the operation was sought from the court. It was held that no one, not even the court, could give the consent — without which the act was tortious. However, in the highly unusual circumstances, the court did grant the declaration.

NOTE: As shown in 25:**5**, assault and battery are also crimes and, under the Offences Against the Person Act 1861, s. 45 (as amended), acquittal or conviction of such offences precludes subsequent civil action.

(c) *The tort of false imprisonment.* This comprises the *unlawful, direct and total deprivation of the freedom of another* for any period, however short. Restraint may be actual or by means of force, threats or other means (e.g. depriving a person of his clothes) but there must be some positive act; thus a mere omission (e.g. failure to release people caught in a broken-down lift) would be insufficient. It is not necessary for the person concerned to be aware of the restraint — which could occur whilst he is asleep, unconscious or drunk. The fact that the detention must be *unlawful* prevents a valid arrest (8:**2**) from being actionable; nevertheless, it is possible for a lawful detention to become unlawful through a change in circumstances. The requirement that the restraint should be *direct* excludes inadvertent imprisonment through negligence, whilst the need for the detention to be *total* means that an action cannot lie if an alternative (albeit inconvenient) means of egress exists —

Sayers v. *Harlow Urban District Council* (1958): On account of a defective lock. S could not open the door to leave a public lavatory cubicle. Attempting to escape, she stood on a revolving toilet roll which rotated, causing her to fall to the ground and suffer injury. The lack of a sufficiently direct act precluded redress for false imprisonment but the Court of

Appeal held the council (which operated the lavatory) 75 per cent liable in negligence.

Weldon v. *Home Office* (1990): Serving a four-year sentence in Leeds Prison, W was taken by prison officers, without good cause and in bad faith, to a strip cell where he was left overnight without his clothes. The Court of Appeal held that he had been deprived of his residual liberty and could bring an action for false imprisonment.

Progress test 19

1. Describe forms of conduct which could constitute trespass to land. **(1)**

2. In the event of trespass to land, examine the occupier's right to use force and the remedies obtainable in civil proceedings. **(2)**

3. Outline possible defences in respect of trespass to land. **(3)**

4. Discuss trespass to goods and conversion. **(4, 5)**

5. At his own request, Lawrence (a commercial analyst) was given a tour of Malcolm's factory. Left unattended for a few minutes, he entered an office and started to examine confidential documents. Finding him there, Malcolm forced him into an adjoining washroom, locked the door and sent for his solicitor. It was an hour before the latter arrived and Lawrence was eventually allowed to leave. What advice do you think the solicitor gave to Malcolm? **(1, 2, 6)**

20

The tort of nuisance

The liability in nuisance

1. The essential elements of private nuisance

There are two types of nuisance — public and private — but, as the former is basically a criminal offence, tortious liability normally arises in respect of *private nuisance*. This involves a *wrongful and indirect interference with another person's use or enjoyment of land* (e.g. by way of noise, fumes, vibrations, etc) or, alternatively, an *interference with another's right in connection with land* (e.g. obstructing a right of way, interference with light, etc). Whereas such conduct overlaps with negligence and with the rule in *Rylands* v. *Fletcher*, it is important to note that *nuisance and trespass are mutually exclusive* (i.e. one cause cannot give rise to both actions). Nuisance differs from trespass in that it is not actionable *per se*; it lies for *indirect* (as opposed to direct) injuries; also it relates to *enjoyment* (as opposed to possession) of land. The essential elements of the interference are that:

(a) *It must be wrongful.* 'A balance has to be maintained between the right of the occupier to do what he likes with his own, and the right of his neighbour not to be interfered with' (*per* Lord Wright in *Sedleigh-Denfield* v. *O'Callaghan* (1940) (20:3(g)). Consequently, to be 'wrongful', the interference must be unreasonable — and therefore substantial. Reasonableness is a question of fact and relevant criteria in respect of the interference might well be its locality, time, duration, frequency and nature. Though malice is not an essential ingredient in nuisance, it could be relevant in assessing whether the defendant had acted reasonably —

Home Brewery Co v. *William Davis & Co* (1987): Percolating unchannelled through HB's land, water descended into a disused osier bed and claypit on WD's adjoining lower land. Having filled in the claypit to build houses, WD then infilled the osier bed, thus forcing water back on to HB's land. It was held that, although an occupier was entitled to let natural, unchannelled water pass through his land, a neighbour was under no obligation to receive it and could take reasonable steps to prevent it entering his property, even though damage might be caused to the other occupier. As the building of the houses was reasonable, the major claim in respect of the claypit could not succeed; however, the infilling of the osier bed (which caused only temporary, but reasonably foreseeable, extra flooding) was actionable.

Christie v. *Davey* (1893): C and D lived in adjoining semi-detached properties and, whenever C gave music lessons, D shouted, shrieked and banged trays on the party-wall. An injunction to restrain this nuisance was granted in view of the fact that D had acted deliberately and maliciously to annoy C. (*See also Bradford Corporation* v. *Pickles* (1895) (20:3(a).)

(b) *It must be indirect.* As shown in 19:1, interfering with another's property by throwing stones on to it, erecting something (e.g. an advertising sign) which projects over it, or burrowing beneath the surface would constitute trespass. Conversely, if the interference was caused by stones falling from a neighbouring ruin, the overhanging branches of a tree — or its spreading roots — then the tort would be nuisance —

Spicer v. *Smee* (1946): When his home was destroyed through fire, caused by defective wiring in the defendant's adjoining bungalow, it was held that the plaintiff could succeed in nuisance.

Tetley v. *Chitty* (1986): A local authority granted a seven-year lease to a go-kart club to operate a track on its land. On account of the nuisance caused by the noise, T and other neighbouring ratepayers sought damages and an injunction, both of which were granted against the council — as it had given permission for the use.

(c) *It must be detrimental to use or enjoyment.* The interference must cause the plaintiff actual (but not merely potential) discomfort or inconvenience, which need not be substantial but must not be infinitesimal. The test is: 'Has the plaintiff suffered *material* discomfort according to plain, simple and sober notions?' Damage to property on the land is actionable but it is not clearly established whether this also applies to personal injury —

> *Allison* v. *Merton, Sutton & Wandsworth Area Health Authority* (1975): Living in a dwelling adjoining the boiler-house of a hospital controlled by MS&W, A (aged 71) had been subjected to a continual, low frequency sound from the boilers, sometimes giving the impression of physical vibrations. This materially interfered with his sleep — inducing depression, nervous agitation and distress — although there was no evidence of injury to health, measurable in medical terms. In respect of past suffering, A was awarded £850 damages and an injunction was granted — but suspended for 12 months, within which MS&W was required to abate the nuisance.

> *St Helen's Smelting Co* v. *Tipping* (1865): Shrubs cultivated by T (the initial plaintiff) were damaged by fumes from a factory operated by StH who contended that, as the locality was an industrial one, T had to accept the situation. However, the House of Lords held that, whereas locality was an important consideration in the case of alleged nuisances related to interference with comfort and enjoyment, it was nevertheless irrelevant where physical damage to property was occasioned; consequently, T was entitled to damages. (*See also* 20:4(**d**).)

(d) *It may relate to a right in connection with land.* Actions can be brought in respect of interference with light, with access of air, with support of land, with private rights of way or for pollution of streams, etc —

> *Bradburn* v. *Lindsay* (1983): One half of a semi-detached house, owned but left unoccupied by L, became derelict, vandalised and eventually demolished by the local authority, with L's consent. Living in the other half and having protested at various stages, B brought an action for

the damage to his home. It was held that L was liable, also
that B was entitled to support in the form of buttresses.

The parties in nuisance

2. The parties to an action for nuisance
In actions for nuisance, the rights and liabilities to sue and be
sued are as follows:

(a) *The interests of plaintiffs.* As nuisance is, by definition, an
interference with the use or enjoyment of *land*, it follows that only
a person with some *title* to the property can sue. An owner-occupier
can therefore always bring an action and a tenant is generally able
to do so; however, if the occupier is not the owner, the latter can
sue only for permanent injury to his property. Those with neither
possession nor proprietary interest in the land affected (e.g.
members of the occupier's family, employees, guests or lodgers)
cannot bring actions in nuisance. Anyone who acquires an interest
in land subject to a continuing nuisance can recover the cost of
remedying damage which occurred prior to his acquisition. In
addition to seeking an injunction and/or damages, the plaintiff can
exercise the self-help remedy of *abatement*. This means that he may
terminate the nuisance himself, without recourse to litigation (e.g.
by cutting branches or roots). In an emergency (e.g. a fire likely
to spread), he may enter the other's land to abate the nuisance;
otherwise, he should first give notice and a reasonable time for the
other occupier to abate it himself. Exercise of the right is a bar to
an action for damages. Local authorities are statutorily
empowered (e.g. under the Control of Pollution Act 1974) to
require the abatement of certain forms of nuisance —

> *Malone* v. *Laskey* (1907): Mrs M and her husband occupied
> property provided by his employers and sublet from L, who
> operated an engine in adjoining premises. The vibrations
> which it created caused a bracket supporting a water tank in
> M's house to collapse and injure her. It was held that,
> although the working of the engine was a nuisance, M could
> not recover, as she had no interest in the property. Note:
> Due to statutory occupancy rights, matrimonial partners
> may nowadays have rights of action.

> *Masters* v. *Brent London Borough Council* (1978): M's father transferred to him the lease of a house affected by the encroaching roots of a tree, for which BLBC was responsible. M sought damages for the cost of remedial work and BLBC contended that he could not recover for anything which accrued before he acquired the leasehold. It was held, however, that the nuisance was continuing at the time of acquisition and therefore the total cost was recoverable.

> *Cope* v. *Sharpe* (1912): Having entered C's land and destroyed heather, to prevent the spread of a fire, S was held to be not liable for trespass.

(b) *The liability of defendants.* Anyone who causes a nuisance by wrongful conduct is strictly liable for its creation and continuance. If the nuisance emanates from land, the occupier is primarily liable, and the owner would be liable only if he was the person who created or authorised the nuisance (*see Tetley* v. *Chitty* (1986) (20:**1(b)**)). An occupier is responsible for nuisances created by his employees, agents, family, guests and independent contractors. Furthermore, he may be liable for failing to act in respect of nuisances which are of natural origin or inherited from predecessors in title, unless he can show that he could not reasonably have identified or abated them. (*See* 20:**3(f)–(g)**) —

> *Greenwood* v. *Portwood* (1984): Cracks in G's walls were partially caused by the roots of a tree belonging to P, his next-door neighbour. Until experts were consulted, the cause was not suspected; it was therefore held that, as there had been no reasonably foreseeable risk, the question of precautions which could have been taken did not arise.

The defences in nuisance

3. The effective defences to an action for nuisance
The following defences can succeed in an action for nuisance:

(a) *The rebuttal of the claim.* It is an adequate defence to prove that the activity complained of is not appreciable or unreasonable — e.g. smoke from an occasional bonfire is not a nuisance. Moreover, occupiers of property enjoy certain absolute rights (e.g. to erect buildings, possibly obscuring a view), which are unlike the making of noise in that they are not limited by the requirements of reasonableness, nor affected by malicious intent —

> *Bradford Corporation* v. *Pickles* (1895): Percolating unchannelled through P's property, water flowed eventually to BC's land, where it was used for their city supply. In an attempt to force BC to buy his land at his price, P started to extract the water. BC's action failed because it was held that extraction from undefined (as opposed to defined) channels was an occupier's absolute right.

(b) *The sensitivity of property or persons.* It is possible to plead abnormal sensitivity on the part of the plaintiff —

> *Robinson* v. *Kilvert* (1889): Heat rising from K's cellar damaged R's abnormally sensitive brown paper on the floor above. It was held, however, that there was no nuisance, as the heat was not excessive and would not have damaged paper generally.

(c) *The consent of the plaintiff.* The consent (as opposed to awareness — *see* 20:**4(a)**) of the plaintiff is a good defence, provided that there is no negligence on the part of the defendant. Thus an occupier may expressly permit another to do what would otherwise constitute a nuisance — e.g. to discharge foul water on to his land. The tenant of part of premises is deemed to accept the risk of nuisance arising from the condition of any part retained by the landlord —

> *Kiddle* v. *City Business Properties Ltd* (1942): K leased part of CBP's premises and heavy rain caused a gutter on the part retained by CBP to flood and discharge water into K's shop. The stock was damaged but there was no negligence by CBP and K's action failed, as he was deemed to have consented to run the risk.

(d) *The passage of time.* Under the Prescription Act 1832, the right to commit a nuisance may be acquired by 20 years' exercise of the acts constituting the nuisance, provided that such exercise is not achieved by violence, secrecy or consent (*see also* 2:**2(d)**). Time begins to run only when the plaintiff becomes aware of the nuisance —

> *Sturges* v. *Bridgman* (1879): For more than 20 years B, a confectioner, had used a pestle and mortar on his Wigmore Street premises, adjacent to the garden of S, a Wimpole Street physician, who had not complained. It was only when S built a consulting room at the end of the garden that the noise and vibration became unacceptable. An injunction was granted and it was held that B could not plead protection by prescription, as no actionable nuisance had existed until the consulting room was built.

(e) *The protection of statutory authority.* It has already been shown in **17:16** that activities which might otherwise constitute nuisance may be sanctioned by Act of Parliament or delegated legislation. However, this protection will be lost if the conduct exceeds the limits permitted by the legislation, or if the nuisance results from the defendant's negligence —

> *Buley* v. *British Railways Board* (1975): Noise arising from BRB's use of a goods terminal at night would have caused actionable nuisance to B, an adjacent householder, but BRB claimed the authority to operate a rail transport system under the Transport Act 1962, s. 3. B sought an injunction but the Court of Appeal held that the onus was on him to show failure by BRB to take reasonable care to avoid greater noise than was inherent in the work; also BRB was under no obligation to conduct operations at a place or time which caused the minimum of interference with private rights.

(f) *The latent defect in property.* Unobservable processes of nature, defects in building materials, etc, may provide a defence in nuisance, unless it can be shown that the defendant knew (or ought to have known) about the danger, and failed to take reasonable steps to avert it —

> *Leakey* v. *National Trust* (1980): As the surface of a hill on NT's land was liable to crack, debris had occasionally fallen on to L's land. In the hot summer of 1976, NT was asked to attend to the danger but declined to do so; whereat a major

landslip occurred, causing damage to L's property. The Court of Appeal upheld NT's liability in nuisance because, although the landslip resulted from natural causes, NT had been made aware of the danger and had failed to take reasonable steps to avert it.

(g) *The act of a third party.* The creation of a nuisance by a trespasser may be a defence, unless it can be shown that the defendant knew (or ought to have known) about it and failed to take reasonable steps to abate it —

> *Sedleigh-Denfield* v. *O'Callaghan* (1904): Without informing O'C, a trespasser on his land put a pipe in a ditch. Three years later it became blocked and S-D's adjacent garden was flooded. As one of his employees had cleaned out the ditch twice-yearly, O'C was presumed to know of the danger and, having done nothing to avert it, he was held liable in nuisance.

4. The ineffective defences to an action for nuisance
The following defences will not normally succeed in an action for nuisance:

(a) *The awareness of the plaintiff.* As shown in 20:3(c) and as illustrated in *Sturges* v. *Bridgman* (1879) (20:3(d)), awareness is not the same as consent. It is no defence to say that the plaintiff was aware of a nuisance and yet went to live near it — 'Whether the man went to the nuisance or the nuisance came to the man, the rights are the same' —

> *Bliss* v. *Hall* (1838): B bought a house near H's tallow chandlery, which emitted noxious fumes. H contended that it had been in operation for three years before B's arrival but the defence failed.

(b) *The benefit of the public.* If a nuisance harms the plaintiff (even slightly), it is normally no defence that it benefits the general public (even substantially) —

> *Kennaway* v. *Thompson* (1980): In 1972 K moved into a house near a lake, where a club had organised motor-boat racing and water-skiing for about 10 years. The frequency and

noise of these activities increased until K sought damages
for nuisance and an injunction. Awarding damages, Mais J
ruled that the public interest was such that it would be
oppressive to grant an injunction. However, the Court of
Appeal held that the public interest should not prevail over
the private interest of the person affected by the nuisance;
consequently, K was entitled to an injunction (restricting
noisy meetings to a limited number of occasions).

(c) *The taking of reasonable care.* Negligence is not a necessary
element in a claim for nuisance and the defendant cannot excuse
himself by showing that he took maximum care. As, by definition,
a nuisance is unreasonable, it can be no defence to plead
reasonable care — or reasonable use of one's property. Apart from
nuisances which are authorised by statute or consent, any activity
which cannot be prevented from being a nuisance cannot be
carried on at all.

(d) *The suitability of place.* In the absence of consent or statutory
authority, it is no defence that the place from which a nuisance
emanates is suitable for the activity complained of, and that no
other place is available. A business which cannot be carried on
without creating a nuisance cannot be conducted at all. If an
alleged nuisance interferes with an occupier's comfort and
enjoyment of his land, locality can be a significant factor — because
'That may be a nuisance in Grosvenor Square which would be none
in Smithfield Market' (*per* Pollock C.B. in *Bamford* v. *Turnley below*).
Nevertheless, in *St Helen's Smelting Co* v. *Tipping* (1865) (20:**1(c)**),
it was held that locality is irrelevant if damage to property has been
occasioned —

> *Bamford* v. *Turnley* (1862): By using his land for burning
> bricks, T caused substantial annoyance to his neighbour, B.
> It was held to be no defence that it was done in a proper
> and convenient place, and was a reasonable use of the land.

> *Laws* v. *Florinplace* (1981): In a residential area, F converted
> a boutique into a sex shop, with illuminated signs describing
> its wares. When the local residents sought damages for
> nuisance and an interlocutory injunction, the latter was
> granted — as it was held that an actionable nuisance existed
> and presented a triable issue.

Progress test 20

1. Compare and contrast trespass and nuisance. **(1)**

2. Outline the essential elements of a private nuisance. **(1)**

3. What are the principal defences that can be pleaded in an action for nuisance? **(3)**

4. Discuss seemingly reasonable arguments that will not be accepted as defences in actions for nuisance. **(4)**

5. Having bought an old house in an isolated village, Pauline complains that her sleep is invariably disturbed in the early hours, by the noise from Oliver's bakery next door. She is threatening to seek an injunction and Oliver consults you, contending that his family has baked on the site for 60 years, that the expense of installing modern equipment and soundproofing would make the price of bread prohibitive in the village, also that Pauline is known to be an insomniac. Advise Oliver. **(3, 4)**

21

The tort of defamation

The grounds for an action

1. The nature of defamation

Defamation involves *wrongfully damaging the reputation of another* by conduct that 'holds him up to hatred, ridicule or contempt' (*per* Blackburn J in *Capital & Counties Bank* v. *Henty* (1882), *below*) or 'tends to lower the plaintiff in the estimation of right-thinking members of society generally' (*per* Lord Atkin in *Sim* v. *Stretch* (1936), *below*). Nowadays, however, neither of these tests is entirely satisfactory. Defamation may be encountered in various forms (e.g. written or spoken words, pictures, effigies, etc) and the law has two basic but conflicting purposes — to enable a person to protect his reputation, also to preserve freedom of speech —

> *Capital & Counties Bank* v. *Henty* (1882): H, a brewery firm, cashed customers' C&CB cheques at the bank's Chichester branch. When a new manager discontinued this facility, they sent out a circular stating that: 'Messrs Henty & Co hereby give notice that they will not receive in payment cheques drawn on any of the branches of the Capital & Counties Bank'. This caused a run on the bank which sued H, alleging an implication that it was insolvent. It was held that the circular was not actionable.

> *Sim* v. *Stretch* (1936): In a telegram to the plaintiff, the defendant said: 'Edith has resumed her service with us today. Please send her possessions and the money you borrowed, also her wages'. The plaintiff sued, claiming that the words were defamatory in suggesting that he had

borrowed money from his housemaid and failed to pay her wages. The action failed, as it was held that the words were not capable of lowering the plaintiff in the estimation of right-thinking members of society generally.

Byrne v. *Deane* (1937): After B was suspected of having informed the police that there were illegal gambling machines on club premises, a lampoon appeared on the club notice board, 'But he who gave the game away, may he byrrn in hell and rue the day'. This was held not to be defamatory because the members would not be right-thinking if an attempt to suppress crime lowered a person in their estimation.

2. The nature of libel

With civil actions for the tort dating back to the sixteenth century, two modes have developed whereby defamation may be committed. These are *libel* and *slander* — and the significant difference between them lies in the fact that, whereas one is actionable *per se*, the other (with certain exceptions) requires proof of damage. In 1975 the *Report of the Committee on Defamation* (under the chairmanship of Mr Justice Faulks) recommended the abolition of the distinction between them. *Libel* is defamation in a *permanent* form (e.g. in writing, printing, painting, carving, etc) and it is actionable *per se*. Under the Defamation Act 1952, s. 1, 'the broadcasting of words (also visual images) by wireless telegraphy shall be treated as publication in a permanent form'. The broadcast must, however, be 'for general reception' — thus defamatory statements during private (e.g. police) transmissions would probably be slander. Under the Theatres Act 1968, s. 4, words published during the course of a play are likewise treated as publication in a permanent form; in this context 'words' includes pictures, visual images, gestures and other methods of signifying meaning but there are certain exceptions to these provisions (e.g. plays performed in a private home) —

Youssoupoff v. *Metro-Goldwyn-Mayer Pictures Ltd* (1934): A film made by MGM falsely imputed that Princess Y had been raped or seduced by the monk Rasputin. It was held that the film was a libel and that Y was entitled to damages, as her reputation could be affected, although no moral discredit was attributable to her.

3.   The nature of slander

Slander is defamation in a *non-permanent* form and it is actionable only on proof of special damage (meaning, in this context, a quantifiable pecuniary loss), *except* in the following cases, where slander is actionable *per se:*

(a)   *The imputation of crime.* Words imputing to the plaintiff the commission of a crime *punishable with imprisonment* are actionable without proof of special damage. The essential feature is the causing of others to shun the plaintiff — and not merely his exposure to criminal prosecution —

> *Webb* v. *Beavan* (1883): Overheard by others outside Gloucester gaol, B said to W 'I know enough to put you in there' and the words were held to be actionable *per se.*

(b)   *The imputation of disease.* Words imputing to the plaintiff an *existing* disease (e.g. AIDS) which would cause others to shun him are actionable without proof of special damage.

(c)   *The imputation of unchastity.* Under the Slander of Women Act 1891, words which impute unchastity, adultery (and now also lesbianism) to any woman or girl are actionable without proof of special damage.

(d)   *The imputation in respect of office, etc.* Under the Defamation Act 1952, s. 2, words calculated *to disparage the plaintiff in any office, profession, calling, trade or business* held or carried on by him are actionable without proof of special damage.

4.   The essential elements of defamation

In libel actions the plaintiff has an absolute right to trial by jury, unless there is likely to be a prolonged examination of documents, in which case the presumption is in favour of trial by a judge alone. In *jury trials,* the *judge* must first decide, *as a matter of law,* whether the statement, etc, complained of is *reasonably capable* of bearing the alleged defamatory meaning; if not, a verdict is entered for the defendant. Where the judge's decision is in the affirmative, the *jury* decides, *as a matter of fact,* whether there was actual defamation. Should it so decide, it also assesses the quantum of damages and, in recent years, a wide variation in awards has caused this function to be criticised. To bring a successful action for libel or slander, the plaintiff must prove three matters in respect of the alleged defamation — i.e. that:

(a) *It was defamatory.* There must be damage to the plaintiff's reputation — thus mere vulgar abuse does not constitute defamation, as it merely injures one's dignity; nor is a statement which simply injures the plaintiff's business (though this may be actionable as injurious falsehood). The test is not the nature of the defendant's intention but the meaning which could be imputed by reasonable persons. Innocent intention is therefore no defence — although it might mitigate damages. Conversely, defamatory intention is not sufficient if others did not appreciate the defamation. An apparently innocent statement may be defamatory on account of *innuendo* (a secondary or hidden meaning, which may arise from surrounding circumstances). However, this must be specially pleaded — in that it must be proved by the plaintiff with supporting evidence — and he cannot base it upon facts which became known afterwards. If an innuendo would have been inferred by reasonable persons, the fact that the defendant was not aware of it is no defence —

Tolley v. *J.S. Fry & Sons Ltd* (1931): Without permission, F published a caricature of T (a well-known amateur golfer), with a packet of their chocolate in his pocket and a limerick alleging that the chocolate was as excellent as T's prowess. It was held that there was an innuendo that T had commercialised his amateur status and he was awarded damages.

Monson v. *Tussauds* (1894): Having been tried for murder in Scotland, M had been released on a verdict of 'not proven'. However, in its 'Chamber of Horrors', T's waxworks exhibition showed an effigy of him with a gun and a depiction of the murder scene. The Court of Appeal held this to be defamatory.

Grappelli v. *Derek Block (Holdings)* (1981): When G (a celebrated jazz violinist) cancelled a series of concerts, booked without his authority by DB (his agents), DB untruthfully told theatre managements that G was seriously ill. They then arranged a further series on dates and in places close to those originally scheduled. G claimed that this was defamatory, because of the innuendo whereby people would think that he had given a false story. The Court of Appeal held that facts which subsequently came into existence could not make the statement about illness defamatory; however, G succeeded in an action for injurious falsehood.

(b) *It referred to the plaintiff.* Reference may be *express* or *latent* (i.e. without directly mentioning the plaintiff by name). The test, therefore, is whether a person to whom the statement, etc, was communicated would reasonably think that it referred to the plaintiff. It is not necessary to show that reasonable persons did in fact think this — but only that the statement was capable of being so understood by reasonable persons. A class of persons (e.g. politicians in general) cannot be defamed as such, unless it is so small and well-defined that the statement must refer to any or every member of it —

Hayward v. *Thompson* (1981): In an article concerning an alleged murder plot, a Sunday newspaper (of which T was the proprietor) stated that 'a wealthy benefactor of the Liberal Party' was involved; subsequently, an article in the next issue referred to H by name. The Court of Appeal held that the words in the first article were capable of imputing guilt, as well as suspicion of guilt, also that it had been right for the jury to consider the second article, in order to identify the person referred to in the first one.

Orme v. *Associated Newspapers Group* (1981): An article in an ANG newspaper concerning the Unification Church in England (the 'Moonies') gave rise to a libel action by O (the leader of the Church). ANG contended that, relating to the Church as a whole, the material was not actionable at the suit of O. However, Comyn J held that the grave charges contained therein must be capable of referring to O, if only because people might say that he must have known what went on.

(c) *It was published.* The plaintiff must prove that the defendant communicated the defamation to at least one person other than the plaintiff (or the defendant's spouse). Publication need not be intentional and it would be sufficient to show that someone other than the plaintiff would be likely to see or hear the defamation (e.g. communication by way of a postcard); nevertheless, it is essential that the recipient should understand its meaning and reference to the plaintiff. Each publication of a defamation gives rise to a separate cause of action, and repetition — even by someone unaware of its defamatory nature — constitutes publication. Innocent dissemination (e.g. by a newsagent, bookseller, etc) does not constitute actionable publication, if the disseminator did not know — and was not negligent in failing to discover — that the material was defamatory —

> *Theaker* v. *Richardson* (1962): Writing to T and accusing her of being a 'lying, low-down, brothel-keeping whore and thief', R sealed the letter in a cheap manilla envelope, addressed it with a typewriter and put it through her letter-box. Thinking that it was an election leaflet, T's husband opened it and read the contents. It was held that there had been publication — as the husband's action was a natural consequence of the conduct by R, who had anticipated that someone other than the plaintiff would open the letter.

> *Bottomley* v. *F.W.Woolworth & Co Ltd* (1932): Amongst many American magazines sold by W was one edition of *Detective Story Magazine*, containing an article defamatory of B. Despite not carrying out periodic inspections of the publications, W was held not liable for the dissemination, as it was unlikely that such inspections would have provided knowledge as to the contents of one particular issue.

The defences to an action

5. The defence of justification

In addition to the appropriate general defences, the defendant in an action for defamation may deny that the matter was defamatory, deny that it referred to the plaintiff, deny publication, also invoke any one or more of a number of special defences. The first to be considered is *justification* — a plea that an allegedly defamatory statement is substantially true. The onus is on the defendant to *prove* the truth (also that of any innuendo, if the statement, etc, is capable of bearing one), whereas the plaintiff does not have to establish falsity. On its own, justification is a dangerous defence because, if it fails, the defendant may suffer heavier damages for persisting in his defamation. The defence is not affected by malice or an improper motive on the part of the defendant — though, under the Rehabilitation of Offenders Act 1974, s. 8, 'spent' convictions may support a plea of justification only in the absence of malicious motive. The defence is also not vitiated by a minor inaccuracy and, if there are several imputations, the Defamation Act 1952, s. 5, makes it sufficient for the defendant to prove the truth of the most important ones, provided that those left unproved do not materially injure the plaintiff's reputation. In similar circumstances, it may be open to the defendant to justify the 'common sting' — i.e. contend that a defamatory statement was justified in a wider sense than that complained of by the plaintiff, provided that the statement could fairly be read in the wider sense which the defendant sought to justify —

> *Williams* v. *Reason* (1988): In a newspaper article, R alleged that W had breached the International Rugby Football Board regulations on amateurism by continuing to play rugby union football after having contracted to write a book about his playing career for £10,000. W's libel action succeeded and, on appeal, R unsuccessfully sought leave to adduce fresh evidence that, whilst an international player, W had received payments for wearing the boots of a well-known manufacturer. Ordering a retrial, the Court of Appeal held that the judge had misdirected the jury and that the sting of the alleged libel was 'shamateurism'. R's article could be taken to allege shamateurism on the part of W in a wider sense than in connection with the book; thus the boot money evidence would be admissible at the rehearing.

6.   The defence of fair comment

The defence of *fair comment on a matter of public interest* will succeed provided that it is based on substantially true facts and that the following conditions are fulfilled:

(a) *It must be fair.* This means that the comment must be an honest expression of the defendant's opinion, made in good faith and the belief of its truth, without malicious distortion. The test is whether a fair-minded person (holding a strong, obstinate or even prejudiced view) could have been capable of making the statement; the fact that another may disagree with it is immaterial —

> *Silkin* v. *Beaverbrook Newspapers* (1958): Lord S alleged that words in a newspaper article suggested that he was an insincere and hypocritical person, who was prepared to sacrifice his principles for selfish reasons of personal profit; and that he was unfit to participate in the House of Lords. Having been directed that the fairness of comment hinged on whether or not the writer had expressed an opinion which he honestly held, the jury returned a verdict for the defendants.

> *Thomas* v. *Bradbury Agnew & Co Ltd* (1906): BA published in *Punch* a very savage review of a book by T. The reviewer harboured personal spite against T and the Court of Appeal held that the defence of fair comment must fail, as it was distorted by malice.

(b) *It must be comment.* The statement must be one of opinion and not of fact. It is often difficult to separate fact from comment and this problem has led to the use of the so-called 'rolled-up' plea — that, 'in so far as the words complained of consist of allegations of fact, they are true in substance and in fact; in so far as they are expressions of opinion, they are fair comment'. The Defamation Act 1952, s. 6, provides that, where a statement consists partly of fact and partly of comment, the defence of fair comment 'shall not fail by reason only that the truth of every allegation of fact is not proved' — if the expression of opinion is nevertheless fair, with regard to the facts that are proved. An attack on a person's moral character cannot be fair comment, as it consists essentially of allegations of fact —

> *London Artists* v. *Littler* (1969): Four leading actors in a West End play presented by L (a well-known impresario) simultaneously gave notice to leave the cast. In a letter released to the press, L wrongly accused LA (who were

responsible for the management of the theatre) of conspiracy. The Court of Appeal held that the defence of fair comment could not succeed, as the allegation of a plot was a statement of fact.

(c) *It must be on a matter of public interest.* 'Public interest' covers the conduct of public persons, the administration of public institutions, even the affairs of private businesses which affect the public at large, also activities which are voluntarily submitted to comment (e.g. acting, writing, painting, composing, speech-making, etc). It is for the judge to decide whether a matter is of public interest and the defence is not available for comments on purely private matters.

7. The defence of absolute privilege

In certain circumstances the public interest demands that a person should be free to say what he thinks fit, without having to consider the possibility of an action for defamation. In the following cases, therefore, the defence of *absolute privilege* protects statements from all legal liability, even if they are untrue and malicious:

(a) *Parliamentary proceedings and publications.* Under Article 9 of the Bills of Rights 1688, no civil action can be brought against an MP for anything said or written which is *a proceeding in Parliament*. This covers words used inside or outside the Houses of Parliament in the course of duty, but not conversations on private matters (even within the Houses). The test is not where the words were used — but whether they occurred in the course of 'a proceeding in Parliament'. Subsequent to the cases of *Stockdale* v. *Hansard* (1839–40), the Parliamentary Papers Act 1840 provided that any proceedings concerning a defamatory matter in a publication authorised by either House can be stayed on production of a certificate from an officer of the House —

> *Church of Scientology of California* v. *Johnson-Smith* (1971): Alleging that JS (an MP) had libelled them when discussing scientology in a TV interview, CSC sued him. He pleaded fair comment and CSC sought to rebut this by showing malice, as evidenced by extracts from *Hansard* of JS's

speeches on the subject in Parliament. It was held, however, that this would infringe parliamentary privilege.

(b) *Judicial proceedings.* As show in 5:2(c), all judges are completely immune from proceedings in respect of statements made by them in the exercise of their judicial functions, and within the limits of their jurisdiction. Statements made by advocates, parties, jurors and witnesses are similarly privileged, and the protection extends to tribunals exercising judicial (but not administrative) functions —

> *Addis* v. *Crocker* (1961): A sued the members of the Solicitors' Disciplinary Committee for libel in their published findings on a disciplinary matter. It was held, however, that publication was absolutely privileged.

(c) *Communications between officers of state.* A statement is absolutely privileged if made by one officer of state to another, in the course of official duty. Examples have included communications between a High Commissioner and the Prime Minister, a Minister and an official, a military officer and his superiors —

> *Dawkins* v. *Lord Paulet* (1869): D, a Coldstream Guards captain, forwarded a communication to P (Major-General, commanding Brigade of Foot Guards) for onward transmission to the Adjutant-General. He then sued P for libel in the covering letter, but this was held to enjoy absolute privilege.

8. The defence of qualified privilege

This covers the matters outlined below, where the public interest does not demand the complete immunity of absolute privilege, but where some extended right of freedom of speech is nevertheless desirable. The privilege is 'qualified' in that the protection it affords can be rebutted by proof of malice; it relates mainly to:

(a) *The statements made in the performance of a duty.* Here the essential requirement is that of reciprocity — a question of law for the judge to determine. On the one side there must be a legal, moral or social *duty* to make the statement and, on the other side, there must be a *corresponding interest* to receive it (e.g. references supplied to prospective employers) —

> *Watt* v. *Longsdon* (1930): Having received a letter accusing W (an employee) of immorality and dishonesty, L (a company director) showed it to the company chairman and also to W's wife. It was held that the publication to the chairman was privileged (as there was a reciprocal duty and interest), but the publication to the wife was not privileged; she had an interest in receiving the letter but L had no duty to show it to her.

(b) *The statements made in protection of a lawful interest.* In this case there need not be any duty to make the statement but reciprocity is still essential, in that there must be an *interest* to be protected and a *duty* to protect it. The interest may be that of the person making the statement or of the general public; consequently, the protection covers letters of complaint about officials, etc —

> *Beach* v. *Freeson* (1971): Having received a number of complaints from his constituents about B (a solicitor), F (an MP) wrote to the Law Society and the Lord Chancellor. It was held that both letters were protected by qualified privilege.

(c) *The fair and accurate reports of public proceedings.* Provided that they are fair and accurate (a question of fact), media reports of parliamentary or judicial proceedings are protected by qualified privilege. Part I of the Schedule to the Defamation Act 1952 extends this protection to reports in respect of the legislatures and courts of the United Kingdom dependencies, also international courts and organisations (e.g. UNO). Part II of the Schedule lists a number of local and private bodies (e.g. trade, professional and sporting organisations, local government authorities, public inquiries, public meetings, company general meetings, etc) but, in these cases, the defence of qualified privilege cannot be raised if the defendant failed to accede to a request to publish a reasonable contradiction or correction —

> *Cook* v. *Alexander* (1973): In a House of Lords debate, a bishop strongly criticised C who had been instrumental in effecting the closure of an approved school. A full report of

the debate appeared in the *Daily Telegraph* and on another page was a 'parliamentary sketch' by A. This emphasised the bishop's attack and referred to 'a rather bumbling reply'. The Court of Appeal held that, having been made fairly and honestly, the parliamentary sketch was privileged.

(d) *The professional communications between solicitors and clients.* On separate occasions, the Court of Appeal has treated this privilege as both absolute and qualified.

9. The offer of amends

A publisher who has exercised all reasonable care with respect to a publication may claim that a defamation contained in it was made innocently *either* because he did not intend to publish the offending words about the plaintiff and did not know of circumstances whereby they might be taken to refer to him *or* because he did not know of circumstances by which apparently innocent words might be understood as defaming the plaintiff. When such conditions are fulfilled, the publisher may (under the Defamation Act 1952, s. 4) make an *offer of amends*. He must also submit an affidavit of the facts he relies on to establish the innocence of the defamation, an offer of suitable correction and apology, and an offer to take reasonable steps to notify recipients of the publication. If the offer is accepted, the aggrieved party may take no further proceedings for defamation but, if it is rejected, it will be a defence for the offeror to show that the publication was made innocently, also that the offer was made without reasonable delay, and has not been withdrawn.

Progress test 21

1. Define defamation and explain, with reference to decided cases, the matters that must be proved for an action to succeed. **(1, 4)**

2. Distinguish between libel and slander. **(2, 3)**

3. Describe the defences of justification and fair comment. **(5, 6)**

4.   Compare and contrast absolute and qualified privilege. **(7, 8)**

5.   Furious at being declared redundant, Rupert telephoned the flat where Stuart, the firm's chief executive, was known to live alone. On the answering-machine he left an angry message, in which he wrongly accused Stuart of financially ruining the company by misappropriating funds. Unbeknown to Rupert, Stuart had just left for a three-week foreign holiday and had arranged for a colleague to visit the flat daily, to collect any messages. As a result, he has now been ordered back from abroad to face an investigation by the directors. Advise Stuart. **(1–6)**

Part four

The criminal law

22
The principles of criminal liability

The nature of general liability

1. The elements of general liability

As shown in 4:1–2, a crime is any *act or omission* that is *prohibited by the law of the state* (generally because it threatens the security, well being or good order of society) and that *gives rise to proceedings*, usually *initiated by the Crown, with a view to punishment*. Crimes may be classified in various different ways — dependent principally upon their *source* (i.e. statutory and common law offences — 2:1(b)–(c)), *mode of trial* (i.e. summary and indictable offences — 4:4(a)–(c)) or *nature* (i.e. non-arrestable and arrestable offences — 8:2(a)). A basic tenet of English criminal law is the maxim *actus non facit reum nisi mens sit rea* (an act does not itself constitute guilt unless the mind is guilty); this means that, to obtain a conviction for a criminal offence, the prosecution normally has to establish:

(a) *The existence of an actus reus.* As mere intent would be insufficient, criminal liability necessitates some act or omission (as outlined in 22:2) on the part of the defendant —

> *R* v. *Deller* (1952): Having signed a document purporting to mortgage his car to a finance company, D traded in the vehicle, representing it as free from mortgage. The document was actually void in law and D had (unintentionally) told the truth. The Court of Appeal therefore held that, as there was no *actus reus*, D was not guilty of false pretences.

R v. *Taaffe* (1984): Having agreed to import currency (which he mistakenly believed to be prohibited), T was convicted of being *knowingly* concerned in the importation of cannabis (a prohibited substance). The House of Lords held that, as no offence would have been committed if the goods had been currency, T's incorrect belief did not convert the importation into a crime.

(b) *The existence of mens rea.* A 'guilty mind' (or, more accurately, 'criminal intention') is normally as essential element of every crime — but it does not mean moral wickedness or criminal depravity. *Mens rea* can be defined as an intention to commit a criminal act *or* recklessness as to the consequences of that act and, in a few instances, it can include mere negligence; further consideration is therefore given to it in 22:3.

2.   The nature of an *actus reus*

An *actus reus* may comprise actual conduct (e.g. the giving of false evidence on oath, which constitutes perjury), the result of conduct (e.g. the causing of death in murder), an omission to perform a legal duty (*see* **(e)** *below*) or even the result of surrounding circumstances (*see* **(d)** *below*). For it to exist:

(a) *It must fulfil all requirements.* In relation to any particular offence, the conduct must embrace all the consequences that must occur (e.g. death in the case of murder), all the circumstances that must exist (e.g. a valid marriage in the case of bigamy) and all the conditions that must be fulfilled (e.g. the requirements for theft — 26:1) —

Chief Constable of Avon and Somerset Constabulary v. *Jest* (1986): Questioned about the taking of a car, J said that he had never been in such a model, but his thumb-print was found on the rear-view mirror. As there was no evidence of possession or control, the justices dismissed charges of taking the vehicle without consent, and the Divisional Court upheld this decision.

(b) *It must be linked to any required consequence.* If the *actus reus* of an offence relates to the result of conduct, a nexus (link) must be established between the act and the result. The fact that this may not be attributable solely to the conduct of the defendant does not necessarily absolve him from liability — but an unforeseeable intervention might, in certain circumstances, preclude his conviction —

> *R* v. *Smith* (1959): In a barrack-room fight, S stabbed a fellow soldier, who was twice dropped to the ground whilst being taken to the medical reception centre. Because of the pressure of other cases, he was incorrectly treated and died — though his chances of recovery would have been good, if he had received a blood transfusion. S's conviction of murder was upheld.

> *R* v. *Dyos* (1979): In a fight involving a number of people, D struck a man on the head with a brick and he died. A pathologist found two main wounds on the head, both of which could 'very probably' have caused death — though there was a 'reasonable and sensible' possibility that the victim might have recovered from the first. It was impossible to tell which one this was and there was no evidence to show that both were caused by D. As it could not be proved that he was responsible for the death, it was held that there was no case to answer.

(c) *It must lack justification.* What might otherwise constitute an offence may be justified on the grounds of protecting property or self-defence (23:6), etc —

> *R* v. *Hill; R* v. *Hall* (1989): The defendants (two women members of CND) had been found in possession of a hacksaw, with which they intended to cut the perimeter fence of a US base in Britain. Their defence was that they wanted to force the UK Government to give up nuclear weapons, in order to protect property from the threat of nuclear war. It was held that the causation was too tenuous for the acts to amount to protection, also that the defendants could not have believed that there was an immediate need to protect their property. The Court of Appeal upheld their conviction of possessing an article with intent to damage property.

(d) *It must be voluntary.* An act may be involuntary (therefore not criminal) on account of automatism (23:3), duress (23:7), the mechanical failure of a vehicle, illness or accident causing loss of consciousness or faculties, etc. There are, however, some very rare cases wherein a defendant (who has performed no voluntary act) may be convicted of an offence through 'surrounding circumstances', which are themselves prohibited —

> *Winzar* v. *Chief Constable of Kent* (1983): Called to remove W, who was drunk at Ramsgate General Hospital, the police placed him in a vehicle on the forecourt in Westcliff Road and took him to the police station. He was then charged with being found 'drunk on the highway called Westcliff Road'. Although his presence there was momentary and not of his volition, the Divisional Court held that it sufficed to show that he was on the highway and 'perceived to be drunk'.

(e) *It may comprise an omission.* An omission can constitute an *actus reus* only when there is a legal (and not merely moral) duty to act — thus no crime would result from passively watching a stranger drowning. Nevertheless, omissions can give rise to certain statutory offences — e.g. failing to stop in the event of a road accident (Road Traffic Act 1972, s. 25) or wilful neglect of children by their parents (Children and Young Persons Act 1933, s. 1). The same applies if anyone undertakes a duty upon which the safety or welfare of others depends —

> *R* v. *Dytham* (1979): D, a police officer in uniform, was near a club exit when a man was ejected, beaten and kicked to death in the gutter. Not having intervened or summoned assistance, D was charged with 'misconduct of an officer' and the Court of Appeal upheld his conviction.

> *R* v. *Stone; R* v. *Dobinson* (1977): S (aged 67, partially deaf and almost totally blind) lived with D (his mistress) and his anorexic younger sister. When the latter became helplessly infirm, no doctor was consulted nor was a visiting social worker informed. On her death from toxemia, S and D were charged with manslaughter and the Court of Appeal upheld their convictions.

3. The nature of *mens rea*

As shown in 22:1(b), *mens rea* normally comprises intention, recklessness or negligence — though, in crimes of strict liability (22:4), it can be said to exist simply through permitting a prohibited result to happen. It is therefore necessary to consider:

(a) *The nature of intention.* Certain offences (e.g. wounding with intent (25:6(b)), murder (25:2), theft (26:1)), also attempts to commit any offence (24:1) are *crimes of specific intent* — wherein a definite intention must be proved beyond reasonable doubt, and mere recklessness or negligence cannot constitute *mens rea*. Other offences (e.g. assault, rape, etc) may be termed *crimes of basic intent*, wherein proof of intention or recklessness (but not negligence) will suffice. The Criminal Justice Act 1967, s. 8, provides that, in determining whether a person has committed an offence, a court or jury shall not be bound in law to infer that he intended or foresaw a result of his actions by reason only of its being a natural and probable consequence of those actions; but it shall decide whether he did intend or foresee that result by reference to all the evidence, drawing such inferences from the evidence as appear proper in the circumstances —

> *R* v. *Pearman* (1985): Stopped by the police, P reversed his car into the police vehicle, accelerated forward, hitting an officer, then drove off. He was convicted of attempt to cause grievous bodily harm with intent, the jury having been directed that he had the necessary intent under the Criminal Attempts Act 1981, s. 1 (*see* 24:1), if he committed a voluntary act foreseeing that really serious bodily harm would result from it. Quashing the conviction, the Court of Appeal held that *forsight of consequences must not be equated with intent — although it is something from which intent may be inferred.*

(b) *The nature of recklessness.* Derived from the two cases cited below, and applicable to differing crimes, there are alternative tests for proof of recklessness. Under the 'Cunningham' criterion (particularly relevant to statutory offences defined as being committed 'maliciously'), recklessness exists *if the defendant was aware of a risk that was not justified and took that risk deliberately.* The 'Caldwell' test (appropriate for statutory offences defined as being committed 'recklessly') establishes recklessness *if, when performing an act that created an obvious risk, the defendant had EITHER given no thought to the possibility of there being such a risk OR had recognised that there was some risk involved and had nevertheless gone on to take it —*

> *R* v. *Cunningham* (1957): Having entered a house, wrenched out the gas meter and stolen the contents, C failed to turn off a tap and left the pipe discharging gas. He was charged with 'maliciously causing to be taken a noxious thing' and Oliver J defined malicious as 'wicked'. Quashing C's conviction, the Court of Appeal held that 'maliciously' in a statutory crime postulates foresight of consequence and the first test above.

> *R* v. *Caldwell* (1982): Pursuing a grievance against the proprietor, C set fire to a hotel and was convicted of arson. He claimed that he was so drunk that the thought that he might be endangering life had never entered his mind. The Court of Appeal quashed his conviction but, reversing this decision, the House of Lords stated the second test above and held the C's failure to give thought to the endangering of life, through self-induced intoxication, was irrelevant.

(c) *The culpability of negligence.* As distinct from recklessness, negligence (which implies conduct, rather that a state of mind) connotes an absence of such care, skill or foresight as a reasonable man would exercise. As *mens rea* and a ground for criminal liability, negligence (not to be confused with 'neglect' — a state of affairs that it creates) does not arise in common law offences other than manslaughter (25:4) and it is found in relatively few statutory crimes (e.g. offences under the Road Traffic Act 1988 relating to objective standards of care).

(d) *The principle of transferred malice.* If A attempts to stab B but misses and kills C, it is accepted that the malice towards B is transferred to C, whom A can be convicted of murdering —

> *R* v. *Latimer* (1886): Quarrelling with another man in a public house, L attempted to hit him with his belt but injured an innocent bystander. The Court of Criminal Appeal upheld his conviction of unlawful and malicious wounding.

R v. *Pembliton* (1874): Outside a public house, P threw a stone at an adversary but missed him and broke a window. His conviction of unlawful and malicious damage, under the Malicious Damage Act 1861, s. 51, was quashed — as the Act required an intention to damage property.

(e) *The irrelevance of motive. Mens rea* must not be confused with motive (the reason why someone wishes a particular event to happen), which is usually irrelevant to the question of criminal liability. Thus an innocent motive does not preclude the existence of *mens rea*, and a wicked motive without *mens rea* will not constitute a crime —

Hills v. *Ellis* (1983): H saw a police officer arresting a man whom he thought was the innocent party in a fight. He took the officer's arm, to draw attention to the fact, and was convicted of obstruction. The Divisional Court upheld the conviction, as all the requirements of the offence had been established and the motive was irrelevant.

The nature of strict liability

4. The elements of strict liability
Proof of the existence of *mens rea* is *not* required in certain *absolute* offences where statutes impose *strict liability* and, to obtain a conviction, it is necessary merely to prove the existence of prohibited circumstances. It may seem unjust to convict someone who has not knowingly acted improperly but it is argued that strict liability is essential when there is an overriding need to prevent conduct detrimental to the welfare of the community and there are difficulties in proving intent. Crimes of strict liability are not easily identifiable. If the definition of an offence contains words such as 'knowingly', 'wilfully', 'maliciously', 'with intent', etc, *mens rea* will probably be necessary. In the absence of express provisions, the need for *mens rea* should be presumed but it can be rebutted. In many cases strict liability is of a regulatory nature, often applying to the so-called 'victimless crimes' (*see* 1:**1(a)**) and tending to reflect topics of public concern at any given time. Common areas in which it is found therefore cover:

(a) *The possession of prohibited items.* Examples include controlled drugs, uncertificated firearms, explosives, forgery equipment, offensive weapons in public places, etc. It would be a defence for the possessor to establish that he was ignorant of the nature (but not merely the quality) of the item —

> *Gibson* v. *Wales* (1983): G was charged with carrying an offensive weapon (a flick knife) in a public place, contrary to the Prevention of Crime Act 1953, s. 1(1)(4). The magistrate held that it was not an offensive weapon *per se* and dismissed the case, as there was no proof of an intent to injure. Allowing the prosecutor's appeal, the Court of Appeal held that a flick knife is offensive *per se* and the onus is on the carrier to show that he had it with him for an innocent purpose.

> *R* v. *Customs and Excise Commissioners, ex parte Claus* (1988): Having entered the green ('nothing to declare') channel, C had a conversation with a Customs officer and then voluntarily handed over 26 dutiable items. He was charged with failure to declare them and the case was dismissed; however, the Divisional Court held that the Customs and Excise Management Act 1979, s. 78, created strict liability on entering the channel and it was irrelevant if a voluntary declaration took place at some later stage.

(b) *The regulation of road traffic.* Examples include speeding, driving with excess alcohol, failure to wear a seat-belt, etc, and sometimes special reasons may provide a defence —

> *Strowger* v. *John* (1974): A motorist left his car locked on a public road and, whilst he was away, the licence holder fell to the floor. He was convicted of failing to display an excise licence, contrary to the Vehicles (Excise) Act 1971, s. 12(4), but successfully appealed. On appeal by the prosecutor, the Divisional Court restored the conviction as no *mens rea* was necessary — though it might have been different if the licence had been removed by a third party.

> *R* v. *Newton* (1974): N was convicted of driving with alcohol over the prescribed limit, having unsuccessfully pleaded that his drinks had been laced — as a special reason for non-disqualification. The Divisional Court dismissed his

appeal, in view of the heavy and important duty on a driver to watch the amount of drink taken. Resulting from the Attorney-General's Reference No.1 of 1975, the person who laces a drink is guilty of procuring (*see* 22:5) the consequent offence.

(c) *The standards of food and drink.* Here strict liability relates not only to the maintenance of hygiene and the giving of proper measures but also the licensing of public houses —

Smedleys v. *Breed* (1974): At a time when one of its factories was producing 500,000 tins of peas per week, S Co was convicted of an offence under the Food and Drugs Act 1955, when one tin was found to contain a dead, sterilised and harmless caterpillar, which resembled a pea. Despite the fact that S Co exercised very high quality control, with a trained inspectorate paid bonuses for detecting extraneous matter, the House of Lords dismissed its appeal, as the offence was one of strict liability.

(d) *The protection of the environment* —

Alphacell v. *Woodward* (1972): A paper mill discharged waste into two tanks beside a river and two pumps were used to remove effluent. However, an overflow occurred when foliage blocked the pump inlets and, although he had not been negligent, the mill owner was convicted of 'causing' polluted matter to enter the river, contrary to the Rivers (Prevention of Pollution) Act 1951, s. 2(1). The House of Lords held that, in the absence of any intervention by a trespasser or Act of God, he had caused the pollution.

R v. *Wells Street Metropolitan Stipendiary Magistrate, ex parte Westminster City Council* (1987): Hired by a company leasing a Grade II listed building to remove furniture, a contractor also took away fixtures and fittings (having been instructed to remove 'everything of value'). Charged with unauthorised alteration to the building, contrary to the Town and Country Planning Act 1971, a director of the company and the contractor were discharged at committal proceedings. However, allowing an application for judicial review, the Divisional Court held that the offence was one of strict liability.

The nature of secondary liability

5. The elements of secondary liability

It is necessary to consider not only *principal offenders* (i.e. those who, by their own conduct or through an agent, directly bring about an *actus reus*) but also *secondary parties* (those who 'aid, abet, counsel or procure' a crime, without being the actual perpetrators). Under the Accessories and Abettors Act 1861, s. 8 (as amended), these are liable to trial and punishment just as if they were principal offenders — though the following factors are relevant to their prosecution:

(a) *The existence of an offence.* If no offence is actually committed, it is not possible to convict anyone of aiding and abetting; however, it is an offence to aid and abet an attempt to commit a crime —

> *R* v. *Quick; R* v. *Paddison* (1973): Pleading that his conduct resulted from diabetes, Q (a mental hospital nurse) was convicted of assaulting a patient. The Court of Appeal quashed his conviction and, consequently, the conviction of P for aiding him by encouragement was also quashed.

> *R* v. *Dunnington* (1984): D was to drive an escape car for two others who intended to commit a robbery but the plan misfired and they were put to flight. All three were convicted of attempted robbery and, upholding their convictions, the Court of Appeal held that, under the Criminal Attempts Act 1981, s. 1(1)(4), to aid and abet a criminal attempt is an offence (whereas to attempt to aid and abet is not one).

(b) *The actus reus of aiding and abetting.* Encouragement in some form is a minimal requirement before anyone can properly be regarded as involved in an offence —

> *R* v. *Bentley* (1953): Accompanied by one Craig, B was in a rooftop chase and, after being taken into custody, he shouted 'Let him have it, Chris', whereat Craig shot and killed a police officer. Both were convicted of murder and Craig, being too young for the death penalty, was committed to life imprisonment, whilst B was hanged.

> *R* v. *Bland* (1988): Because she lived in one room with her

co-defendant (who was charged with possession of a controlled drug, with intent to supply), B was prosecuted for the same offence. Quashing her conviction, the Court of Appeal held that there was no evidence of active or passive assistance. This required more than mere knowledge that the principal defendant was drug-dealing and there needed to be some element of encouragement or control.

(c) *The mens rea of aiding and abetting.* It must be shown that the defendant knew that his conduct would be of assistance to the principal offender and that the latter would cause the *actus reus* with the appropriate *mens rea* —

> *R* v. *Bainbridge* (1960): B had purchased oxy-acetylene cutting equipment and had supplied it to others who used it to cut the bars of a bank window. B stated that he suspected that it might be used for some illegal purpose but did not know that it was to be used for a bank robbery. Upholding his conviction, the Court of Criminal Appeal held that it was sufficient to show that the defendant knew that a crime of the *type* committed was intended but, if an offence of a totally different nature had been undertaken, the supplier would not have been a party to it.

> *R* v. *Anderson and Morris* (1966): A and M went in search of one Welch, A being armed with a knife of which M denied any knowledge. Welch died of stab wounds after A had been seen punching him, with M standing behind Welch's back, apparently not taking any part. A was convicted of murder and M of manslaughter. Quashing M's conviction, the Court of Criminal Appeal held that, where two persons embark on a joint enterprise, each is liable for acts done in pursuance of it (including any unusual consequences) but, if one of them goes beyond what has been tacitly agreed as part of the common enterprise, his co-adventurer is not liable for the consequences of the unauthorised act.

(d) *The actus reus of counselling.* The word 'counsel' in the Accessories and Abettors Act 1861, s. 8, does *not* connote any causal connection between the counselling and the principal offence. To establish an offence under the Act, it is simply necessary to show that there was counselling and that the principal offence was committed by the person counselled, acting within the scope of his authority and not by accident —

> *R* v. *Calhaem* (1985): Allegedly having counselled another to murder a woman, C was convicted of murder (under s. 8 of the 1861 Act). Having pleaded guilty, the murderer had given evidence at C's trial that he had decided not to kill the victim, but had gone berserk and done so. Upholding C's conviction, the Court of Appeal stated the principles outlined above.

(e) *The impeding of apprehension.* Under the Criminal Law Act 1967, s. 4(1), as amended, it is an offence for anyone, knowing or believing another to be guilty of an arrestable offence, to do 'without lawful authority or reasonable excuse, any act with intent to impede his apprehension or prosecution' —

> *R* v. *Donald and Donald* (1986): The defendants were convicted of assisting another to commit a robbery by having sheltered him, knowing that he was responsible for the offence. Although he had not stood trial, the prosecution had adduced evidence of his involvement and the Court of Appeal upheld the convictions.

The nature of vicarious liability

6. The elements of vicarious liability
As shown in 17:10, vicarious liability means the responsibility of one person for the acts of another and, in so far as the criminal law is concerned, it relates principally to:

(a) *The liability of employers.* In respect of crimes committed by employees in the scope of their employment, an employer is *strictly* liable for absolute offences (22:4); he is also *vicariously* liable for the common law offences of public nuisance and criminal libel, together with (non-absolute) statutory offences *where authority has been totally delegated to an employee* — but not if general supervision is retained — or merely for aiding, abetting or attempt —

> *Sopp* v. *Long* (1970): The licensee of the Windsor Station Buffet was the Secretary of British Transport Hotels, who

delegated his authority through a chain of managers to a
manageress. When whisky was sold in short measures at the
buffet, he was convicted of an offence contrary to the
Weights and Measures Act 1963. Upholding the conviction,
the Divisional Court held that only the licensee could sell
and, by being absent from the premises, he sold through his
employee.

Essendon Engineering Co v. *Maile* (1982): When one of its
vehicle testers was convicted of deliberately issuing a false
MoT certificate, contrary to the Road Traffic Act 1972,
s. 171, EE was also convicted of the same offence. Quashing
the company's conviction, the Divisional Court held that the
tester could have made EE guilty of a crime requiring *mens
rea* only if the company had given him full discretion to act
independently of its instructions — and there was no
evidence to support this.

(b) *The liability of corporations.* A limited company is as criminally
liable as a human being for offences punishable with a fine (i.e. all
crimes except those for which a non-pecuniary sentence is fixed
by law). Its liability may therefore be *strict* (in the case of absolute
offences), *vicarious* (as an employer) or *direct* (in respect of conduct
by those who control its actions — e.g. directors) —

R v. *ICR Haulage Co Ltd* (1944): ICRH was convicted of a
common law conspiracy to defraud and the Court of Appeal
held that the acts of the managing director were those of
the company — thus his fraud was its fraud.

Tesco Supermarkets v. *Nattrass* (1972): Although it had set up
an elaborate system of supervision, TS was convicted of an
offence contrary to the Trade Descriptions Act 1968, as a
'special offer' poster had been unjustifiably displayed,
because a store manager had failed to check the work of his
staff, in accordance with his duties. The House of Lords
held that, as the store manager was not involved in the
central direction of TS's activities, it was entitled to be
acquitted.

(c) *The liability of partners.* One partner is not liable for the criminal
acts of another unless it can be shown that they acted in concert —

Bennett v. *Richardson* (1980): Having travelled on partnership business in a defective van, hired by the partnership and driven by his partner, a blind man was charged with permitting the use of a defective vehicle on the road. The justices dismissed the information and, upholding their decision, the Divisional Court held that the only persons who could be charged with the offence were the driver or his employer — but not his partner.

Parsons v. *Barnes* (1973): B was convicted of an offence under the Trade Descriptions Act 1968, as his partner had signed B's name upon an invoice, on partnership notepaper, for the repair of a roof by 'turnerising', despite the fact that this process had not been used. Although not present when the work was done, B had attended an initial inspection of the roof when turnerising was discussed. Dismissing B's appeal, the Divisional Court held that it was justifiable to conclude that the partners had acted in concert throughout.

(d) *The liability of parents.* Courts have powers to require parents: to attend proceedings involving their children under 16 (in future this will be their duty, unless it would be unreasonable); to pay fines imposed on their children under 17; also to exercise proper care and control of their children under 18 (fines being imposable on parents who unreasonably refuse to do so).

Progress test 22

1. In connection with criminal offences, explain the significance of intention and recklessness. **(3)**

2. Justify the existence of strict liability. **(4)**

3. Examine the adequacy of the law relating to the criminal liability of accomplices. **(5)**

4. 'It is not sensible to make one person liable for the crimes of another.' Discuss. **(6)**

5. Although Alec was three months under the age for a licence, Bob lent him his motor-cycle for a trial run around the neighbourhood. Seeing two youths walking in the road, Alec recognised one as Cyril — a boy who had bullied him at school. Accelerating, he drove towards him but collided with David, the other youth, who fell to the ground, hitting his head on the kerb. A passing motorist took David to the local hospital, where the overworked staff failed to diagnose head injury and sent David home after treatment for minor abrasions; two days later he died. Assess all criminal liability.   **(1–5)**

23
The nature of general defences

The defences of a mental nature

1. The defence of insanity

'Insanity from a medical point of view is one thing; insanity from the point of view of the criminal law is a different thing' (*per* McCardie J). Moreover, when the sanity of a defendant is in question, medical evidence is given but the issue is determined by the jury. The matter arises in the following circumstances.

(a) *The issue of fitness to plead.* In criminal prosecutions, at any time before the opening of the defence case, the defendant may be found *unfit to plead* (i.e. incapable of understanding the proceedings). The issue may be raised by the defence (in which case the burden of establishing unfitness is on the defendant and must be proved on a balance of probabilities), the prosecution (where the burden is on the prosecution and must be proved beyond reasonable doubt) or the judge (with the burden on the prosecution). The matter is tried by a specially empanelled jury and, if the defendant is so found, an order may be made detaining him 'during Her Majesty's pleasure' and the power to discharge him from such detention may be exercised only with the consent of the Home Secretary. Under the Criminal Appeal Act 1968, s. 15, the defendant may appeal against a finding of unfitness —

> *R* v. *Berry* (1977): B, a paranoid schizophrenic, was found unfit to plead by a jury which had not been directed as to the matters that they should consider. Allowing his appeal, the Court of Appeal held that the judge must give clear

directions to the jury that they must consider the defendant's ability to instruct counsel, to understand the evidence and to give evidence himself. A state of high abnormality is not necessarily conclusive of unfitness.

R v. Webb (1969): In W's trial for indecently assaulting a girl, the prosecution wished to adduce evidence that he was unfit to plead but, hoping to get an acquittal by challenging the prosecution's case, the defence objected. The issue was tried before arraignment and, being found to be under a disability, W was ordered to be detained. Quashing the finding of disability, the Court of Appeal held that the nature of the supposed disability and the defendant's interests were the factors to be considered; furthermore, weight should have been given to the chances of a successful defence — especially where there would not have been confinement in a hospital if the defendant had been found not guilty.

(b) *The issue of guilt.* Every person is presumed to be sane and to possess a sufficient degree of reason to be responsible for his crimes. However, this presumption may be rebutted by the defence with evidence that satisfies the jury, on a balance of probabilities, that the defendant was insane at the time of the offence charged. The question is determined in accordance with the criteria set out in the M'Naghten Rules (*see* 23:**2**).

(c) *The issue of diminished responsibility.* In cases of murder only, it is possible, under the Homicide Act 1957, s. 2(1), to plead diminished responsibility (enabling the defendant to be convicted of manslaughter) if it can be shown that *he was suffering from such abnormality of mind (whether arising from a condition of arrested or retarded development of mind, or any inherent causes, or induced by disease or injury) as substantially impaired his mental responsibility for his acts and omissions in doing, or being a party to, the killing.* If the defendant pleads diminished responsibility, the prosecution may adduce evidence to prove insanity (Criminal Procedure (Insanity) Act 1964, s. 6) —

R v. Byrne (1960): B, a sexual psychopath, killed a young woman and pleaded diminished responsibility. Stable J directed the jury that, if they found only that B suffered from perverse sexual urges that were impossible or very difficult to resist, that would not bring the case within s. 2(1) of the 1957 Act. Allowing B's appeal against conviction of murder, and substituting a verdict of manslaughter, the Court of Criminal Appeal held that 'abnormality of mind' meant a mind so different from that of ordinary human beings that the reasonable man would term it abnormal. This was sufficiently wide to cover the ability to exercise willpower to control physical acts.

R v. *Tandy* (1988): After consuming nearly a whole bottle of vodka, T strangled her daughter and, being charged with murder, she pleaded diminished responsibility. Upholding her conviction, the Court of Appeal held, that, to substantiate her plea, she needed to establish three elements: that she was suffering from an abnormality of mind at the time of the offence; that the abnormality was induced by the disease of alcoholism, also that it substantially impaired her mental responsibility. To provide a defence under s. 2(1) of the 1957 Act, a craving for drink or drugs must be such as to make consumption involuntary; a state of alcoholism resulting from voluntary drinking is insufficient.

2. The criteria of the M'Naghten Rules

These resulted from the acquittal in 1843 of Daniel M'Naghten, who had killed Sir Robert Peel's secretary, Drummond, instead of the Prime Minister. The matter caused such wide dissatisfaction that the House of Lords (not in its appellate capacity) sought the opinion of the judges. Their view was that: *To establish a defence on the ground of insanity, it must be clearly proved that, at the time of the committing of the act, the party accused was labouring under such a defect of reason, from disease of mind, as not to know the nature and quality of the act he was doing; or, if he did know it, that he did not know what he was doing was wrong.* When the defendant is thus found to be insane, the Criminal Procedure (Insanity) Act 1964, s. 1, provides that a verdict of *not guilty by reason of insanity* shall be returned and there is detention during Her Majesty's pleasure; however, under the Criminal Appeal Act 1968, s. 12, there is a right of appeal against this verdict. Judicial interpretation of the M'Naghten Rules has related to:

(a) *The disease of mind.* This implies a mental condition, as opposed to its physical cause. 'The law is not concerned with the brain but with the mind, in the sense that "mind" is ordinarily used, the mental faculties of reason, memory and understanding. . . . In my judgment, the condition of the brain is irrelevant and so is the question of whether the condition of the mind is curable or incurable, transitory or permanent' (*per* Devlin J in *R* v. *Kemp* (1957)) —

> *R* v. *Hennessy* (1989): Requiring daily insulin for diabetes and experiencing stress from marital and employment problems, H was charged with taking a motor vehicle without consent. He claimed that he was suffering from hyperglycaemia through not having taken his insulin for several days, and did not know what he was doing. The judge held that, through a disease of the mind, he was incapable of forming the necessary *mens rea* and was insane within the meaning of the M'Naghten Rules. Changing his plea to guilty, H appealed against the ruling. Dismissing the appeal, the Court of Appeal held that hyperglycaemia caused by high blood sugar levels was an inherent defect that was a disease of the mind.

> *R* v. *Smith* (1982): Charged with having an offensive weapon and threatening to kill, S pleaded that her conduct was attributable to pre-menstrual syndrome but she was convicted. Dismissing her appeal, the Court of Appeal held that there was no defence in law of irresistible impulse. This case bears out the widely held view that the M'Naghten Rules constitute an unsatisfactory basis for the law of insanity.

(b) *The nature and quality of the act.* It is necessary to show that the defendant did not know the physical quality of his act. If a person commits an offence under an insane delusion as to existing facts, but is not in other respects insane, his liability will be the same as if the facts were real —

> *R* v. *Sullivan* (1983): Charged with inflicting grievous bodily

harm on a friend, S pleaded that he was recovering from an epileptic seizure at the time. The judge ruled that the defence amounted to a plea of insanity and S changed his plea to one of guilty. The House of Lords held that the ruling was correct. Although, in medical terms, epilepsy might not be considered a disease of the mind, the effect was such as to cause a defect of reason so that S did not know the nature and quality of the act he was doing, and was thus insane for the purpose of a verdict of 'not guilty by reason of insanity'.

(c) *The unawareness of wrong-doing.* If the defendant was aware of the nature and quality of his act, insanity can be established only if it can be shown that he did not know that it was contrary to the law or wrong 'according to the ordinary standard adopted by reasonable men' —

R v. *Windle* (1952): W gave his certifiably insane wife a fatal dose of 100 aspirins. There was some evidence that he was suffering from a form of communicated insanity but, after telling the police what he had done, he added that he supposed he would hang for it. Devlin J ruled that there was no evidence of insanity to go to the jury and the Court of Appeal held that this was correct.

3. The defence of automatism

Automatism has been defined (by Lord Denning in *Bratty* v. *Att. Gen. for Northern Ireland* (1963)) as *an act done by the muscles, without any control by the mind, such as a spasm, a reflex action or a convulsion, or an act done by a person who is not conscious of what he is doing, such as an act done whilst suffering from concussion or whilst sleep-walking.* If an *actus reus* involves some positive act on the part of the defendant, it must be willed by him; therefore, in a state of automatism, his actions would be involuntary and consequently not punishable. Automatism due to mental disease constitutes *insane automatism* (with the M'Naghten Rules applying and the burden of proof upon the defendant). If, however, it is due to some other cause (e.g. sleep-walking), it is *non-insane automatism* and, should this be raised, the burden of disproving it is on the prosecution —

R v. *Bailey* (1983): In a hyperglycaemic state, having failed to take food after insulin, B (a diabetic) wounded another person. The jury was directed that B could not rely on the defence of automatism, as his state was self-induced, but the Court of Appeal held that this was a misdirection. Self-induced automatism, other than that brought about by alcohol or dangerous drugs, may be a defence to crimes of basic intent, unless the prosecution can prove a necessary element of recklessness. In the instant case, the prosecution should have been prepared to show that B knew of the effects of failure to take food after insulin, or that such effects were common knowledge.

R v. *Isitt* (1978): After being involved in an accident, I drove off in a dangerous manner. Pleading at his trial that he had driven without conscious thought, he adduced medical evidence that the accident had left him in a state of 'hysterical fugue'. Upholding his conviction, the Court of Appeal held that, although insanity and automatism could provide a defence to a charge of dangerous driving, I had clearly been driving purposefully, albeit with a mind possibly closed to moral inhibitions.

4.   The defence of intoxication
    Though not a defence in itself, intoxication (through drink or drugs) may negate *mens rea* and a distinction needs to be drawn between:

(a) *The effects of involuntary intoxication.* Involuntary intoxication (e.g. through the 'lacing' of drinks) may be a mitigating factor in offences *not* of strict liability — see *R* v. *Newton* (1974) (22:**4(b)**). Addiction to drink or drugs, which makes consumption involuntary, may give rise to insanity within the M'Naghten Rules, or constitute diminished responsibility in cases of murder — see *R* v. *Tandy* (1988) (23:**1(c)**).
(b) *The effects of voluntary intoxication.* Self-induced intoxication, existing at the time when the intention to commit an offence is formed, may negate the necessary purposive element in *crimes of specific intent* (22:**3(a)**). A drunken intention is nevertheless an intention and it is for the jury to decide whether, at the material time, the defendant had the requisite intent (not merely whether

he was capable of forming it). In *offences of basic intent,* the reckless or intentional consumption of drink or drugs does not provide any defence — and might itself constitute adequate *mens rea.* The effect of voluntary intoxication inducing a mistake of fact is illustrated in *R* v. *O'Grady* (1987) (23:5) —

> *DPP* v. *Majewski* (1976): Convicted of various assaults, M had pleaded that he was suffering from the effects of drink or drugs at the time. Dismissing his appeal, the House of Lords held that the rule at common law was that self-induced intoxication could not be a defence to a criminal charge in which no special intent was necessary; that rule was not altered by the Criminal Justice Act 1967, s. 8 (*see* 22:**3(a)**).

> *R* v. *Hardie* (1985): After taking several Valium tablets when his relationship with a woman broke up, H started a fire in her flat whilst she was in another room. Charged *inter alia* with 'intent to endanger life and recklessness', he was convicted. However, allowing his appeal, the Court of Appeal held that the normal rule did not apply to soporific or sedative drugs, and the jury should have been left to consider whether the taking of the Valium was itself reckless.

5. The defence of mistake

A mistake of *fact* (but *not* law) may afford a defence to crimes which are *not* of strict liability, if it negates *mens rea* or a requisite intention or recklessness —

> *R* v. *Williams (Gladstone)* (1984): W was convicted of assaulting a police officer who failed to produce a warrant card and whom W mistakenly believed to be assaulting a youth. Quashing his conviction the Court of Appeal held that the jury should have been directed that: (i) the burden of proving the unlawfulness of W's actions lay on the prosecution; (ii) if W had acted under a mistake as to the facts, he should be judged according to his mistaken view; (iii) the reasonableness of W's belief was material to the question whether the belief was held at all but, if it was held, its reasonableness was irrelevant to guilt or innocence.

> *R* v. *O'Grady* (1987): Charged with the murder of a man, O'G pleaded that, being intoxicated, he had mistakenly

believed that he was being attacked. The jury was directed that, in such circumstances, he was entitled to defend himself in so far as was reasonable. He was convicted of manslaughter and the Court of Appeal held that, in respect of self-defence, reliance could not be placed on a mistake of fact induced by voluntary intoxication.

See also *R* v. *Deller* (1952) and *R* v. *Taaffe* (1984) (22:**1(a)**).

The defences of a coercive nature

6. The defence of self-defence

Under the Criminal Law Act 1967, s. 3(1), 'A person may use such force as is reasonable in the circumstances in the prevention of crime, or in effecting or assisting in the lawful arrest of offenders or suspected offenders or of persons unlawfully at large'. Whether force is 'reasonable' is a question of fact for the jury in each particular case and is related to the question of whether it would have been possible to prevent the evil by some other means. The 'prevention of crime' could well cover the protection of oneself, one's family or one's property from violence. If the defendant claims to have acted in self-defence, the onus is on the prosecution to disprove it —

R v. *Georgiades* (1989): When the police went to arrest his brother, G (a heroin dealer) was seen on a balcony with a loaded gun. Charged with possession of firearms and ammunition with intent to endanger life, he pleaded that, not having seen police in uniform, he thought he was being attacked. Allowing his appeal, the Court of Appeal held that it was a defence to show that the intent to endanger life was for a lawful purpose and the judge should have put this issue to the jury.

R v. *Hussey* (1924): Given an invalid notice to quit, H refused to vacate his rooms and, when his landlady with two friends attempted to force open his barricaded door, he fired through a broken panel and injured one of them. Quashing his conviction of unlawful wounding, the Court of Appeal held that the distinction between self-defence and defence of one's property had not been drawn to the jury's attention and, in defence of his house, a man need not retreat — because that would be giving up the dwelling to his adversary.

7.   The defence of duress

Duress is a defence in its own right (i.e. it does not involve a mere denial of *mens rea*) and it exists if threats of death or of immediate and serious physical injury to the defendant or his family (but not simply damage to property) justify any criminal act other than murder. If such evidence is adduced, the onus is on the prosecution to negate the defence (e.g. by showing that the defendant had the opportunity to escape from the threat) and not upon the defence to establish it. The test is whether, in the same situation, a sober person of reasonable firmness, with characteristics similar to those of the defendant, would have responded in the same way. Akin to duress (with coercion by persons) is the defence of *necessity* (with duress of circumstances) —

> *R* v. *Shepherd* (1988): With others, S had entered premises and had stolen goods. Charged with burglary, he claimed that, having joined the enterprise willingly, he had subsequently lost his nerve but had participated because he and his family were threatened with violence. Quashing his conviction, the Court of Appeal held that, if violence was not contemplated at the time of the voluntary participation, the defence of duress was available to S. However, it would be no defence for one who joined (or failed to take the opportunity to escape from) a group known to use violence.

> *DPP* v. *Jones* (1990): After drinking at a public house and on being attacked by a man in the car park, J took refuge in his car and drove two miles home. Charged with driving with alcohol over the prescribed limit, he raised the defence of necessity akin to duress and the justices dismissed the information. Allowing the prosecutor's appeal, the Divisional Court held that, as J had not ascertained whether he was being pursued, the defence did not justify his driving all the way home.

8.   The defence of dominating authority

It is possible for *mens rea* to be negated by compliance with the orders of a superior and, in the Armed Forces, it would appear that 'an officer or soldier acting under the orders of his superior, not being necessarily or manifestly illegal, would be justified by his orders' (*per* Willes J in *Keighley* v. *Bell* (1866) —

> *Johnson* v. *Phillips* (1976): Sitting in his car, a motorist refused to comply with the order of a police officer to reverse the wrong way down a one-way street. He was convicted of obstructing a police officer in the execution of his duty and, dismissing his appeal by way of case stated, the Divisional Court held that a police officer has power to direct a motorist to disobey traffic regulations in the interests of preserving life or property and, in doing so, he is acting in the execution of his duty.

> *R* v. *Thomas* (1816): Acting under orders to keep all boats at a distance, T (a Marine) shot and killed a boatman who persisted in approaching his ship. Finding T guilty of murder, the court held that the homicide would have been justifiable 'if the act had been necessary for the preservation of the ship'.

The capacity of minors

9. The defence of incapacity
In respect of criminal liability, the capacity of minors (persons under 18) falls into three categories:

(a) *Children under the age of 10.* Under the Children and Young Persons Act 1963, s. 16, there is a conclusive presumption that a child under the age of 10 cannot be guilty of any criminal offence — though he or she may be placed in care —

> *Walters* v. *Lunt* (1951): Parents who took a tricycle from their seven-year-old son could not be convicted of receiving stolen goods, as the boy was incapable of stealing. They could nevertheless have faced other charges.

(b) *Children aged 10 but under 14.* In this age-range there is a presumption that a child is *doli incapax* (incapable of evil) but this may be rebutted by proof of *actus reus* and *mens rea*, with a 'mischievous discretion' (i.e. a realisation by the child that what he was doing was seriously wrong). The burden of rebutting *doli incapax* lies on the prosecution — with evidence of previous convictions and character being admissible. There is an irrebuttable presumption that a boy under 14 cannot be convicted of rape or other offences involving sexual intercourse; however, he can be convicted of abetting another to commit such offences, and of indecent assault —

> *IPH* v. *Chief Constable of South Wales* (1987): Convicted of criminal damage to a van (which was pushed into a post, with its windows smashed and paint scratched), H (aged 11) had admitted to having pushed it, and that his action would cause damage. Allowing his appeal, the Divisional Court held that there was no evidence that H knew that what was done was seriously wrong and more than naughtiness or childish mischief.

> *R* v. *Coulbourn* (1988): Having fatally stabbed a fellow-schoolboy, C (aged 13 years 9 months) was convicted of murder. Though the judge had not directed the jury on the presumption of *doli incapax*, he dealt with capacity in the summing up. Upholding the conviction, the Court of Appeal held that the evidence showed that C understood the serious nature of his actions and there had not been a miscarriage of justice.

(c) *Young persons aged 14 or over*. From the age of 14 a minor is presumed to be fully responsible for his actions, but is still subject to special sanctions (*see* 7:1) —

> *R* v. *R (SM)* (1984): A few days after R (aged 15) was arrested for a series of burglaries, petrol bombs were thrown at a house occupied by people whom R suspected of tipping off the police. He said that the bombs were intended to frighten but not to injure and, at his trial for arson with intent, the judge rejected the submission that the required 'recklessness' should relate to someone of his age and characteristics, rather than the ordinary prudent man. The Court of Appeal upheld this ruling.

Progress test 23

1. Explain what is meant by 'unfit to plead' and 'diminished responsibility'. **(1)**

2. 'It is impossible to justify the retention in the criminal law of archaic rules perpetuating an unsound and unacceptable interpretation of insanity.' Discuss. **(2)**

3. Distinguish between automatism and intoxication. **(3, 4)**

4. Compare and contrast the defences of self-defence and duress. **(6, 7)**

5. Incorrectly believing that his elderly father had suffered a heart attack, Eric was driving him to a hospital when he was caught in a speed trap and warned that he would probably be prosecuted. On the way home he stopped at a public house where he met an acquaintance, Fred. The latter told Eric that his affair with a married woman would be revealed to his wife if he did not drive the get-away car for an intended burglary. Having consumed numerous drinks, Eric agreed to do so and was subsequently arrested when the plan went wrong. He now seeks your advice. **(4, 5, 7)**

The nature of inchoate offences

The offence of attempt

1. The elements of attempt

In most cases a criminal offence has three preliminary offences (attempt, incitement and conspiracy — to commit the main offence) associated with it. Each of these exists as an independent offence in itself and there is no need for the main offence to be actually committed; consequently they are often referred to as *inchoate* (i.e. undeveloped) offences. In some instances attempt (e.g. to pervert the course of justice) is not in fact inchoate but is instead a full substantive offence. In its preliminary sense, attempt was formerly a common law crime but this was abolished by the Criminal Attempts Act 1981 which applies to every offence triable on indictment except conspiracy, aiding, abetting, counselling or procuring an offence, assisting offenders and concealing arrestable offences. Section 1(1) of the Act provides that *if, with intent to commit an offence to which this section applies, a person does an act which is more than merely preparatory to the commission of the offence, he is guilty of attempting to commit the offence.* From this can be drawn:

(a) *The nature of the actus reus.* There must be some act that is sufficiently connected with the ultimate offence so as to be *more that merely preparatory.* Whether an act fulfils this requirement is a question of fact for the jury if the judge decides that there is evidence from which it could make such a finding. If possible, it is also necessary to identify where merely preparatory acts terminate and the defendant embarks on the substantive offence —

R v. *Gullefer* (1987): In order to get a greyhound race declared void, so that he could recover his stake money, G climbed on to the track to distract the dogs. Quashing his conviction of attempted theft, the Court of Appeal held that, on the facts, G's conduct was not an attempt to steal that had gone beyond the merely preparatory.

R v. *Widdowson* (1986): Buying a motor-cycle, W had completed a hire-purchase proposal form (used by the finance company for checking credit-worthiness) in the name of his next-door neighbour. Quashing W's conviction of attempting to obtain services dishonestly, the court of Appeal held that, being not more than merely preparatory, his act could not be categorised as attempt. If the finance company had responded favourably, W would still have had to complete an agreement form, in order to obtain any services.

(b) *The nature of mens rea.* It must normally be established that there was an *intent* to commit the ultimate offence and, as shown in *R* v. *Pearman* (1985) (22:**3**(a)), this is not the same as foresight of consequences. Under the 1981 Act, s. 1(2), *a person may be guilty of attempting to commit an offence to which this section applies even though the facts are such that the commission of the offence is impossible*; furthermore, under s. 1(3), *if the facts of the case had been as he believed them to be .... he shall be regarded as having had an intent to commit that offence* (e.g. attempt to kill with a defective gun or to steal from an empty pocket). In general, recklessness is no substitute for intent but in *R* v. *Khan* (1990) the Court of Appeal held that attempted rape may be committed by a man who is reckless as to whether a woman consents; this is because the attempt (and its necessary intention) relates to the physical activity (the intercourse), whilst recklessness applies to the absence of consent —

R v. *Shivpuri* (1986): S was convicted of attempting to be knowingly concerned with and harbouring a controlled drug, namely heroin. In a police interview he had admitted to possession of drugs and, in a statement under caution, he had said that he deeply suspected the substance to be heroin. On analysis it was found to be a vegetable substance similar to snuff but the Court of Appeal upheld the conviction. Dismissing S's appeal, the House of Lords held that the impossibility of the crime was no defence for a person charged with criminal attempt.

R v. *O'Toole* (1987): Barred from a public house and having made remarks indicating an intention to damage it, O'T had splashed petrol around the vestibule. He pleaded that it was spilt by accident and the judge directed the jury that, if they were satisfied that O'T attempted to damage, they should then proceed to consider whether he intended to damage the property or was reckless as to whether it be damaged. Allowing O'T's appeal, the Court of Appeal held that there was no room for recklessness when the alleged offence was attempt.

The offence of incitement

2.   The elements of incitement

Incitement can be an integral part of a substantive statutory offence (e.g. incitement to disaffection) but, in its preliminary sense, it is a common law offence to incite another to commit a crime (other than conspiracy) and it is triable summarily or on indictment (depending on the mode of trial for the main offence). It is immaterial whether it is possible for the ultimate offence to be committed or whether it was in fact undertaken.

(a) *The nature of the actus reus.* This is an express or implied, spoken or written suggestion, persuasion or threat, which is communicated to the intended person or persons. Involving some passive element of pressure or persuasion, incitement must be distinguished from aiding and abetting (*see* 22:5) which necessitates active participation —

R v. *Sirat* (1986): Seeking the death or serious injury of his wife, S urged another man to pay a (non-existent) person to do or procure the act. Quashing his conviction of incitement to cause grievous bodily harm, the Court of Appeal held that S may have been convicted of a non-existent offence for which he was not charged (incitement to incite to cause grievous bodily harm).

(b) *The nature of mens rea.* This is an intention by the defendant (albeit unaware of the criminality involved) that his persuasion should result in another person committing a crime. Incitement must be distinguished from *entrapment* — which is the inducement of someone to commit a crime with the intention of effecting a prosecution —

> *R* v. *Willis* (1976): Acting on information received about a drugs syndicate, a police officer telephoned an intermediary who said that he could supply cocaine. The officer offered to buy some and, when W and others handed it over, they were arrested. Dismissing their appeals against convictions of conspiracy to supply drugs, the Court of Appeal held that there is no defence of entrapment in English law and the *agent provacateur* had not encouraged a crime that would not otherwise have been committed.

> NOTE: Under the Police and Criminal Evidence Act 1984, s. 78, the court has a discretion to exclude evidence likely to have an adverse effect on the fairness of a trial.

The offence of conspiracy

3.   The elements of common law conspiracy

Formerly this comprised an agreement (and not merely an intention or acquiescence) by two or more persons to do an unlawful act, or a lawful act by unlawful means, with the requisite *mens rea* being the intention to carry out the agreement, coupled with knowledge of those facts which make it unlawful. Creating the statutory offence of conspiracy (*see* 24:4), the Criminal Law Act 1977 abolished the common law offence apart from:

(a) *The conspiracy to defraud.* As this can be both a common law and a statutory offence, the demarcation between the two has given rise to substantial conflict of judicial opinion —

> *R* v. *Cooke* (1986): Convicted of the common law offence of conspiracy to defraud, C (chief steward on the Paddington-Penzance train) had conspired with others to sell privately acquired beverages (in washed up plastic cups

belonging to the British Railways Board), without accounting for the proceeds. Quashing the conviction, the Court of Appeal held that the use of the cups constitutes a substantive offence (under the Theft Act 1968), conspiracy for which must be charged as such, and not as a common law conspiracy. Reversing this decision, the House of Lords upheld the conviction because conspiracy to defraud might be charged at common law regardless of the fact that the evidence might additionally disclose a substantive offence.

R v. *Levitz, Mbele and Vowell* (1989): Having set up a device enabling telephone calls (mostly from abroad) to be made without payment, L, M and V were convicted of conspiracy to defraud British Telecom. Quashing their convictions, the Court of Appeal held that there was little or no evidence of an agreement to commit fraudulent conduct (the calls being from abroad) beyond an agreement to commit statutory offences under the Theft Act 1968 and Telecommunications Act 1984.

(b) *The conspiracy to corrupt public morals or outrage public decency.* This involves a common law offence resurrected in *Shaw* v. *DPP* (1962) from the eighteenth century —

Knuller (Publishing, Printing & Promotions) v. *DPP* (1973): K published the *International Times*, a magazine containing advertisements inviting readers to meet the advertisers for the purpose of homosexual practices, in some cases for money. Although the Sexual Offences Act 1967 had legalised homosexual acts in private by consenting adults, the House of Lords upheld a conviction of conspiracy to corrupt public morals on the grounds that this offence could be committed by encouraging conduct that though not itself illegal, might be calculated to corrupt public morals.

4. The elements of statutory conspiracy
The Criminal Law Act 1977, s. 1(1), provides that *if a person agrees with any other person or persons that a course of conduct shall be pursued which .... will necessarily amount to or involve the commission of any offence or offences by one or more of the parties to the agreement or .... would do so but for the existence of facts which render the commission of*

the offence or any of the offences impossible, he is guilty of conspiracy to commit the offence or offences in question. It is a matter for the judge to decide whether the evidence against each defendant is markedly different — thus making it possible for the jury to convict one and acquit the other.

(a) *The nature of the actus reus.* This is the agreement that must involve two or more persons and it cannot exist if a defendant is the intended victim of the offence, or if the only other person(s) with whom he agrees (both initially and at all times during the currency of the agreement) are his spouse, a person under the age of 10 or an intended victim of the offence —

> *R* v. *McDonnell* (1965): It was held that M could not be guilty of conspiracy with a company of which he was a director and the sole person responsible for its acts.

(b) *The nature of mens rea.* This is the intention of the defendant to play some part in a course of conduct that, to his knowledge, would amount to or involve the commission of an offence. It is not necessary, however, that there should be an intention on the part of each conspirator that the offence should actually be committed. If it can be committed without knowledge of 'a particular fact or circumstance' (e.g. sexual intercourse with a girl who is not known to be under 16), there cannot be a conviction of conspiracy unless the fact or circumstance is known to the defendant. *Mens rea* must be such as to recognise the innocence of those who agree to a course of conduct in order to expose and frustrate the criminal purpose of others —

> *R* v. *Anderson* (1985): Remanded in Lewes prison and expecting to be released on bail, A agreed to participate in a plan to free a cell-mate. He was to supply two others with diamond wire, for cutting metal bars, and would be paid £20,000. On his release he received £2,000 but was then injured in a road accident and took no further part. The House of Lords upheld his conviction of conspiracy to effect the escape of a prisoner, contrary to the Criminal Law Act 1977, s. 1.

> *R* v. *El-Ghazal* (1986): Having knowingly introduced two people to each other, so that one should acquire cocaine,

E-G was convicted of conspiracy unlawfully to possess cocaine, contrary to the Criminal Law Act 1977, s.1. The Court of Appeal upheld his conviction as he knew the purpose of the introduction.

Progress test 24

1.   Examine the Criminal Attempts Act 1981, s. 1(1)   **(1)**

2.   Discuss the offence of incitement.   **(2)**

3.   'Legal uncertainty in the distinction between common law and statutory conspiracy to defraud has been unreasonably costly.' Discuss.   **(3)**

4.   Examine the Criminal Law Act 1977, s. 1(1).   **(4)**

5.   Employed by an electronics company and contacted by a stranger who offered him £60,000 for a secret component, George persuaded Hugo, a storeman, to leave his jacket on a table for 10 minutes with his keys in a pocket. Before George could do anything, however, a suspicious security officer had discovered and impounded the keys. Assess criminal liability. **(1, 2, 4)**

The nature of offences against the person

The offences of a fatal nature

1. The *actus reus* of murder

Murder (the fixed penalty for which is life imprisonment) is committed *if a person of sound mind unlawfully kills any human creature in being and within the Queen's peace, with malice aforethought, so that death occurs within a year and a day.* The *actus reus* is the causing of death and, for this to constitute murder:

(a) *It must be committed by a person of sound mind.* The defence of insanity and the plea of diminished responsibility are summarised in 23:**1–2**. *See also R* v. *Coulborn* (1988) 23:**9(b)**).

(b) *It must be unlawful.* Lawful homicide may occur if death is caused when a person uses 'such force as is reasonable in the circumstances in the prevention of crime, or in effecting or assisting in the lawful arrest of offenders or of persons unlawfully at large' (Criminal Law Act 1967, s. 3(1) — *see* 23:**6**).

(c) *It must concern a human creature in being.* An infant is considered as 'in being' when it has an existence independent of its mother — i.e. when totally extruded from the mother's body and alive — though the umbilical cord need not have been cut. Death of an infant born alive from injuries inflicted in the womb may constitute murder or manslaughter. The infliction of injuries that prevent an infant from being born alive is a separate offence (e.g. child destruction or procurement of a miscarriage).

(d) *It must be within the Queen's peace.* Nowadays this covers all persons in Her Majesty's territories except rebels and alien enemies actually engaged in hostile operations against the Crown. In practice, British courts have jurisdiction over murders committed by aliens on British territory (including ships and aircraft) or by British citizens anywhere in the world —

> *R* v. *Page* (1954): Having killed an Egyptian national in Egypt, P, a British soldier, was convicted of murder by a court martial. Upholding the conviction, the Courts Martial Appeal Court criticised the statement in the *Manual of Military Law* that it must be proved in the case of murder that the victim was within the Queen's peace, and that the army carries the Queen's peace with it, wherever it goes.

(e) *It must cause death within a year and a day.* It must be proved that the victim died within a year and a day of the acts committed by the defendant and, if there was a series of acts, the time runs from the last one. Death occurring outside this period is presumed attributable to some other cause; consequently a question could arise over criminal infection with AIDS. The chain of causation is considered in 22:2(b).

2. The *mens rea* of murder

The *mens rea* of murder is *malice aforethought* and this means *an intention to kill or to cause very serious bodily harm.* As stated in *R* v. *Pearman* (1985) (22:3(a)), intention may be inferred from (but must not be equated with) foresight of consequences. In *R* v. *Hancock and Shankland* (1986) (*below*), the House of Lords held that a jury should be directed that the likelihood of a consequence being foreseen is in proportion to its degree of probability and, if it was foreseen, it is more likely to have been intended —

> *R* v. *Hancock and Shankland* (1986): A block of concrete pushed off a bridge by H and S (striking miners) fell on to the motorway below, killing the driver of a taxi taking a miner to work. H and S were convicted of murder but the Court of Appeal substituted convictions for manslaughter and the House of Lords dismissed the Crown's appeal.

> *R* v. *Nedrick* (1986): Having poured petrol through a house letter box and set it alight, N caused the death of a child. Admitting the arson, he claimed that he did not want anyone to die and the judge directed the jury that foresight equated with intention. Quashing a conviction of murder,

and substituting one for manslaughter, the Court of Appeal held that the direction was clearly wrong.

3. The elements of voluntary manslaughter

Manslaughter (punishable with any sentence — from absolute discharge to life imprisonment) is found in two forms — voluntary and involuntary. Voluntary manslaughter connotes an unlawful killing *with the mens rea necessary for murder* but mitigated under the Homicide Act 1957 in the following ways:

(a) *The plea of diminished responsibility* (s. 2(1) of the 1957 Act). This is outlined in 23:1(c).

(b) *The defence of provocation.* The defence of duress (23:7) is not available to a defendant charged with murder but it must be distinguished from provocation. Whereas in duress the words or actions of one person break the will of another, in provocation they break his self-control. Under s. 3 of the 1957 Act 'where on a charge of murder there is evidence on which the jury can find that the person charged was provoked (whether by things done or by things said, or by both together) to lose his self-control, the question whether the provocation was enough to make a reasonable man do as he did shall be left to be determined by the jury; and, in determining that question, the jury shall take into account everything, both done and said, according to the effect which, in their opinion, it would have on a reasonable man.' It should be emphasised that provocation is a defence only to a charge of murder and, if successful, it results in a conviction of manslaughter but not an absolute acquittal. Moreover, if the judge decides that there is some evidence of provocation, he must direct the jury to decide whether the defendant was actually provoked and whether a reasonable man, with characteristics similar to those of the defendant, would have responded in a like manner, if so provoked —

> *R* v. *Doughty* (1986): Losing his temper with his baby who had persistently cried for several hours, D put cushions over the child's head and knelt on them. The infant died and D was convicted of murder, with the judge having refused to allow the defence of provocation to be put to the jury. Quashing the conviction and substituting one of manslaughter, the Court of Appeal held that, on account of

the causal link between the crying of the baby and D's response, s. 3 of the 1957 Act was mandatory.

R v. *Sawyer* (1989): Having fatally stabbed another man in the chest, S had admitted to the police that, in accusing the other of stealing his girocheque, he had lost his temper. He denied this admission, which might have substantiated provocation and, refusing leave for him to appeal against conviction of murder, the Court of Appeal held that the judge would have been wrong if he had put the issue to the jury on such a slender basis.

(c) *The survival from a suicide pact.* Under s. 4(3) of the 1957 Act, a suicide pact is 'a common agreement between two or more persons, having for its object the death of all of them, whether or not each is to take his own life'. If a party to such a pact survives, s. 4(1) of the Act provides that 'it shall be manslaughter and shall not be murder for a person, acting in pursuance of a suicide pact between him and another, to kill the other or be party to the other being killed by a third person'.

4.   The elements of involuntary manslaughter
Involuntary manslaughter connotes an unlawful killing *without the mens rea necessary for murder* and basically it falls into two main categories:

(a) *The acts of constructive manslaughter.* Constructive manslaughter exists when the defendant commits *an unlawful act* (i.e. a criminal offence), which a reasonable and sober person would consider to be *dangerous* (i.e. likely to cause physical injury, however slight). In view of the principle of transferred malice (22:**3(d)**), it is not necessary for the act to have been directed at the deceased —

R v. *Watson* (1989): In the process of burgling a flat, W and another verbally abused the occupier, who had a weak heart and died 90 minutes later. The Court of Appeal held that the unlawful act of burglary existed, also that a reasonable and sober bystander would have immediately noticed the occupier's vulnerability; thus, if his death resulted from an act that the bystander would have considered dangerous, then manslaughter would have occurred.

R v. *Arobieke* (1988): After quarrelling with another man,
A was seen walking along a railway platform looking into a
train that had been boarded by the other person. The latter
then jumped down on to the tracks and was fatally
electrocuted. Quashing A's conviction of manslaughter, the
Court of Appeal held that merely looking into a train,
without knowing whether another party was on it, did not
constitute an unlawful act.

(b) *The acts of criminal negligence.* Criminal negligence is of a much
more serious nature than that which would give rise to liability in
tort (*see* 18:1) and for manslaughter there must be proof of gross
negligence. The test is whether a reasonable person would have
considered that the defendants's conduct was such as to create an
obvious and serious risk of causing physical injury to another; if
not, any negligence would be insufficiently grave. As shown in *R*
v. *Stone*; *R* v. *Dobinson* (1977) (22:2(e)), an unlawful omission can
equate to gross negligence if the defendant is under a legal duty
to act —

R v. *Seymour* (1983): Driving a lorry to push his car,
S crushed to death a woman who was getting out of it.
Upholding his conviction for manslaughter, the House of
Lords held that, in such circumstances, the jury should be
directed that they must be satisfied that the defendant drove
in such a manner as to create an obvious and serious risk of
causing physical injury to some other person who might
happen to be using the road. *See also R* v. *Caldwell* (1981)
(22:**3(b)**).

The non-fatal offences of a physical nature

5.   The elements of assault
Outlined in 19:6(a)–(b) is the common law distinction between
assault (intentionally putting another person in reasonable fear of
immediate violence) and battery (intentionally causing contact
with the person of another). In addition to being a tort, assault is
also a crime, with aggravated derivatives shown in **(b)** and **(c)** *below*.
It is therefore necessary to distinguish:

(a) *The nature of common assault.* Under the Criminal Justice Act

1988, this is only a summary offence and, although assault may be limited to its strict definition above, it has also acquired a broader connotation that embraces battery. For assault in its narrower sense, the *actus reus* is the creation in the mind of another (possibly even by mere words) the belief that unlawful force is to be used immediately against him — and the *mens rea* is the intention to create that belief. For battery, the *actus reus* is the application of the slightest force (with no need for any resultant harm) and the *mens rea* is the intention to apply that force. The main defences to such a prosecution are self-defence (23:6), lawful and reasonable chastisement (e.g. of children) and consent. As merely touching a person could constitute battery, consent is constantly being impliedly given to potential offences (e.g. by participation in contact sports) but it cannot be a defence to a charge of assault occasioning actual bodily harm (*see* **(b)** *below*) and it can be negated if the conduct was unreasonable, if there was vitiation by fraud or ignorance, or if there was a likelihood of resultant death —

> *Logdon* v.*DPP* (1976): Demanding the payment of money, which he alleged was owed to his client, L showed a gun (which he said was loaded) to a VAT official and threatened to hold her hostage. When he saw her shaking, he handed over the weapon, which was a replica. He was convicted of assault and, upholding the conviction, the Divisional Court held that the offence involved a threat of unlawful force committed when, by a physical act, the threatener intentionally or recklessly caused the threatened person to believe that such force was about to be inflicted on him.

> *R* v. *Jones*; *R* v. *Campbell* (1986): In a school game two boys were seriously injured after being thrown in the air by J, C and others. Prosecuted for assault, they claimed that they had not foreseen such serious injury but they changed their pleas to guilty after the judge declined to give a direction that they should be acquitted if the jury thought that they indulged in 'rough and undisciplined' play with no intent to injure and in the genuine belief that the victims consented. Allowing their appeals, the Court of Appeal held that, even if far-fetched, such a defence should have been left to the jury and pleas had been changed only because of the ruling.

(b) *The nature of assault occasioning actual bodily harm* Under the Offences Against the Person Act 1861, s. 47 (as amended), it is an offence to commit an assault (in the broader sense) on another, thereby causing actual bodily harm. The *actus reus* is the assault or battery leading to the harm and the *mens rea* is an intention to commit the assault or recklessness (as determined by the *Cunningham* test — 22:3(b)). 'Bodily harm' means hurt or injury calculated to interfere with a person's health or comfort —

> *R* v. *Spratt* (1990): Having wounded a young girl with two air-pistol pellets fired from a window, S pleaded guilty to s. 47 assault but claimed that he was unaware of the child's presence and gave no thought to the risk. Appealing against conviction, he contended that his plea did not reveal *mens rea*. Quashing the conviction, the Court of Appeal held that the *mens rea* for s. 47 required that S should have foreseen that the particular type of harm would result and yet had gone on to take the risk of it. Mere failure to give thought to the possibility of risk was insufficient and the basis of the plea did not amount to the admission of an offence.

(c) *The nature of assault on a police officer.* Under the Police Act 1964, s. 51(1), it is an offence to assault a constable (or anyone assisting him) in the execution of his duty. The *mens rea* is the intention to assault (in its broader sense) and there is no need for knowledge that the person concerned was a constable (which here includes a prison officer) or that he was acting in the execution of his duty — though the onus is on the prosecution to prove that he was so acting —

> *Weight* v. *Long* (1986): After an argument, L's girlfriend walked off and he followed her, to see if she was all right and to ask the way home. Whilst he was so doing, he was twice approached by a constable and, on the second occasion, he punched and kicked the officer. Acquitting L of a s. 51(1) offence, the justices held that the officer had not been acting in the execution of his duty, as he had no reason to believe that an offence had been (or was being, or would be) committed. Allowing the prosecutor's appeal, the Divisional Court held that a constable was acting in the

execution of his duty if his intention in attempting to speak to someone was in pursuit of the preservation of peace or prevention of crime. *See also DPP* v. *Hawkins* (1988) (8:**2(b)**).

6.   The elements of wounding

In its broader sense, assault may result in wounding or the infliction of grievous bodily harm (i.e. serious injury). To constitute a wounding there must be a breach of the continuity of the skin — consequently, even when a bone is fractured, there can be no wounding if the skin is unbroken. Under the Offences Against the Person Act 1861 there are two relevant crimes and it is therefore necessary to distinguish:

(a) *The nature of unlawful and malicious wounding.* Under s. 20 of the 1861 Act, it is an offence *unlawfully and maliciously to wound or inflict any grievous bodily harm upon any other person, either with or without any weapon or instrument.* The *actus reus* is the unlawful wounding or infliction of grievous bodily harm, with *unlawful* connoting a lack of consent or self-defence. The *mens rea* is the fact that the defendant acted *maliciously* — i.e. foresaw that some physical harm to another would be the consequence of his act — though he need not actually have foreseen that the harm would be as grave as that which occurred. A defendant charged with this crime can be convicted of the lesser offence of assault occasioning actual bodily harm —

> *R* v. *Parmenter* (1990): Convicted of four offences of inflicting grievous bodily harm on his infant son, P had claimed that he was inexperienced with small babies and did not realise that his handling of the child (confirmed by a paediatrician as being not inappropriate for a three to four year old) was totally unsuitable for one newly-born. Substituting a conviction for assault occasioning actual bodily harm, the Court of Appeal held that the jury had been inadvertently misled into thinking that they had to determine whether P 'ought to have foreseen' (as opposed to 'actually foresaw') the consequence of his acts.

> *W (a minor)* v. *Dolbey* (1989): Pointing an air-rifle at another, W was twice told not to do so but, mistakenly believing the fact, he said that the gun was unloaded. Pulling the trigger,

he caused injury and, convicting him of malicious wounding, the justices held that ignoring the risk of the gun being loaded was recklessness amounting to malicious intent. Allowing W's appeal, the Divisional Court considered the *Cunningham* test (22:**3(b)**) and held that, in the circumstances, recklessness as to whether the gun was loaded could not amount to malice.

(b) *The nature of wounding with intent.* Under the Offences Against the Person Act 1861, s. 18, it is an offence *unlawfully and maliciously, by any means whatsoever, to wound or cause any grievous bodily harm to any person, with intent to do some grievous bodily harm to any person or with intent to resist or prevent the lawful apprehension or detaining of any person.* The *actus reus* is thus virtually the same as that of unlawful and malicious wounding, though the use of the word *cause* (as opposed to *inflict*) removes a need for assault by the defendant (thus the releasing of a fierce dog against the victim would be sufficient). To establish *mens rea,* it must be proved that the defendant acted with the specific intent of causing grievous bodily harm or preventing arrest (thus mere recklessness would be insufficient). The offence is punishable with life imprisonment —

> *R* v. *Stubbs* (1989): Involved in a fight and using a knife, which he carried for his work, S stabbed another man in the stomach. Charged with wounding with intent, he claimed to have been so drunk that he could not remember what he did. As the Crown and judge accepted a plea to unlawful and malicious wounding, S was sentenced to 30 months' imprisonment. Allowing the appeal, the Court of Appeal held that, in the circumstances, the drunkenness had not been so extreme as to justify the reduction of a s. 18 charge to s. 20. *See also R v. Pearman* (22:**3(a)**).

The non-fatal offences of a sexual nature

7. The elements of rape

Under the Sexual Offences Act 1956, s. 1, it is an offence for a man to rape a woman and the Sexual Offences (Amendment) Act 1976 provides that *a man commits rape if he has unlawful sexual intercourse with a woman who, at the time, does not consent to it and, at the time, he knows she does not consent, or is reckless as to whether she consents to it.* The *actus reus* is the unlawful sexual intercourse with a non-consenting woman and the *mens rea* is the knowledge that there is no consent or recklessness as to whether it exists. In a prosecution for rape it is therefore necessary to prove:

(a) *The act of unlawful sexual intercourse.* The intercourse is deemed complete upon proof of penetration of the vagina by the penis and it is not necessary for the hymen to be ruptured or for there to be emission of seed. The slightest penetration will suffice and, if none is proved, the defendant may be charged with attempt. The intercourse must be unlawful; consequently, from 1736 it was accepted that a husband could not be guilty of rape upon his wife — unless, in latter years, there existed a divorce decree, judicial separation or injunction. However, in *R* v. *R (a husband)* (1991), the Court of Appeal held that a rapist remained a rapist subject to the criminal law irrespective of his relationship with his victim. This was certified as a point of law of general public importance and leave was given for appeal to the House of Lords.

(b) *The absence of consent.* Consent may range from actual desire to reluctant acquiescence and the issue should not be left to the jury without further direction. A conviction does not require proof that the victim put up any resistance but consent is vitiated if the rape was effected by fraud, force or the inducement of fear — or if the victim did not understand the nature of the act —

> *R* v. *Olugboja* (1981): O and another man forced two girls to a bungalow where O told one that he was going to have intercourse with her. She asked him to leave her alone but did what he told her. The House of Lords held that, although no specific threats had been made, the girl had submitted through fear of what might happen if she did not, and the intercourse was non-consensual.

> *R* v. *Birchall, Pollock and Tatton* (1986): An educationally subnormal 15-year old girl with a mental age of 11 attended a party and consumed a considerable quantity of alcohol. She was placed on a bed fully clothed and found by B, P and T who all had sexual intercourse with her. Charged with rape, they claimed that she had consented but, giving evidence, she denied this and the prosecution argued that,

being insensible, she had been incapable of consenting. Allowing the appeals, the Court of Appeal held that the jury should have been directed about the need for corroboration of the girl's evidence.

(c) *The existence of knowledge or recklessness.* For a conviction of rape, the prosecution must prove that the defendant knew that the woman did not want sexual intercourse or was reckless as to whether or not she wanted it. The jury should be directed that if, albeit mistakenly, he genuinely believed that she wanted intercourse, he should be acquitted. In considering whether his belief was genuine, they should take into account all the circumstances and ask themselves whether he had reasonable grounds for such a belief. If they cannot find such grounds, he should be convicted; likewise, if they decide that he could not have cared less whether or not the woman consented, but carried on regardless, he should be found guilty of reckless rape —

> *R* v. *Fotheringham* (1989): Claiming that he was so drunk that he mistook the babysitter for his wife, F was convicted of raping her. Dismissing his appeal, the Court of Appeal held that self-induced intoxication was no defence, whether the issue was intention, consent or mistaken identity.

> *R* v. *Breckenridge* (1984): Convicted of attempted rape, B appealed on the ground of misdirection and, allowing the appeal, the Court of Appeal held that, in reckless rape, the jury must be directed that they can convict only if they conclude that the defendant's attitude as to whether the complainant consented was that he could not care less.

8. The elements of unlawful sexual intercourse

Under the Sexual Offences Act 1956, ss. 5, 6(1) and 7(1), it is an offence for a man to have unlawful sexual intercourse with a girl under the age of 13 and, subject to certain exceptions, with a girl under 16 or with a woman who is a defective. In the case of a girl under 13 the offence is one of strict liability — thus belief that she was older is no defence and her consent is immaterial (though absence of it could give ground for a rape charge). If a girl is between 13 and 16, it is a defence for a man to show that he had reasonable cause for believing that she was his wife (though the marriage would be invalid) or that he was under the age of 24 and had not previously been charged with a like offence and had reasonable cause for believing her to be 16 or over —

> *R v. Taylor, Roberts and Simons* (1977):T, R and S were convicted of unlawful sexual intercourse, having engaged in various repeated sexual acts with a 14-year old girl, described as 'undoubtedly a wanton' and 'treated as the village whore'. Upholding their convictions, the Court of Appeal held that consent was no defence.

> *R v. O'Grady* (1978): Having received suggestive letters from a 14-year old girl, O'G (who was of the same age group) succumbed to her advances and had intercourse with her. He was sentenced to three months at a detention centre but the Court of Appeal held that, when the parties are in the same age-group and both willing, a custodial sentence would be inappropriate.

9.   The elements of indecent assault

Under the Sexual Offences Act 1956, ss. 14–15, it is an offence for any person (male or female, including boys under 14) to make an indecent assault upon a male or female. The essentials of indecent assault are:

(a) *The nature of the actus reus.* There must be an intentional or reckless assault (in either its narrow or broader sense — 25:5) in circumstances of indecency (probably meaning an overt sexual element). Consent is no defence if it has been obtained by fraud, if the intended or probable consequence of the assault is the infliction of bodily harm, or if the consenting party is under the age of 16 or mentally defective —

> *R v. Thomas* (1985): Having invited her to kiss him, T rubbed a schoolgirl's skirt but walked away when she objected. Quashing his conviction of indecent assault, the Court of Appeal held that indecency could not properly be inferred from such evidence and it was not necessarily sufficient to show an act that a child was demonstrably reluctant to accept.

R v. *Hall* (1988): Charged with indecent assault on a female ex-student with a mental age of 9, H was principal of a college for the mentally-handicapped. Admitting the assault, he argued that the victim had consented and was not 'defective', as she was only moderately impaired. Upholding H's conviction, the Court of Appeal held that a mentally handicapped woman is 'defective' if she suffers severe impairment of intelligence and social function, by comparison with persons of normal development.

(b) *The nature of mens rea.* If, on a charge of indecent assault, the facts are just as consistent with an innocent interpretation as with a guilty one, proof of an indecent intention is required and, in these circumstances, proof of motive is admissible. However, if the facts of the assault are incapable of being regarded as indecent, no undisclosed intention on the part of the defendant can make the assault indecent —

R v. Court (1988): Having struck a 12-year-old girl about 12 times on her buttocks outside her skirt, C was asked by the police for his reasons and replied 'I don't know — buttock fetish'. He was convicted of indecent assault and, dismissing his appeal, the House of Lords enunciated the principles outlined above.

R v. Pratt (1984): Having forced two boys to undress, P claimed that his sole motive was to search for cannabis, which he thought they had taken from him. It was held that an indecent intention had to be proved by the prosecution.

Progress test 25

1. Describe the *actus reus* and *mens rea* of murder. **(1, 2)**

2. Distinguish between voluntary and involuntary manslaughter. **(3, 4)**

3. Compare and contrast the various offences of assault and wounding. **(5, 6)**

4. Examine the essential elements of rape. **(7)**

5. Ivor was driving a power boat, towing Jason who was water-skiing, when his attention was distracted by a girl sunbathing on the beach. As a result, the boat suddenly veered off course and Jason's skis hit Karen, who was swimming nearby and who drowned. Late that night Leslie, Karen's fiancé who had been drinking heavily, threw a petrol bomb through Ivor's bedroom window but it failed to ignite. Assess any criminal liability. **(3, 4, 5, 6)**

The nature of offences against property

The essentials of theft, robbery and burglary

1. The *actus reus* of theft

Under the Theft Act 1968, s. 1, *a person is guilty of theft if he dishonestly appropriates property belonging to another with the intention of permanently depriving the other of it.* The *actus reus* is the appropriation of property belonging to another, thus it is relevant to examine:

(a) *The nature of appropriation.* Under s. 3(1) of the 1968 Act, *any assumption by a person of the rights of an owner amounts to an appropriation.* This means that a person effects an appropriation when he commits any act relating to the property that only an owner can do —

> *R* v. *Morris*; *Anderton* v. *Burnside* (1983): In supermarkets, M and B each removed labels from goods and replaced them with ones showing lower prices, which they paid at the check-out. Both were convicted of theft and, dismissing their appeals, the House of Lords held that the changing of the labels was something that only an owner could do; therefore, there had been an appropriation within s. 3(1).

> *R* v. *Navvabi* (1986): Having opened various bank accounts in false names, N obtained gaming chips at casinos with cheques supported by a banker's card and drawn on empty accounts. Allowing his appeal against conviction of theft, the Court of Appeal held that the use of a cheque and card in these circumstances was not an appropriation within s. 3(1).

(b) *The nature of property.* Under s. 4 of the 1968 Act, 'property' *includes money and all other property, real or personal, including things in action (see* 15:5) *and other intangible property.* In effect, it includes gas and water but not electricity (the dishonest use of which is provided for in s. 13). Land cannot be stolen except by a person who holds property on trust for another *or* who is not in possession of the land and appropriates anything severed from it *or* who is a tenant and appropriates all or part of a fixture or structure let to be used with the land. The picking of wild mushrooms, flowers, fruit or foliage is not theft unless it is for reward — though there may be an offence under the Wildlife and Countryside Act 1981. Similarly, wild creatures not tamed or ordinarily kept in captivity cannot be stolen — but under Schedule 1 to the 1968 Act it is an offence to take or kill deer in enclosed land or to take fish from water that is subject to private rights; furthermore, poaching is covered by other statutes —

> *R v. Kohn* (1979): For his own purposes, K, an accountant, drew various sums from a company account, using company cheques. The Court of Appeal upheld his conviction of theft as there was an appropriation of the cheques themselves and also of things in action (i.e. debts owed by a bank to a customer whose account is in credit or overdrawn within agreed limits).

> *Oxford* v. *Moss* (1979): M, a university student, obtained a proof of his examination paper, which he photocopied and intended to return. Upholding his acquittal of theft, the Divisional Court held that confidential information was not tangible property and therefore it could not be stolen.

(c) *The nature of possession.* Under s. 5 of the 1968 Act, *property shall be regarded as belonging to any person having possession or control of it, or having in it any proprietary right to interest* or if it has been received from another for a particular purpose (e.g. a contribution to a fund) *or* if it has been obtained by another's mistake (e.g. receiving a £10 note tendered in mistake for £5, or a debt mistakenly repaid twice over) —

> *R* v. *Turner* (1971): to evade payment, T removed his car from the garage where it had been repaired, without telling the proprietor. Upholding his conviction of theft, the Court of Appeal held that the property was in the possession or control of the garage.

R v. *Davis* (1989): Having received two housing benefit cheques sent in error, instead of one, D cashed both and was convicted of theft. The Court of Appeal held that the cash received represented the 'proceeds' of property obtained by another's mistake, within s. 5(4).

2. The *mens rea* of theft

The *mens rea* of theft has two components:

(a) *The proof of dishonesty.* In this context a person acts dishonestly if his conduct would be regarded as dishonest by the ordinary standards of reasonable people, and he realises that it is so regarded. Under s. 2 of the 1968 Act, the appropriation may be dishonest even if the defendant is willing to pay for the property (e.g. leaves behind money even greater than its value). However, it would *not* be dishonest (and the defendant could make 'a claim of right') if he believed that he had a legal right to deprive the other of the property *or* that the other would have consented if he had known of the appropriation and the circumstances *or* that the owner could not be discovered by taking reasonable steps —

> *R* v. *Small* (1988): Charged with stealing a car, S claimed that he thought it had been abandoned, as it had been left unmoved for some days with no petrol, also a flat tyre and battery. The judge's direction to the jury was in effect that an unreasonably held belief in abandonment could not be an honest belief. Quashing S's conviction, the Court of Appeal held that the jury should have been directed to consider whether, according to the standard of reasonable and honest people, the act was dishonest — and, if so, whether S realised that his conduct was dishonest by that standard.

> *R* v. *Robinson* (1977): Charged with robbing a man whose wife owed him £7, R was convicted of theft, the judge having directed the jury that the defence necessitated an *honest* belief in a legal right. Quashing the conviction, the Court of Appeal held that it did not have to be an honest belief.

(b) *The intention of permanently depriving.* Under s. 6 of the 1968 Act, a person is to be regarded as having the intention of permanently depriving another of his property *if his intention is to treat the thing as his own, to dispose of regardless of the other's rights;* thus a borrowing may be sufficient if it is *for a period and in circumstances making it equivalent to an outright taking or disposal.* In view of a frequent absence of intention permanently to deprive, s. 12(1) of the 1968 Act creates a separate offence for the temporary appropriation of motor vehicles (taking a conveyance without consent or authority — *see* 22:2(a)) —

> *R* v. *Velumyl* (1989): Having taken £1,050 from his employer's safe, without authority and contrary to company rules, V (a manager) claimed that he lent the money to a friend and expected to return it on the following Monday. Upholding his conviction of theft, the Court of Appeal held that, not intending to return the actual notes and coins that he had taken, V had the requisite intention of permanently depriving.

> *R* v. *Lloyd*; *R* v. *Bhuee*; *R* v. *Ali* (1985): Films taken from a cinema by the projectionist were copied on to video cassettes by his associates and returned before their absence had been noticed. L, B and A were charged with conspiracy to steal and, quashing their convictions, the Court of Appeals held that there was no theft, as the borrowing had not been for such a period or in such circumstances as to amount to an outright taking or disposal. There would have to have been an intention to return the thing taken in such a changed state that it had lost all its goodness or virtue.

3. The elements of robbery

Under s. 8(1) of the 1968 Act, *a person is guilty of robbery if he steals, and immediately before or at the time of doing so, and in order to do so, he uses force on any person or puts or seeks to put any person in fear of being then and there subjected to force.* For a conviction of robbery (really an aggravated theft and punishable with life imprisonment), it is therefore necessary to prove:

(a) *The act of stealing.* If any of the elements necessary for theft should not exist, then there cannot be a conviction of robbery;

similarly, all of the defences open to one charged with theft are available also for robbery —

> *Corcoran* v. *Anderton* (1980): Two men attempted to snatch a woman's handbag and, striking her in the back, the first tugged at the bag, which fell to the ground. The woman screamed and the men ran away. Convicted of robbery, C (the second man) appealed on the ground that, as there had been no appropriation of the bag, his conduct could not have exceeded attempt. Upholding the conviction, the Divisional Court held that the tugging could amount to a sufficient degree of control to constitute appropriation.

(b) *The use of force.* Accidental force or slight physical contact will not suffice but the force may nevertheless be minimal. The fact that it can be used 'on any person' means that it may be effected against someone other than the one whose property is stolen (e.g. holding a person hostage or at gun-point) —

> *R* v. *Maxwell* (1990): After his business partner (one Lewis) had walked out with a computer and 40 discs, M offered a group of men £1,500 to retake the discs at the house of one Richardson (where Lewis was living). During the raid the Richardsons suffered extreme violence, as a result of which M and the others were convicted of robbery. M had argued that he would have pleaded guilty to burglary but was innocent of robbery, as he had never intended the use of violence. When the jury sought direction, the judge stated that burglary was not an alternative charge (but failed to mention the possibility of theft). The House of Lords upheld the conviction.

> *R* v. *Clouden* (1987): Having approached a woman from behind, C wrenched her basket down from her hands and escaped with it. Convicted of robbery, he appealed on the ground that force had been used on the property but not the person of the woman. Upholding his conviction, the Court of Appeal held that whether force was used in order to steal was an issue for the jury.

(c) *The timing of force.* The use of force must occur *immediately before or at the time of* the stealing. Thus force used to acquire information needed for a theft to be committed some time later, or used after a theft had been completed, would not convert it to robbery —

> *R* v. *Donaghy and Marshall* (1981): After D and M threatened the life of a mini-cab driver, he drove them to London, where they stole £22 from him. It was held that, in order to convict of robbery, the jury had to be satisfied that the defendants gave the impression by their manner that they were continuing the threats at the time of the theft.

4. The elements of burglary

Under s. 9(1) of the 1968 Act, a person is guilty of burglary if: (*a*) he enters any building or part of a building as a trespasser, with intent to commit offences of stealing anything in the building, of inflicting on any person therein grievous bodily harm, of raping any woman therein, or of doing unlawful damage to the building or anything therein; also (*b*) if, having entered any building or part of a building as a trespasser, he steals or attempts to steal anything, or inflicts or attempts to inflict on any person therein any grievous bodily harm. Within the meaning of the Act, it is therefore necessary to examine:

(a) *The nature of an entry.* The word 'enters' is not defined in the Act and can give rise to various possible interpretations. At common law there has been held to be entry if any part of the defendant's body crosses the threshold or if there has been the insertion of an instrument for effecting the main offence (e.g. a butterfly-net to remove valuables), but not if the instrument is used solely for gaining entry —

> *R* v. *Brown* (1985): Convicted of burglary, B had broken a shop window and rummaged about with the top half of his body inside the window. Upholding his conviction, the Court of Appeal held that there had been a substantial and effective 'entry'.

(b) *The nature of a building.* The word 'building' covers dwellings, factories, offices, shops, etc., also (under s. 9(3) of the 1968 Act) 'an inhabited vehicle or vessel' regardless of whether a person living therein is present or absent. The words 'part of a building' provide for situations where someone has a right to be in one part but not another —

Norfolk Constabulary v. *Seekings and Gould* (1986): Convicted of attempted burglary, S and G had entered two articulated lorry trailers, which were being used as temporary storage space on a building site. They were fitted with steps and supplied with electricity but, on appeal, it was held that they were not buildings within s. 9(3).

R v. *Walkington* (1979): Charged with burglary, W had been seen to enter the counter area of a department store and open the drawer of a till (which was empty). The judge directed the jury to decide whether the counter area was 'part of a building', whether W had knowingly entered it as a trespasser and whether at that time he intended to steal. Upholding W's conviction, the Court of Appeal held that a person entering premises intending to steal is guilty of an offence irrespective of the fact that there is nothing in the premises worth stealing.

(c) *The nature of a trespasser.* For a conviction it is essential to prove that the defendant must have known (or be reckless as to the fact) that he entered a building without consent or by fraud —

R v. *Collins* (1973): At 4 am a girl awoke and saw on her window sill a naked, blond young man. Concluding that he was her boyfriend, she invited him in and sexual intercourse took place. When she turned on the light, she realised that it was not her boyfriend — but C, who was convicted of burglary with intent to commit rape. The Court of Appeal quashed the conviction as the jury had not been directed to consider whether C knew he was entering without an invitation or was reckless whether he did so or not.

R v. *Jones*; *R* v. *Smith* (1976): Entering a bungalow belonging to the father of one of them, J and S stole two television sets. Convicted of burglary, they appealed on the ground that a person such as a son, with general permission to enter, could not be a trespasser. Upholding their convictions, the Court of Appeal held that, as the permission given had been exceeded, the jury were entitled to find that they were trespassers.

(d) *The nature of the intent.* The *mens rea* is the intent of stealing (*see R* v. *Walkington* (1979) 26:**4(b)**), inflicting grievous bodily harm (*see* 25:**6**), raping a woman (*see* 25:**7**) or unlawfully damaging the building or its contents (*see* 26:**10**) —

> *R* v. *Bozickovic* (1978): Having been seen leaving a flat that he had no right to enter, B was charged with burglary with intent to steal. Nothing had been stolen or disturbed and B claimed to have been too drunk to know what he was doing. A submission of no case to answer was allowed.

> *R* v. *Jenkins* (1983): Charged with burglary in that 'he inflicted grievous bodily harm on .... therein', J was found guilty of the lesser offence of assault occasioning actual bodily harm. Allowing his appeal, the Court of Appeal held that, on such a charge, it is not open to the jury to convict of the lesser offence.

5. The elements of aggravated burglary

Under s. 10(1) of the 1968 Act, *a person is guilty of aggravated burglary if he commits any burglary and at the time he has with him any firearm or imitation firearm, any weapon of offence or any explosive.* Under s. 10(1)(b), *'weapon of offence' means any article made or adapted for use for causing injury to or incapacitating a person, or intended by the person having it with him for such use.* For a conviction, the prosecution must therefore prove that the defendant had the weapon with him with the intent of causing injury to some person but need not show that he intended to use it in the course of the burglary —

> *R* v. *Stones* (1989) Arrested whilst running away from a house that had been burgled, S was found to be carrying a kitchen knife, which he said was for self-defence. He was charged with aggravated burglary and the judge directed the jury that it was sufficient to show that S was carrying a weapon of offence during the burglary, with the intention of using it on some person. The Court of Appeal upheld his conviction.

> *R* v. *Francis* (1982): Entering a house armed with sticks, which they discarded, F and another then stole property. They were convicted of aggravated burglary, with the jury

having been directed that the prosecution needed only to prove that they were armed when they entered the premises. Substituting convictions for burglary, the Court of Appeal held that there had been a misdirection. Unless they intended to steal when they entered, they were guilty of aggravated burglary only if they had a weapon with them at the moment when they stole.

The essentials of deception and blackmail

6. The obtaining of property by deception

Under s. 15(1) of the 1968 Act, an offence is committed when a person *by any deception dishonestly obtains property belonging to another, with the intention of permanently depriving the other of it.* With an obtaining by deception substituted for an appropriation, this is therefore similar to theft and both offences may be committed on the same facts, with the proviso that the requirements of dishonesty and an intention of permanently depriving are fulfilled. For a conviction of obtaining property by deception, it is necessary to examine:

(a) *The nature of deception.* Under s. 15(4) of the 1968 Act, '*deception means any deception (whether deliberate or reckless) by words or conduct, as to fact or as to law, including a deception as to the present intentions of the person using the deception or any other person.* There must therefore be some form of misrepresentation which the maker knows to be untrue or which he makes not caring whether it be true or false. In this context, recklessness thus connotes indifference as to truth or falsity; consequently, mere negligence would not be sufficient. A deception as to 'present intentions' could arise from a situation where one person obtains money from another by falsely pretending that he will do some work for it. In all cases the deception must be the operative cause of the obtaining —

> *R* v. *King; R* v. *Stockwell* (1987): Falsely describing themselves as representing a firm of tree surgeons, K and S told a householder that essential work to trees was necessary to prevent damage to the gas mains and house foundations. They were convicted of attempting to obtain property by deception and, dismissing their appeals, the Court of Appeal held that, if the attempt had succeeded, it

would have been for the jury to decide whether the deception had been an operative cause of obtaining money.

R v. *Gilmartin* (1983): Obtaining supplies with post-dated cheques, which he knew would be dishonoured, G (a stationer) was convicted of dishonestly obtaining goods by deception. Upholding his conviction, the Court of Appeal held that the deception was by conduct — i.e. falsely representing that each cheque was a good and valid order for the payment of the sum specified.

(b) *The nature of dishonesty.* In *R* v. *Ghosh* (1982) (*below*) the Court of Appeal held that dishonesty in this context characterises a state of mind, as opposed to a course of conduct; consequently there cannot be a conviction if a person makes a representation that he believes to be true — even though he ought to have known it to be false. A jury should therefore be directed to determine whether, according to the ordinary standards of reasonable and honest people, what was done was dishonest; if this is so, they must then decide whether the defendant must have realised that what he was doing was dishonest by those standards —

R v. *Ghosh* (1982): G, a surgeon, was alleged to have falsely represented that money was due to him for an operation that had been performed on the National Health by someone else. Upholding his conviction of deception, the Court of Appeal stated the principle outlined above and it has been followed in subsequent cases.

R v. *Price* (1990): Charged with obtaining services and evading a liability by deception (*see* 26:**7(c)–(d)**), P claimed to have thought that he was the beneficiary of a trust fund and that his conduct was honest — although most people might not have agreed. The recorder directed the jury that they all knew what constituted dishonesty and they had to decide whether P had falsely purported that he had the means to pay. Upholding his conviction, the Court of Appeal held that a *Ghosh* direction was not appropriate in all cases and applied only where a defendant might have believed that what he was alleged to have done was in accordance with the ordinary person's idea of honesty.

(c) *The nature of obtaining.* Under s. 15(2) of the 1968 Act, *a person is to be treated as obtaining property if he obtains ownership, possession or control of it, and 'obtain' includes obtaining for another, or enabling another to obtain or retain.* It is therefore sufficient to obtain ownership without possession or vice versa —

> *R v. Ashbee* (1989): Having conspired with others to obtain British passports by fraudulent use of birth certificates and application forms, A was convicted of obtaining property by deception and sentenced to four years' imprisonment. He appealed on the ground that the maximum sentence should have been that for the offence of making a false application for a passport. Dismissing his appeal, the Court of Appeal held that falsely applying for a passport was different from obtaining (and subsequently using) one.

(d) *The nature of property.* The meanings of 'property' and 'belonging to another' are as shown in 26:**1(b)**–**(c)** —

> *R v. Davies* (1982): Having persuaded two residents of an old people's home to endorse cheques drawn in their favour and to hand them over to him, D was convicted of obtaining property by deception. Upholding his conviction, the Court of Appeal held that, as the residents had not appreciated what they were signing, the property in the cheques remained with them and did not pass to D; consequently he could be guilty of dishonestly obtaining 'property belonging to another'.

(e) *The nature of the intention.* The 'intention of permanently depriving' is the same as in 26:**2(b)** —

> *R v. Atwal* (1989): Having obtained credit and charge cards from companies without the ability or willingness to pay for purchases made against them, A was charged under s. 15(1). It was held that the offence was made out if a card was dishonestly obtained by deception and if, at the time of obtaining it, the defendant had the intention of cheating the company. In such circumstances he would be intending to

treat the card as his own to dispose of regardless of the
rights of the owner.

7. The other derivatives of deception

Under the Theft Act 1968 and the Theft Act 1978 there are
four other offences involving deception:

(a) *The obtaining of a pecuniary advantage by deception*. Under s. 16(1)
of the 1968 Act, an offence is committed when a person *by any
deception dishonestly obtains for himself or another any pecuniary
advantage*. This means dishonestly obtaining credit or some other
form of financial advantage. Section 16(2) of the 1968 Act now sets
out two cases (a third having been repealed) in which a pecuniary
advantage is to be regarded as obtained. The first covers the
situation where a person is allowed to borrow by way of overdraft,
or to take out any policy of insurance or annuity contract, *or* obtains
an improvement of the terms on which he is allowed to do so. The
second covers the situation where a person is given the
opportunity to earn remuneration or greater remuneration in an
office or employment *or* to win money by betting —

R v. *Lambie* (1981): Having exceeded the £200 limit of her
credit card, L was asked to return it to the bank but
continued to use it . She was convicted of the evasion of a
debt by deception and, upholding her conviction, the House
of Lords held that the presentation of the card had been a
representation of her authority to make a contract on the
bank's behalf.

R v. *McNiff* (1986): By making false statements, McN
obtained the provisional tenancy of a public house, which
took effect on his being granted a justices' licence. Allowing
his appeal against conviction under s. 16, the Court of
Appeal held that an opportunity to apply for an 'office' in
which remuneration will be earned does not amount to 'an
opportunity to earn remuneration'.

(b) *The procuring of the execution of a valuable security by deception*.
Under s. 20(2) of the 1968 Act, it is an offence when a person
*dishonestly, with a view to gain for himself or another, or with intent to
cause loss to another, by any deception procures the execution of a valuable
security*. A 'valuable security' includes any document creating,
transferring, surrendering or releasing a right in or over property,

or authorising the payment of money or delivery of any property, or the satisfaction of any obligation —

> *R* v. *Beck* (1985): Using forged stolen travellers' cheques and a Diner's Club card stolen in England, B obtained cash and goods in France. Even though they knew they were forgeries, the English bank and company honoured the bills. Dismissing B's appeal against conviction under s. 20, the Court of Appeal held that 'procure' means to cause or bring about (in this case to compel the bank and company to pay on the securities), also that the honouring of the debts constituted an 'execution' within the jurisdiction.

(c) *The obtaining of services by deception.* Under s. 1 of the 1978 Act, *a person who by any deception dishonestly obtains services from another shall be guilty of an offence.* There is an obtaining of services where the other is induced to confer a benefit by doing some act, or causing or permitting some act to be done, on the understanding that the benefit has been or will be paid for —

> *R* v. *Halai* (1983): To obtain a mortgage, H made false statements to a building society's agent and used post-dated cheques (which he knew would be dishonoured) to pay for a survey and open a savings account. Falsely representing that cash had been paid into the account, he withdrew £100 from it. Upholding his conviction, the Court of Appeal held that by deception he had obtained a service from the agent, a benefit from the survey and £100 from the building society.

(d) *The evasion of liability by deception.* Under s. 2 of the 1978 Act it is an offence if, by deception, a person *dishonestly secures the remission of the whole or part of any existing liability to make a payment — whether his own liability or another's OR with the intent to make permanent default in whole or in part of an existing liability to make a payment, or with intent to let another do so, induces the creditor or any person claiming payment on behalf of the creditor to wait for payment (whether or not the due date for payment is deferred) or to forgo payment OR dishonestly obtains an exemption from, or abatement of, liability to make a payment.* In this context 'liability' means a legally enforceable liability and the provisions would not apply to a liability, which has not been accepted or established, to pay compensation for a wrongful act or omission. Furthermore, a person induced to take in payment a cheque, or other security for money, by way of conditional satisfaction of a pre-existing liability, is treated not as being paid but as being induced to wait for payment —

> *R* v. *Firth* (1990): By failing to notify a hospital of patients' private status, F (a consultant gynaecologist) avoided being billed for NHS hospital services. Dismissing his appeal against conviction under s. 2, the Court of Appeal held that evading liability could be an act of either commission or omission.

8. The elements of blackmail

Under the Theft Act 1968, s. 21, blackmail is committed when a person *with a view to gain for himself or another, or with intent to cause loss to another, makes any unwarranted demand with menaces*. There cannot be an 'attempt to blackmail' and the essential elements of the offence are:

(a) *The nature of gain or loss.* Under s. 34(2) of the 1968 Act, gains and losses must be in money or other property and may be temporary or permanent. Moreover, 'gain' includes keeping what one has — as well as getting what one has not, also 'loss' includes not getting what one might get, as well as parting with what one has —

> *R* v. *Bevans* (1988): Holding a gun, B confronted a doctor who visited his house and demanded an injection, which was administered. Charged with blackmail, he argued that the offence related only to economic interests. Upholding his conviction, the Court of Appeal held that the substance injected was property and constituted a 'gain', in that B obtained something which he did not previously have.

(b) *The nature of an unwarranted demand.* Under s. 21(1) of the 1968 Act, *a demand with menaces is unwarranted unless the person making it does so in the belief ... that he has reasonable grounds for making the demand and ... that the use of the menaces is a proper means of reinforcing the demand.* If the defendant pleads that the demand was not unwarranted, the prosecution must show that he made it without the belief outlined. The factual question of his belief should be left to the jury and it does not matter what a reasonable man would have believed. Provided that a demand is made, it is immaterial whether it is oral or written, whether it is complied with or even whether it is heard. If a demand is made in a letter, the offence is committed when it is posted —

> *R* v. *Forrester* (1988): Owed a large sum of money by a woman, F wrote to her under a false name demanding £18,000 for the publication rights of an article in which he had described her previous occupation as a brothel-keeper. Having said that it would otherwise be sold to a newspaper, F claimed that he was entitled to the money and that there was nothing wrong in telling the truth to a newspaper. Convicted of blackmail, he was sentenced to 18 months' imprisonment but the Court of Appeal held that, in view of his honestly held belief about being entitled to the money, the sentence should be reduced to 12 months, of which six months would be suspended.

(c) *The nature of menaces.* The word 'menaces' does not mean that there must necessarily be threats of violence, as it is sufficient for something unpleasant or detrimental to be threatened. Under s. 21(2) of the 1968 Act, it is immaterial whether the menaces relate to action to be taken by the person making the demand. The threats may be veiled, as opposed to express, but must be such as to alarm an ordinary person of normal stability and courage — though it is not necessary to show that the intended victim did in fact become alarmed —

> *R* v. *Harry* (1974): Writing to 115 shopkeepers, H (the treasurer of a college rag committee) invited them to pay £1–5 for posters 'to protect you from any Rag activity which could in any way cause you inconvenience'. A count of blackmail was withdrawn from the jury as the threat was not 'of such a nature and extent that the mind of an ordinary person of normal stability and courage might be influenced or made apprehensive, so as to accede unwillingly to the demand'.

The essentials of handling stolen goods and criminal damage

9. The handling of stolen goods

It is an offence dishonestly to handle stolen goods and, under the Theft Act 1968, s. 22(1), *a person handles stolen goods if (otherwise than in the course of stealing), knowing or believing them to be stolen goods, he dishonestly receives the goods, or dishonestly undertakes or assists in their retention, removal, disposal or realisation by or for the benefit of another person, or if he arranges to do so*. It is therefore necessary to examine:

(a) *The nature of stolen goods*. Under s. 34(2)(*b*) of the 1968 Act, 'goods' should be taken to mean money and all other property except land, but including things severed from land by stealing. 'Stolen goods' comprise property acquired not only by theft but also by blackmail and deception. Under the Police and Criminal Evidence Act 1984, s. 74, the prosecution may be allowed to prove the conviction of the thief, in order to establish that the goods are in fact 'stolen'. Under s. 24(3) of the 1968 Act, stolen property may cease to be stolen if restored to the person from whom it was stolen, if transferred to some other lawful possession (e.g. that of the police) or if the person from whom it was stolen ceases to have any right to restitution. If a handler of stolen goods exchanges them for money or other property, then both the stolen goods and the money (or other property) become 'stolen goods'. If, however, stolen goods come into the possession of an innocent party and are then exchanged for something else, the property acquired in exchange does not become 'stolen goods' —

> *Greater London Metropolitan Police Commissioner* v. *Streeter* (1980): A man stole four cartons of cigarettes from his employers and loaded them into a company lorry. However, the security officer found them, marked them and informed the police, who followed the lorry to S's shop. S was charged with handling stolen goods but the magistrate upheld a submission of no case on the ground that the delivered goods were not stolen because the security officer had brought them back into the owner's possession. Allowing the prosecutor's appeal, the Divisional Court held that neither the security officer nor the police

had purported to exercise possession or control; they had merely waited to see what would happen. The case would therefore be remitted to the magistrate to continue the hearing.

(b) *The nature of the knowledge or belief.* In *R* v. *Hall* (1985) the Court of Appeal held that 'knowledge' exists when the defendant is told by someone with first-hand knowledge (the thief) that goods are stolen; on the other hand, 'belief' is something short of knowledge, where there could be no other reasonable conclusion in the light of all the circumstances. However, there must be more than mere suspicion and it is insufficient to show that the defendant *ought to have believed* that goods were stolen —

> *R v. Toor* (1987): For a very low price and without being given a receipt, T (a grocer) purchased stock destined for an airline. Convicted of handling stolen goods, he appealed, claiming a misdirection as to knowledge or belief. The Court of Appeal held that it might often be advisable (particularly where 'suspicion' is concerned) to give the jury a *Hall* direction, but this is not always necessary if the issue is one of 'belief'. It is sufficient for the jury to be directed that this can be inferred if it is the only inference that can be drawn from the facts.

(c) *The nature of dishonest receiving.* It must be proved that the defendant (or his agent or employee, acting on his behalf) obtained possession or control of the goods after a dishonest appropriation had been completed — as handling cannot occur *in the course of stealing*. It is insufficient to 'receive' a person who has stolen goods in his possession — moreover, receiving cannot occur while he still retains possession (e.g. during negotiations for the disposal of the goods) —

> *R v. Park* (1988): As cheques for large sums of stolen money had been 'laundered' through his bank account, P (a solicitor) was convicted of handling stolen goods. He appealed on the ground that arrangements in respect of the money had been made prior to its theft. Allowing the appeal, the Court of Appeal held that an essential ingredient of handling stolen goods was that the goods should already have been stolen.

(d) *The nature of retention, removal, disposal or realisation.* In these cases it is necessary to prove that the acts were done 'by or for the benefit of' another person — thus the disposal of the goods for the thief's own benefit would not make him a handler —

> *R* v. *Bloxham* (1982): Not knowing that it was stolen, B bought a car for £1,300 but did not receive any documents; he later suspected theft and sold the vehicle for £200. Quashing his conviction for handling, the House of Lords held that a purchaser could not be 'another person'.

10. The elements of criminal damage

Under the Criminal Damage Act 1971, s. 1, *a person who without lawful excuse destroys or damages any property belonging to another, intending to destroy or damage any such property, or being reckless as to whether any such property would be destroyed or damaged, shall be guilty of an offence.* The 1971 Act abolished the common law offence of arson but s. 1(3) provides that *an offence committed under this section by destroying or damaging property by fire shall be charged as arson.* Under s. 2 it is an offence for someone to make to another person a threat, intending that the other person would fear it would be carried out, to destroy or damage any property belonging to that other or a third person, or to destroy or damage his own property in a way that he knows is likely to endanger the life of that other or a third person. It is also an offence under s. 3 for a person to have anything in his custody or under his control, intending without lawful excuse to use it, or cause or permit another to use it, to destroy or damage any property belonging to some other person, or to destroy or damage his own or the user's property in a way which he knows is likely to endanger the life of some other person. The essential elements of a s. 1 offence are:

(a) *The nature of lawful excuse.* Under s. 5(2) of the 1971 Act, a defendant is treated as having a lawful excuse if, at the time of the alleged offence, he believed that the person(s) whom he believed to be entitled to give consent to the destruction or damage had (or would have) given such consent. There is also a lawful excuse if the defendant has effected destruction or damage in order to protect property, believing it to be in immediate need of protection and that the means of protection were or would be reasonable, having regard to all the circumstances. A mistaken belief by the defendant that the property is his own is considered in **(c)** *below* —

> *R* v. *Appleyard* (1985): Having fraudulently set fire to a store belonging to a company of which he was managing director, A was convicted of arson. He appealed on the ground that he must have been taken to have consented to the damage but the Court of Appeal held that he was not entitled to consent to a fraudulent purpose. *See also R* v. *Hill*; *R* v. *Hall* (1989) (22:**2(c)**).

(b) *The nature of destruction or damage.* In this context 'destroy' means simply rendering property useless for its intended purpose, whilst 'damage' connotes non-trivial harm, which does not have to amount to rendering useless —

> *Cox* v. *Riley* (1986): By deliberately erasing the program from a printed-circuit card, R rendered a computerised saw inoperable. Convicted of criminal damage, he appealed on the ground that the erasure did not constitute damage but the Divisional Court upheld his conviction.

(c) *The nature of property.* Under s. 10 of the 1971 Act, the destruction or damage must be caused to real or personal property of a tangible nature — including money, wild creatures (but not wild flowers) and land. It is treated as 'belonging to another' if someone else has custody or control of it, or has any proprietary right or interest, or has a charge on it. However, no offence is committed if a person destroys or damages property belonging to another in the honest but mistaken (though not necessarily justifiable) belief that it is his own —

> *R* v. *Smith* (1974): Charged with causing criminal damage to property, S claimed that he honestly but mistakenly believed it to be his own. As the judge ruled that such belief could not constitute a lawful excuse, he was convicted but the Court of Appeal allowed his appeal.

(d) *The nature of intent and recklessness.* The tests for intent and recklessness are as outlined in 22:3**(a)**–**(b)**, but s. 1(2) of the 1971 Act creates an aggravated offence where, in addition to the normal intent, the defendant was 'intending by the destruction or damage to endanger the life of another, or being reckless as to whether the life of another would be thereby endangered' —

> *Chief Constable of Avon and Somerset Constabulary* v. *Shimmen* (1987): Wishing to demonstrate his prowess and control to his friends, S pretended to kick a shop window but did not intend to make contact with it. He broke the window and the justices acquitted him of criminal damage on the basis that, perceiving the risk, he had assessed it as minimal on account of his skill. Allowing the appeal, the Divisional Court held that S had recognised the risk and was reckless.

Progress test 26

1. 'Robbery is really aggravated theft'. Discuss.   **(1, 2, 3)**

2. Describe the offence of burglary and the manner in which it may be aggravated.   **(4, 5)**

3. Compare and contrast the different offences involving deception.   **(6, 7)**

4. Explain what must be proved to obtain a conviction for handling stolen goods.   **(9)**

5. Knowing that the resident owner had gone ashore, Mike boarded a converted barge, secured alongside a tow-path on which he left his nephew, Norman, as a look-out. Having taken various items, including an expensive camera, Mike started a small fire in a cabin, to obliterate fingerprints, and then departed. As a reward for his help, he gave the camera to Norman who sold it to his friend Oscar for £5, explaining that he had found it in some bushes. Assess all criminal liability. **(1, 2, 4, 9, 10)**

Appendix
Examination technique

1.   Revise for the examination — remembering that it is not devised to ascertain the full extent of your knowledge or to trap you into errors. Its purpose is to provide a reasonable range of questions to verify whether you have read, understood and absorbed the elements of the syllabus — also whether you have brought to bear on your reading some intelligent and critical appreciation of your own. More is demanded than the mere regurgitation of memorised extracts from textbooks.

2.   Read through the whole examination paper, including the instructions contained in the heading. Five or ten minutes spent in thoughtful assessment can save you wasted effort and subsequent anguish.

3.   Select the questions which you intend to answer. It is not always wise to choose those that appear to be easiest, as it is always better to select the ones on which merit can be shown.

4.   Divide the total time by the number of answers required, allowing five to ten minutes for reading through the script at the end. When the time apportioned to each question has elapsed, the next *must* be started. If you submit four fulsome answers when in fact five are required, you impose on yourself a handicap of twenty per cent.

5.   Analyse each question, making certain that you appreciate whether more than one point has been raised.

6.   Answer the question that has been set and do not write an answer to a question in the same field which you would have preferred to have set.

7.   Make a 'skeleton' of each answer, with brief headings. Assemble in a logical order the principles and facts that you intend to use.

8.   Avoid irrelevance; this does not gain any marks and often results in a lower mark than might otherwise have been awarded for the relevant matter that is included.

9.   Memorise statutes and cases but bear in mind that it is always the *principle* that matters. The examiners will give credit in 'problem' questions if they are tackled in the right way — even though the answer arrived at may not be the one which is expected. You need to be able to identify the relevance of facts, to apply appropriate legal rules thereto and to evaluate judicial reasoning.

10. Present your work in such a way that the examiner finds it a joy to mark. He is a human being, who appreciates legibility and clarity — combined with clear, concise and exact communication.

Index